A Da Capo Press Reprint Series

**FRANKLIN D. ROOSEVELT
AND THE ERA OF THE NEW DEAL**
GENERAL EDITOR: FRANK FREIDEL
Harvard University

MIGRANT FAMILIES

Division of Research
Work Projects Administration

Research Monographs

Works Progress Administration
Division of Social Research
Research Monograph XVIII

MIGRANT FAMILIES

By John N. Webb
and Malcolm Brown

DA CAPO PRESS • NEW YORK • 1971

A Da Capo Press Reprint Edition

This Da Capo Press edition of *Migrant Families* is an unabridged
republication of the first edition published in Washington, D.C., in 1938.
It is reprinted by permission from a copy of the original edition owned
by the Harvard College Library.

Library of Congress Catalog Card Number 76-165605

ISBN 0-306-70350-5

Published by Da Capo Press, Inc.
A Subsidiary of Plenum Publishing Corporation
227 West 17th Street, New York, N.Y. 10011

Manufactured in the United States of America

MIGRANT FAMILIES

WORKS PROGRESS ADMINISTRATION

F. C. Harrington, *Administrator*

Corrington Gill, *Assistant Administrator*

DIVISION OF SOCIAL RESEARCH

Howard B. Myers, *Director*

MIGRANT FAMILIES

By

John N. Webb

and

Malcolm Brown

•

RESEARCH MONOGRAPH XVIII

1938

UNITED STATES GOVERNMENT PRINTING OFFICE, WASHINGTON

Letter of Transmittal

WORKS PROGRESS ADMINISTRATION,
Washington, D. C., December 27, 1938.

SIR: I have the honor to transmit a report on the characteristics and activities of the depression migrant families which received relief from the transient program of the Federal Emergency Relief Administration.

A high degree of population mobility is a basic necessity in America. As long as the American economy continues to expand, population redistribution to fit the changing concentration of resources will be essential. Rapid changes in industrial technique require a continual shifting of workers among the industrial areas of the country. Varying birth rates in different parts of the country produce a population flow from the regions of high natural increase toward the regions where the increase is less. Soil erosion and the increasing mechanization of agriculture are constantly releasing great numbers of small farmers and agricultural workers for industrial employment in the cities. In the West large-scale agriculture requires an army of migratory agricultural workers who travel great distances to piece out a year's work at short-time harvest jobs.

During good times, when migrants reestablish themselves in a new community with little difficulty, the desirability of population movement is not questioned. During a depression, on the other hand, the same sort of population movement frequently entails a relief problem. As a result, distress migration is generally disapproved by the resident population. This disapproval is expressed concretely in the multifarious State legal residence requirements that exclude newcomers from the usual types of relief benefits in the local governmental units.

In 1933, recognizing that the State residence requirements created a no man's land in which large numbers of needy migrants were ineligible for relief, the FERA set up a uniform requirement of 1 year's residence for general relief throughout the United States. Through the Federal transient program the FERA assumed responsibility for those persons who could not meet this requirement. On this basis the transient program gave care (in addition to the unattached) to some 200,000 different migrant families, containing approximately 700,000 individuals, during the 2 years of its operation.

By examining the experience of the transient program, this report has been able to isolate a number of widely-held misconceptions about transients and transient relief. Analysis of the reasons why migrant families left home and of their subsequent travels reveals that they were not—as is so commonly believed—irresponsible and degraded groups addicted to chronic wandering. On the contrary, a large majority of them were habitually settled and self-supporting families dislodged by the depression and seeking reestablishment elsewhere. The families left home not only because they were in distress but also because of a reasonable expectation of an improved status at their destination. Their travels rarely took them beyond the region with which they were familiar and frequently took them no farther than into an adjoining State. Half the families had moved no more than once before receiving transient relief; afterwards, a large majority remained in the same transient bureau where they had first registered until they found work.

Of particular significance in this connection is the evidence in this study that migrant families were reabsorbed from the transient relief program at a rate considerably higher than the rate for workers on general relief. This fact suggests that the migration of the families studied aided them materially in working out their economic problems, even though public assistance was temporarily required in the process.

The report finds that the transient relief problem is essentially an urban-industrial problem which has in recent years been complicated by migration of destitute drought-refugees. In spite of the belief that depression migration is a one-way movement in which certain States are exclusively contributors, while other States are exclusively recipients, it is revealed that the migration of the families studied usually involved a more or less balanced interchange between the States.

The report concludes from the evidence presented that future efforts toward providing relief to nonresidents should recognize that migrants in need are not essentially different from residents in need. The solution of the transient relief problem would therefore appear to lie in the direction of making the regular work relief and general relief programs accessible to nonresidents by means of reducing or eliminating State legal settlement requirements which artificially create the "transient" as a separate category. The experience of the past, however, warns against the presumption that the initiative in working out this solution will come from the individual States. Transiency is a national problem, and Federal leadership is essential in achieving a solution which would take into account both the needs of distressed migrants and the interests of the individual States.

The study was made by the Division of Social Research under the direction of Howard B. Myers, Director of the Division. The collection and analysis of the data were supervised by John N. Webb, Coordinator of Urban Surveys. The report was prepared by John N. Webb and Malcolm Brown. Special acknowledgment is made to M. Starr Northrop and Jack Yeaman Bryan, who assisted in the analysis of the data, and to Katherine Gordon, who assisted in the preparation of the tables.

Respectfully submitted.

CORRINGTON GILL,
Assistant Administrator.

COL. F. C. HARRINGTON,
Works Progress Administrator.

Contents

FIGURES

Migrant Families

INTRODUCTION

Dᵢₛₜᵣₑₛₛ **DISTRESS MIGRATION** was one of the problems that confronted the Federal Emergency Relief Administration when in 1933 it undertook the wholly new task of active cooperation with the States in extending aid to the unemployed. Through the transient relief program the FERA made available—for the first time on a national scale—immediate and adequate assistance to the needy nonresident. Little was known at that time of the nature of depression migration, and one of the important, though incidental, services of the transient program was to call attention to the problem of the migrant unemployed and to provide a means by which this problem might be studied.

The background of this study is the transient relief program of the Federal Emergency Relief Administration. The principal purpose of this report is to make available information—parallel in its details to the discussion of unattached transients in *The Transient Unemployed* [1]—about the migrant families which registered at transient bureaus. In addition the report attempts to relate the distress migration of families to the larger fields of labor and population mobility.

NONRESIDENT FAMILIES IN NEED

Although transiency has been a recognized social problem for a generation, the problem of nonresident families in need was not clearly demarked until the operation of the transient program. Prior to the transient program it was not generally known that any considerable number of needy families were migrating, and depression migrants were believed to consist almost entirely of unattached men and boys. So little was known of family migration that the early plans for the transient relief program were principally for providing congregate shelters in cities and camps outside the cities for unattached men. The relatively small proportion of family registrations and cases under care in transient bureaus (see ch. IV) during 1934 was, in large part, the result of a lack of facilities for family care.

---

[1] See Webb, John N., Research Monograph III, Division of Social Research, Works Progress Administration, Washington, D. C., 1935.

The underestimation of family distress migration during early years of the depression partly grew out of the fact that family mobility was less spectacular than the mobility of unattached persons. Needy families did not ride the freight trains or congregate at the railroad yard limits where they would have attracted attention at every town along the main-line railroads. Instead they moved largely by automobile so that, except for the general state of disrepair of their cars and the frequent protrusion of personal belongings from the sides, they differed little in appearance from many nonmigrant travelers on the highways.

Another reason for the failure to note family migration was the cautious nature of their travels. All the families studied here were interstate migrants; yet, in the majority of cases they moved relatively short distances. More often than not they migrated within the same general area in which they had been residing. Usually they went to places where they were known or had relatives and friends who might help them. Accordingly, migrant families did not appear as strangers completely unfamiliar with the country.

Most important of all is the fact that a substantial proportion of the families which received aid from transient bureaus made their application for assistance after the completion of migration. These families had often lived in the new community for several months before they found it necessary to ask for aid. Before the initiation of the transient program, the problem of these families would have been known only to social service workers.

The transient relief program brought the problems of needy migrant families to light by granting assistance not only to (1) the migrants who were in need while en route but also to (2) those whose need developed after they had reached their destinations but who could not get resident relief before the expiration of the time required for establishing legal residence in the new community. For this latter group of families transient relief was, in effect, little different from resident relief. Their appeal for special assistance did not arise out of distress connected with the act of migration itself, but from the fact that some specified period of time had not yet been served in the new community.

IMPLICATIONS OF GOVERNMENT AID

The registration figures of the transient relief program justify an estimate that—in addition to the unattached transients—some 200,000 different migrant families, containing approximately 700,000 individuals, were assisted by the transient program during the slightly more than 2 years in which the program was operated. Even granting that many families later returned to their original place of residence, it is clear that the families assisted by the transient program made up a population movement of considerable importance.

The role of the Government in assisting these needy migrant families had little or no effect in initiating their mobility. Very few of the families (or the unattached either) migrated for the purpose of obtaining transient relief. The effects of the transient program upon population movement were felt after migrants were already on the road and frequently after their migration had been completed. The transient program did not create depression mobility, but it was itself created to cope with the fact of depression migrants in need.

The basic purpose of the transient program was to relieve a particular category of distressed persons. The depression demonstrated that people will migrate regardless of the danger that they may become ineligible for normal relief assistance. The difficulty of obtaining local public assistance did not "prevent" the migration of distressed families before the initiation of the transient relief program; it did, however, increase the distress of the migrants who failed to establish themselves at their destination. Because the Federal Government extended assistance to migrants who failed to reestablish themselves after leaving home, it did indirectly affect the population movement itself. In that respect the migration studied here differs from the unassisted distress mobility before 1933 and in previous depressions, when aid to transients was meager and was given with reluctance.

RELATION BETWEEN NORMAL AND DEPRESSION MIGRATION

Basically, migration represents population movement in response to real or fancied differences in opportunity. In periods of prosperity this fact is never questioned. Migration in good times is obviously the response to a greater opportunity in some community other than the one of residence. In periods of depression, however, the opportunities of prosperous times, and particularly the economic opportunities, approach the vanishing point in all communities. Nevertheless, *relative* opportunity remains the motive force back of depression migration, even though the response on the part of the migrant was largely the result of comparing the fact of no opportunity in the place of residence with the hope of some opportunity in another community. During the prosperous 1920's, for instance, differences in opportunity precipitated a large scale movement of workers from rural areas to the cities, and during the early 1930's many of these workers went back to the land because even the limited opportunities in the country were greater than in the cities.

There are two complementary forces at work in any migration and particularly in a depression migration. In the first place there is the expulsive force in the community of residence, and in the second place there is the attractive force in the place of destination. When unfavorable conditions prevail the expulsive forces receive most attention, and when conditions are favorable the attractive forces are most likely to be noted.

Such expulsive forces as unemployment, underemployment, and low wages were obviously an important cause of depression migration. They were not, however, the only forces at work. The apparent ease with which solvent families move from one community to another during prosperous times has by a careless analogy been carried over and applied to depression migrants. Actually, migration is far from a simple operation even in the best of times; and the force required to uproot a settled family and initiate a migration during a depression is far greater than is generally realized. In the migration studied, an essential part of the motivation was the fact that the families were usually drawn to a particular destination by attractions which gave the appearance of being reasonably substantial.

Trial and error are necessarily involved in most migrations. There is an element of uncertainty in any change of the environment and circumstances under which a living is obtained. Detailed knowledge of the social and economic conditions in the new community (and of their probable development in the future) would be necessary if the element of risk in migration were to be removed; and such information is seldom available to migrants or, for that matter, to anyone else.

The element of uncertainty in migration explains why attempts to find a more desirable place to live frequently end in failure. Undoubtedly the risks of leaving a community that is known for one that is unknown, or less well known, vary with favorable and unfavorable economic conditions; but the risk remains in some degree even in the best of times. There is some wasted effort in migration at any time and the loss increases when conditions become adverse.

The migration under consideration in this report occurred during a period of widespread unemployment. Moreover, the migrants studied had, at the time of observation, been unsuccessful in their efforts at relocation. However, the fact that migration had failed to achieve its purpose does not warrant the conclusion that the migrants studied were a residual group of failures. On the contrary, the evidence suggests that—granted an upturn in employment—most of the families could have been expected to gain the objective of their migration and resume economic self-support. Indeed, there was little to distinguish the families which received relief as transients—in either their behavior or social characteristics—from families in the general population which take part in normal population movements except that transient relief families are temporarily in need of public assistance.

During good times migration in search of economic opportunity liquidates itself without a great deal of need for public assistance.

During a depression, on the other hand, essentially the same sort of population movement entails a relief problem. As a result, distress migration is disapproved by the resident population, and tenuous moral distinctions between normal and distress migration get wide acceptance. These distinctions have little objective basis. The "normal" mobility of prosperity becomes "mobility in trouble" in a period of depression. Transiency has been aptly described as being in essence simply "the trouble function of mobility."[2]

PROBLEMS IN MEASURING MIGRATION

Because of the complexity of motivation, including, for example, the weighing of alternatives by the individual, migration is difficult to explain. Distress alone will not account for the migration of the families assisted by the transient program, nor do the risks of depression migration explain why some distressed families moved and others did not. For some families the distress of unemployment was offset partially by the relative security of local relief; for others, the risks of migration were outweighed by the opportunities that might be found. Only through direct contact with the migrant can the important factor of motivation be appraised.

The term *migration* is applied within a wide range of mobility. At the lower end the range stops just short of absolute stability; i. e., just short of the situation where a person was born, reared, and resided continuously in only one community.[3] At the other end of the range migration approaches the constant mobility of such groups as the migratory-casual workers who live and work on the road from one year to the next.[4] Between these two extremes are to be found the great bulk of the migrants who in the course of time bring about the fundamental changes in population distribution. Obviously then, the

[2] Wickenden, Elizabeth, "Transiency = Mobility in Trouble," *The Survey*, Vol. LXXIII, No. 10, October 1937, pp. 307–309.

[3] Moves within a community were excluded from the definition of migration used in the study, although such moves are a special type of migration and deserve more attention than they have received. Clearly, intracity moves could not be excluded on the basis of distance traveled alone, since within large metropolitan areas, such as New York or Los Angeles, it is possible to travel distances greater than those separating many communities from their nearest neighbor. There are good reasons for the decision to exclude moves within cities when the entire country is under consideration. The unit of measurement in spatial changes must necessarily be some recognized civil division, and the city unit serves that purpose without the loss of essential information and without undue complications in statistical tabulation. The city unit also serves as a rough distinction between urban and rural in such important matters as the origins and destinations of migrants.

[4] See Webb, John N., *The Migratory-Casual Worker*, Research Monograph VII, Division of Social Research, Works Progress Administration, Washington, D. C., 1937.

term *migration* covers many types of population movement. It becomes increasingly important that these types be identified and their interrelationship studied.

SOURCE OF INFORMATION

In the main the information presented in this report is based upon a representative sample of 5,489 migrant families selected from the total number receiving care in transient bureaus during September 1935. All the families considered in this report were interstate migrants. The sample was drawn from 85 cities located in 39 States and the District of Columbia (fig. 1). The cities were chosen to provide the wide geographical distribution necessary to the inclusion of all types of migrant families, as well as to take account of differences resulting from variations in size of city and from variations among the States in transient relief programs. The number of families selected in each State was proportionate to the number of families under care in each State during July 1935. A system of random selection was applied within each city to insure freedom from bias in choosing the families to be interviewed.

Through no fault of the method applied in selecting the sample, the families included do not provide a full representation of depression migrants. The unattached persons who received care at transient bureaus are of course excluded. Since the characteristics and behavior of the unattached differed markedly from those of the families, extreme caution must be exercised in applying to the unattached the generalizations that will be drawn from the study of the families.

There was a distinct urban bias in the transient relief population as a whole, and that bias appears in the group of families studied. Transient bureaus were necessarily located in cities and particularly in large cities, because the main routes of travel converge on centers of population. As a result migration involving exchange or redistribution of rural population was much less likely to come into contact with the transient program than was the migration of urban population.

Still another limitation of the sample as representative of all types of depression migration grows out of the fact that these families were selected at a time when the transient relief program had been in operation for about 2 years. During this period of time there was some tendency for families to "pile up" on transient relief in some areas where the slowness of economic recovery retarded their absorption into the resident population. Where this occurred, there was some tendency toward overrepresentation of the less successful depression migrants.

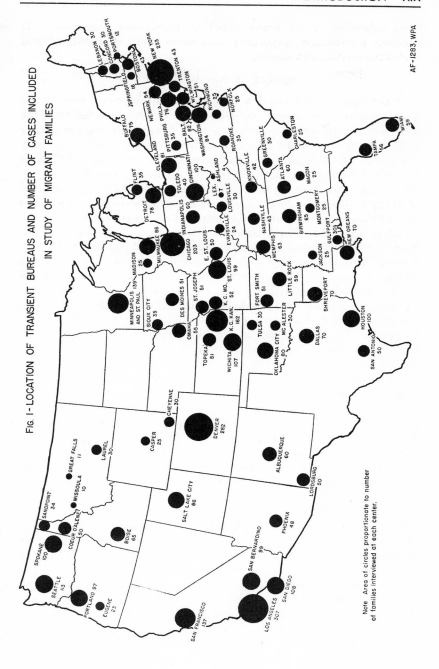

FIG. I - LOCATION OF TRANSIENT BUREAUS AND NUMBER OF CASES INCLUDED IN STUDY OF MIGRANT FAMILIES

AF-1283, WPA

Note Area of circles proportionate to number of families interviewed at each center.

ORGANIZATION OF THE REPORT

In view of the complexity of motivation in depression migration and its importance to an understanding of this movement, the first chapter deals with reasons for migration. The second chapter examines the origins and destinations of these families with particular emphasis upon the extent to which redistribution of population resulted from the movement of the families studied. For the purpose of determining whether the presence of these families on transient relief was the result of habitual instability, an examination is made in chapter III of the mobility of these families prior to the migration that led to need for transient bureau assistance. With these aspects of migration established, it is possible in chapter IV to consider the effect of the transient relief program upon distress migration. The personal characteristics of migrant families in terms of such familiar social classifications as age, sex, color, and race is the subject of the fifth chapter; and an analysis of their employability, occupational and industrial attachment, and duration of unemployment is presented in chapter VI. In chapter VII the more important findings of the report are reconsidered in terms of the larger problem of population mobility of which the depression migration of needy families is shown to be a distinct and important type.

SUMMARY

ALTHOUGH TRANSIENCY has been a recognized social problem for a generation, the problem of nonresident families in need was not fully realized until the operation of the transient relief program of the Federal Emergency Relief Administration, which gave care to a total of roughly 200,000 families containing approximately 700,000 individuals during 2 years of its operation, from September 1933 to September 1935. The transient program brought to light the full extent of the problem of needy migrant families. It extended aid to the depression migrants who were in need while on the road. It also aided those migrants to a new community whose need arose before the expiration of the time required to establish residence. Transient relief took over the no man's land of responsibility created by the tradition of residence requirements for relief eligibility.

Distress migration is disapproved by the resident population, and as a result tenuous distinctions have been drawn between migration under normal and under distress conditions. These distinctions have little objective basis. There was little to distinguish families which received transient relief—in either behavior or social characteristics—from families in the general population which have taken part in the "normal" mobility which is considered to be a characteristic of the American people. The normal mobility of good times becomes "mobility in trouble" in a period of depression.

REASONS FOR MIGRATION

At first glance it may seem impossible to reduce the causes of so complex an action as migration to simple terms for analysis. The complexity of the descriptions, however, is reduced by the fact that reasons for migration are composed of two complementary factors: the reason for leaving one specific place and the reason for selecting another specific place as destination.

The 5,489 migrant families which were interviewed in transient bureaus to form the basis for this study reported that economic distress was the principal reason for leaving their last settled, self-supporting residence. Unemployment was the most important cause of distress, and as a reason for leaving settled residence it by far out-weighed the combined effects of business and farm failures, inadequate earnings, and inadequate relief. Ill-health requiring a change of climate was second to unemployment as a displacing force.

The complaint that migrant families were on the road to see the country "at no expense" to themselves had little basis in fact. Nearly all the families were in more or less acute distress at the time they left their last settled residence.

Very few of the families with a settled residence set out with no destination at all or with such vague destinations as "eastern Colorado" or "the cotton-fields" in mind. Moreover, those families which did intend to migrate to a specific, predetermined place rarely reported an unreasoning choice of destination. The families generally migrated only when the probability of an improved status appeared to be high. More than half the families chose a destination in which there were close personal connections more or less obligated to assist them. Another large group chose its destination because of such specific facts as letters of recommendation to employers, the purchase of farms or homes, and employment-office direction. Altogether, four-fifths of the families had a definite contact at their destination.

What the families hoped for at their destinations was a solution to the basic problems which had confronted them at their former residence. Four-fifths of the families sought economic betterment, principally employment and, to a less extent, help from relatives. Among the remainder the chief objectives were healthful climate and the desire to rejoin relatives.

The reasons for leaving settled residence and for selecting a destination did not vary greatly in the different sections of the United States. Unemployment was the principal expulsive force in every State except North Dakota and South Dakota, where farming failure was of principal importance. Inadequate earnings and inadequate relief showed no significant regional variation. The principal regional variation in the objectives sought at destination was in the proportion of health-seekers, who were particularly attracted to Arizona, California, Colorado, and New Mexico.

The families were neither particularly adventurous nor, on the other hand, irresponsible in undertaking the migration which later necessitated aid from transient bureaus. The essence of the migration studied is contained in the fact that the families were, in general, distressed groups which saw a reasonable solution to their problems through migration to another community.

ORIGINS AND MOVEMENTS

The FERA records of the 30,000 migrant families under care in transient bureaus on June 15, 1935, show that migrant families tended to move relatively short distances. Only 3 percent of the families made full transcontinental moves. The preponderance of short-distance moves places the much-discussed depression movement to the West coast in a new perspective. Although the transcontinental migrations of families were by far the most spectacular, they were actually much less important numerically then the short migrations in all parts of the United States.

A considerable amount of family mobility consisted of a balanced interchange between the States. Rarely was there a large movement from any given State to another without a substantial counter movement. Net population displacement was thus only a fraction of the population movement. Two-thirds of all the movement resulted in the balance of losses and gains within each of the States, and, in terms of population displacement, was canceled. The remaining one-third of the movement was net displacement.

In the belief that they were moving toward regions of greater opportunity, many of the families moved to communities from which families like themselves were at the same time departing because of a lack of opportunity. It would thus appear that a large part of the movement dissipated itself in waste motion. Such a conclusion is not without value in demonstrating the disparity between desirable social goals and uncontrolled social behavior. This conclusion, however, has little relevance, in view of the concrete realities facing depression-stricken families.

Migrant family displacement showed clear geographical trends. The westward flow of families into Kansas, Colorado, California, Washington, Oregon, and New Mexico far exceeded all other net movement, and the general direction of the net movement for the entire United States, with the exception of the Southeast, was consistently toward the West. In the South the greater part of the net movement was northward to Illinois, Ohio, New York, and Michigan. Negroes played an important part in this movement.

There was a striking similarity between these trends and the displacement of families in the general population between 1920 and 1930. In both periods the predominating tendency was a westward movement, and the chief destination in both was California. The emigration from the Cotton States was principally northward in the two migrations. In both there was a net movement out of the less industrialized Eastern States into the more highly industrialized Eastern States.

The most important differences between the displacement of the general population in the 1920's and that of migrant families were the greater movement of families from the Great Plains States, particularly Kansas and Oklahoma. Washington, Oregon, and Idaho were exceedingly important as migrant family destinations, though they received little net gain from the internal migration of the general population in the 1920's.

Throughout the United States on June 30, 1935, 1 migrant family was under care in FERA transient bureaus for each 910 families in the total population, or 1.1 migrants per 1,000 resident families. Because of the wide variety of social and economic conditions in the various regions of the country, the rate of emigration from many States fell exceedingly far above and below this national average. Nevada, for example, contributed migrant families to other States at a rate 35 times the contribution of New Hampshire. The States from which the families emigrated most readily were mostly Western States. All the States with exceptionally high emigration rates lay west of the Mississippi. Several Southern States, particularly Arkansas and Florida, had family emigration rates above the national average. Migrant families emigrated least readily from the densely populated northeastern and north central regions of the United States.

When the migrant family intake of the various States was adjusted to State population, it was found that Idaho, at one extreme, had 1 family under transient bureau care for each 100 population families, while South Dakota, at the other extreme, had 1 family under care per 30,000 population families. In proportion to the resident population the problem of needy migrant families was most serious in Idaho, followed by New Mexico and Colorado. California ranked as fourth and was closely followed by Washington, Wyoming, and the District of Columbia. Most of the States with the highest rate of immigration were States lying west of the Mississippi River.

Migrant families tended to emigrate most readily from those States which had normally been contributing the greatest proportion of their population to other States before 1930. Migrant families tended to seek out those States into which the population had largely been flowing before 1930. There was, however, no consistent relationship between high family emigration rates and a high intensity of resident relief, nor between high family immigration rates and a low intensity of relief.

The origins and destinations of migrant families were both predominantly urban. The families moved mostly from city to city, rather than from farm to farm or between urban and rural places. The origins and destinations of 56 percent of the families were both urban, but both were rural for only 8 percent.

All States, with the single exception of South Dakota, contributed fewer migrant families from rural places than the rural composition of their population would have warranted. In spite of the 1934 drought and in spite of the chronic agricultural problem in such States as Alabama, Georgia, Oklahoma, and Texas, families from these States originated chiefly in urban places. It would appear, therefore, that in the United States as a whole the migrant family relief problem was basically urban and industrial rather than rural and agricultural.

THE PROBLEM OF "CHRONIC WANDERING"

Chronic wandering, at one extreme of mobility, is the aimless type of movement characteristic of persons to whom stability has become either impossible or unattractive. Migration, at the other extreme, is the purposeful and socially necessary type of mobility which has stability as its immediate object. Plainly, public assistance furthers readjustment more easily among migrants than among wanderers.

Examination of family mobility between January 1, 1929, and the date at which the families first registered at a transient bureau reveals that few of the families were habitual wanderers. Over one-half had maintained one residence for 3 years or more, and four-fifths had maintained one residence for at least 1 year. Thus, not more than one-fifth of all the migrant families could be considered to have been highly mobile before they received transient relief.

When family mobility is considered in terms of moves rather than length of residence, it is found that one-fifth had lived in only one place between 1929 and first transient relief and three-fifths had lived in no more than three places. Very few of the families reported any substantial gaps of mobility between their various residences.

The record of family moves shows that the more recently a family was married, the more mobile it was in relation to the length of time it had been formed. Family mobility tended to be greatest soon after marriage and before the families had gained a foothold in a community.

The families which were settled and self-supporting before 1929 became progressively more mobile between 1929 and 1935. But the families which were not settled were as mobile in 1929 as they were in the years that followed. In part, the consistently high mobility of this small group of families resulted from the pursuit of migratory-casual occupations. Except for this minority group, there is little doubt that the families had by and large been habitually settled and self-supporting until a short time before their first transient bureau registration.

Two-fifths of all migrant families first applied for transient relief in the community where they had been residing. Thus, in spite of the generally accepted belief that the nonresident relief problem is one of assisting persons on the road, actually, a large number of families had already completed their migration before applying for transient relief.

EFFECTS OF THE TRANSIENT PROGRAM

The transient program was frequently condemned for "encouraging transiency." Transient bureaus, it was held, aided migrants to "blithely skip from one camp to another, seeing the country while the Government footed the bill." The wide acceptance of such opinions is not difficult to understand. A small part of the migrant family population did consist of chronic wanderers, and the extreme case, because of the attention it attracted, was accepted as proof that all needy migrants were irresponsible and undeserving. The evidence presented in this report indicates that these opinions were unfounded.

In the first place there was relatively little movement of families from bureau to bureau. At the time this study was made three-fourths of the families had registered only at the transient bureau where they were interviewed, and only one-tenth had registered at three or more bureaus.

In the second place families came into and left transient relief at a fairly rapid rate. Monthly closing rates averaged 30 to 60 families for each 100 families under care in the transient program. This could only mean that the same families were wandering from bureau to bureau or that the migrant family population was continually in process of renewal. Since the movement between bureaus was small, it must be concluded that the migrant family population was rapidly changing in membership. Roughly 20 to 40 percent of each month's family case load left the transient relief program each month. The closing rate on resident relief during the same period was 5.6 percent. Allowing for families closed from transient bureaus to the resident relief rolls, and even for the possibility that many other families may have received resident relief later, the turnover of migrant families through normal economic adjustment would still appear to be many times higher than the turnover rates on resident relief.

Transient relief appears to have been a stabilizing influence upon families uprooted by the depression. It did not encourage wandering. On the contrary, it prevented aimless wandering by relieving the needs which were its cause. Stabilization, however, did not mean unlimited dependence upon the transient program for support. Transient relief provided necessary but interim assistance to migrants who in most instances had definite objectives and who were frequently only temporarily in need. The transient program not only provided immediate relief to a distressed group, but it also assisted materially in the solution of the problems that gave rise to the distress.

In judging the value of the transient program, it should be kept in mind that the transient program defined and took over the no man's land of responsibility which had been created by the tradition of the legal settlement requirements for local relief in the various States. The extent of the needs which would otherwise have been largely unmet can be inferred from a summary of the multifarious and frequently stringent restrictions governing eligibility for resident relief benefits.

Typical poor laws provide that a migrant would not be eligible for local relief unless he had lived within the State continuously, with intent to establish permanent residence, and without public assistance for at least 1 year; and in 10 States the residence must have lasted from 2 to 5 years. The migrant's legal status was further complicated by statutes in 19 States providing for loss of legal settlement in the State of origin. These provisions often caused migrants to lose settlement status in one State before it could be acquired in another. A large number of families were, indeed, without legal residence in any State. This fact does not reflect any particular degree of mobility among the families so much as it demonstrates the efficiency with which the settlement laws operate to penalize needy migrants.

Whether or not severe residence requirements do protect a State from an influx of needy nonresidents is still a debatable question. But in many cases the only reasonable solution of distress is through migration. At this point residence requirements and economic forces meet in a head-on collision, which can only be avoided by broadening the concept that people actually do "belong" in a particular place even though that place may be unable to provide them with the opportunity to make a living.

PERSONAL CHARACTERISTICS

Comparison of the personal characteristics of migrant families with those of families in the general and nonmigrant relief populations reveal several important selective factors at work in the migration studied:

1. Youth was a clearly defined characteristic of the economic heads of migrant families. One-half were under 35 years of age, and four-fifths were under 45. In contrast only one-third of the heads of all resident relief families were under 35, and only three-fifths were under 45. Among male heads of families in the general population about one-half were under 45. This distribution indicates the presence of many infants and school-age children in the migrant families; and, indeed, four-fifths of the children in these families were under 15 and one-third were under 5 years of age.

2. Migrant families were small families. Well over half contained only two or three members. The average family size was 3.1 persons, significantly less than the size of both resident relief families and families in the general population (excluding 1-person families).

3. Migrant families were preponderantly native-born white families. By comparison with the general population, foreign-born and Negro migrant family heads were underrepresented. These two minority groups were overrepresented, however, in the resident relief popu-

lation, showing that although more frequently victims of the depression, these groups nevertheless tended to remain immobile. During recent decades the foreign-born have tended to settle in large industrial centers and to group themselves according to racial or national ties. These ties have acted as deterrents to migration, despite limited economic opportunity and recurring unemployment. Moreover, local prejudice outside the highly industrialized areas makes the migration of distressed foreign-born persons more difficult than of the native-born. Custom and prejudice operate to restrict the mobility of Negro families just as effectively.

4. There was a small incidence of separation, widowhood, and divorce among the family groups. Among migrant family heads the proportion that were separated, widowed, or divorced was less than that found in the general population.

5. Migrant family members had a higher level of schooling completed than the heads of either the urban or rural resident relief population. Some of the difference between the school attainment of migrant and resident relief families is attributable to the youth of the migrant group and to the underrepresentation of Negroes. In any event, it is clear that migration was not caused by lack of education.

OCCUPATIONAL RESOURCES

Well over half of the economic heads of migrant families were fully employable. One-third were employable with certain handicaps, consisting principally of chronic illness, physical handicaps, and age. One-ninth of the economic heads were totally unemployable; women heads with dependent children made up a majority of this group, which also included the aged and totally disabled.

Thus, a majority of the economic heads of migrant families were able to work, willing to work, and within the preferred age-range for private employment. Because of physical handicaps and age, the employability of the next largest group was qualified to some extent. There remained a small group of families with unemployable heads; for these families, it is clear that public assistance through old-age and disability benefits and aid to dependent children was the only means by which stability could be assured.

In terms of main class of usual occupation, migrant family heads were markedly "higher" than the heads of resident relief families, and they compared favorably with the gainful workers 10 years of age and over in the general population. There were fewer unskilled and more skilled workers among migrant family heads than among either the resident relief population or the gainful workers in the 1930 Census. White-collar workers were also overrepresented among migrant family heads by comparison with resident relief workers, though they were greatly underrepresented by comparison with gainful workers in the general population.

The greatest number of skilled and semiskilled migrant family heads were building and construction workers. Among the unskilled migrant family heads, manufacturing, agriculture, and domestic service were represented in about equal proportion. The principal white-collar groups were farm owners, salesmen, storekeepers, musicians, technical engineers, and clergymen.

In terms of usual industry, migrant family economic heads were underrepresented in agriculture by comparison both with the economic heads of resident relief families and with gainful workers in the general population. This underrepresentation reflects the basically urban background of the families in transient bureaus. Migrant family heads reported a larger proportion usually engaged in trade and professional service than heads of resident relief families. Otherwise, the two groups showed about equal representation in the broad industrial classifications.

It is significant that the great majority of the families were not usually migratory workers. The detailed occupational and industrial analysis reveals, however, that a large proportion of the family heads customarily followed pursuits that permitted migration with little loss. There was, for example, a large concentration of skilled workers in building, of semiskilled machine operators, and of unskilled workers, such as restaurant cooks, whose occupations can be followed equally well over a wide area.

Long unemployment involves a deterioration of skill which lowers the probability of reemployment. Accordingly, the information on the family heads' usual occupation and industry is qualified by the lapse of time since they last worked.

The average time elapsed since the migrant family heads' last employment at their *usual* occupation was 18.5 months. It was substantially less than the average duration of 30.3 months as reported in sample studies of urban workers on resident relief in 1934, or the average of 40.6 months for a sample of WPA workers in April 1936. The average time elapsed since the family heads' last job at *any* occupation was 7.8 months. For urban workers on relief the average was 22.7 months, and for WPA workers in the last quarter of 1935 it was 24.0 months. It is indicated that many families, while not usually migratory-casual workers, had turned to migratory-casual work after beginning migration. This fact not only implies low earnings on the road but also a lowered occupational status, and it qualifies to some extent the relatively high distribution of family heads in terms of main class of usual occupation.

The analysis of the occupational resources of migrant families suggests the probability of their return to self-support. Beginning with the families with unemployable economic heads, it is clear that if these families were to be absorbed by the new community of residence, it would be on the basis of a transfer of the relief obligation from the old community to the new. It should not be overlooked, however, that such a transfer was frequently socially desirable.

Many of the families with handicapped economic heads were well-equipped occupationally. Some of these families, however, had migrated to communities where their health might be improved but where the opportunities for securing adequate employment were not promising.

For the remaining and majority group, the fully employables, there appears to be little question that their migration could achieve the purpose of reestablishment in the new community.

Chapter I

REASONS FOR MIGRATION

DURING AND after the operation of the Federal transient program there was widespread public discussion of the effects of distress migration. Usually, however, these discussions have been concerned only with the real and imagined effects of this migration upon the resident population. Little effort was made to understand the real point of view of the migrants themselves. This neglect has given rise to popular acceptance of strange theories about the causes of migration, theories which prevent any understanding and hinder any solution of the problem. It seems plain that an understanding of distress migration must include some knowledge of what it meant to the migrant. The depression migrants' own point of view is clearly revealed in the causes the families reported in explaining their migration.

Although there is a considerable body of information available on the generalized causes of population mobility, little is known of the way in which these causes directly affect individuals. In order to learn the individuals' own explanation for the migration which eventually led to relief at transient bureaus, two questions were asked each of the families interviewed for this study:

(1) Why did you leave the community where you last maintained a settled, self-supporting residence?

(2) Why did you select one particular place, to the exclusion of other places, as your destination?

The answers to these questions are the basis for the present chapter.[1]

---

[1] The reasons for migration could not be determined for about one-fifth of the 5,489 families included in this study. It was impossible, by definition, to derive reasons for the migration of the families which had no settled residence. This group of families consisted of those which had not been settled and self-supporting since 1929 and of those which had not been settled and self-supporting since the time the families were formed, if this event occurred after 1929. Although these families must be excluded from the study of reasons for migration, they are the subject of special analysis in ch. III.

At first glance it may seem impossible to reduce the description of so complex an action as depression migration to simple terms for statistical analysis. With a small number of cases this would be true, but examination of many descriptions reveals that they tend to form patterns and that each pattern centers around one common reason that predominates throughout the entire class of similar situations. Moreover, the complexity of the answers which the families gave was reduced by recognizing that the reasons for migration are necessarily composed of two complementary factors: the reason for leaving one specific place and the reason for selecting another specific place.

The problems involved in statistical presentation of the reasons for migration will be evident from an examination of the families' own statements. At the end of this chapter will be found typical reasons reported by 15 typical families. A review of two histories in which particularly complex circumstances are involved will illustrate both the complexity of motivation and the method by which the complexity has been reduced. The Krugers, for example (see history 6, p. 23), migrated from Chicago to San Antonio, Tex., because of (1) unemployment, (2) inability to get resident relief, (3) eviction, and (4) free transportation to San Antonio. The fact that a friend who was driving to Texas was willing to take them with him does not explain the Krugers' move from Chicago, although it *does explain* the selection of their destination. Economic distress arising out of difficulty in obtaining employment or relief and culminating in eviction for nonpayment of rent was the expulsive force that explains why the Krugers were ready to leave Chicago.

The Mosher family (see history 9, p. 23) had long wanted to leave Alabama for the North, but it was not until the death of a brother in Chicago that their move finally took place. The fact that the Moshers had difficulty making a living on an Alabama farm, plus the inadequacy of the relief they received, explains why they wished to leave Alabama; and the death of a relative in the North explains their selection of a particular destination.

The first step in the analysis was to differentiate between the reasons for leaving settled residence and the reasons for selecting a particular destination. The cause of migration always presents two aspects, either directly or by implication. In terms of the place of origin, the cause of migration manifests itself as economic or personal *inadequacies* associated with the community of origin. This aspect may be isolated as the reason for leaving settled residence.[2] In terms of

---

[2] Reason for leaving settled residence was defined as the force, associated with the community of settled residence, which made the families susceptible to the idea of moving.

the place of destination, the cause of migration consists in the expected *advantages* associated with the community of destination. In this aspect the cause of migration is manifested as the reason for selecting a particular destination.[3]

The reason for leaving one place and the reason for selecting another were, of course, two sides of the same coin. It must be remembered that neither reason by itself contains the full explanation of migration. Although the two sets of reasons are tabulated separately, each contains but part of the explanation and the complete explanation must consider both. Moreover, it is important to note that the inadequacies of the place of origin and the advantages of the place of destination were not absolute, but relative to each other. In earlier internal American migrations the "inadequacy" of the places of origin consisted to a large degree in the substantial advantages of cheap land and speculation in new country and in the extensive job opportunities that resulted from the rapid expansion of industry. After 1929, however, this situation was reversed, and destinations frequently came to have advantages only by comparison with the desperate conditions which existed in the communities in which migrants had been settled.

The reasons for leaving settled residence and the reasons for selecting a particular destination, although considered separately, involved special complexities in the reports of many families. In most cases, however, these complexities were merely different aspects of the same general circumstances. In both of the family cases that have been cited, the generic reason for leaving a settled residence was economic distress. For the Krugers, this distress manifested itself as unemployment, inadequate relief, and finally as eviction. Because it was not possible to classify all three of these related circumstances, the one which came last in point of time was selected.[4] The Krugers' reason for leaving settled residence, accordingly, was classified as eviction; and the fact of eviction carries the implication of the other economic difficulties even though they are not specified.[5]

---

[3] Reasons for selection of destination were classified in two ways: first, according to the nature of each family's contact at the destination; and second, according to the basic and secondary objective sought by each family at the destination.

[4] The logic of this distinction lay in the fact that it isolated "the last straw" as a principal reason.

[5] A few families reported a complex reason in which the different factors were not generically related as in the instance cited above. For example, a few families reported that in addition to being unemployed, the health of some member was injured by the climate at the place of settled residence. When such unrelated circumstances were reported, the reason for migration which was classified does not carry the implication of the additional reasons reported by the families. However, a separate tabulation showed only 15 percent of the families reporting this type of complex reason for migration.

REASONS FOR LEAVING SETTLED RESIDENCE

During the depression the transient problem led many newspapers to express the fear that the country was being "overrun" by "dead-beats" who should be promptly "sent home" and made to stay there. The same line of comment was usually accompanied by a special theory that the motivation behind distress migration was the migrants' moral incompetence to maintain stability. The families were said to have left home because they enjoyed travel; and when the FERA transient program reached full operation, the phrase "at Government expense" was added to this explanation.

More realistic answers to the question of why the families migrated are suggested in the 15 case histories. A number of families, as the histories show, had no "homes" at which they could have stayed or to which they might have been returned (see histories 10 and 15, pp. 24 and 25). Nearly all the families which started migration from a settled residence reported frankly that the situation at their settled residence, as far as their own prospects were concerned, had become quite hopeless.[6]

These 15 histories indicate several of the particular sources of this dissatisfaction, such as unsuccessful search for work, inability to earn a living on farms, inadequate relief, unwillingness to be a burden upon relatives, and ill-health. A comprehensive view of the relative importance of these and other basic reasons for leaving settled residence is presented in table 1.

A Distress Migration

The charge that migrant families were out to see the country at no expense to themselves had little basis (table 1). Nearly all the families were in more or less acute distress at the time they left settled residence. Only 6 percent of the families were in no particular difficulties. Of these the majority had jobs that required traveling; the remainder simply left their jobs and businesses and proceeded to another place that appeared to have greater advantages.

Economic difficulty was by far the most important of the basic reasons for migration. More than two-thirds of the families were primarily in economic distress, chiefly through long unemployment, inadequate earnings, the loss of farms or businesses, and inadequate relief. The size of this group clearly stamps the movement as being, above all, a migration of depression-stricken families.

About one-fourth of the families were in personal distress of varying seriousness. The most important single difficulty listed in this group was illness necessitating a change to a different climate or to a com-

---

[6] Migrant families usually protested vigorously against returning to the locality of settled residence (see histories 5, 6, 9, and 11, pp. 22, 23, and 24).

Table 1.—Reason Migrant Families Left Settled Residence

Reason for leaving settled residence	Migrant families
Total	4,247
	Percent distribution
Total	100
Economic distress	69
Unemployment [1]	40
Inadequate earnings [1]	7
Unable to work in particular community [1]	3
Farming failure [1]	8
Business failure [1]	3
Inadequate relief	3
Unwilling to be on relief [1]	1
Evicted from home	2
Relatives unable to continue support	1
Miscellaneous economic difficulties	1
Personal distress	25
Ill-health [1]	11
Domestic trouble [1]	6
Disliked separation from relatives or friends	4
Community disapproval [1]	1
Personal dislike of community [1]	2
Miscellaneous personal difficulties	1
Not in distress	6
Job required traveling	3
Left job	2
Left farm	*
Left business	1
Other	*

* Less than 0.5 percent.

[1] For detailed breakdown see appendix table 1.

NOTE.—81 families, whose reason for leaving settled residence was not ascertainable, are not included.

munity in which medical care was available; and of somewhat less importance were domestic trouble, the desire to rejoin relatives because of homesickness or because the relatives needed help, and the desire to leave a community in which a member of the family had died.

It should be remembered that the hard-and-fast division of the families into those whose distress was primarily either economic or personal often oversimplifies complex motives. Personal difficulties doubtless lay at the root of the economic distress of many families, especially of those which reported that they were ashamed to apply for relief or that their relatives could no longer support them.

It is probable that to an even greater extent economic hardships were the cause of personal distress reported by the families. Much of the domestic trouble shown in table 1 consisted of quarrels between a family and its relatives over the sharing of living expenses. All the families which migrated because of dislike of the community were also unemployed. The instances of desertion and divorce were often directly related to the inability of the economic head to support his family, and community disapproval was more often than not the result of antisocial behavior growing out of unemployment.

Several of the classifications shown in table 1 require detailed analysis and clarification.

Unemployment

Unemployment was the most frequently reported reason for leaving settled residence. Two-fifths of the families migrated primarily because they saw no prospect of further work in the community in which they had once considered themselves permanent residents.

Obviously the fact of unemployment does not by itself explain the migration of these families. Most of the millions of American families which were unemployed during the depression did not go to other States in search of work. An equally important part of the explanation of the migration of these families lies in the advantages they expected at their destinations.

The great majority of the families reporting unemployment as their basic reason for leaving settled residence attributed their unemployment directly to the depression itself, rather than to long-time trends in industry or accidental events (appendix table 1). Almost three-fourths of them explained that they were unemployed because of depression retrenchment at the place they usually worked (see history 5, p. 22) or because of the slack demand for their skill—usually related to construction—in the community in which they had been settled (see history 6, p. 23). The remainder was divided about evenly into two groups. One group of family heads had lost their jobs through events not directly related to the depression—through discharge for cause, the retirement of managers whose favorites they were, or through nepotism (see history 1, p. 21). The other group attributed their unemployment to causes which would probably have necessitated migration regardless of the depression—to the completion of a job of definite duration in seasonal occupations, to the effects of the drought, or to the migration of industry.

Inadequate Earnings

A number of families reported that they had been more or less regularly employed until the time they left their settled residence, but that they were dissatisfied with the amount of their earnings (table 1). Most of these families added that they were actually unable to live on the income their jobs provided. The cause of their low earnings was attributed most frequently to a reduction to part-time work. Less important causes were seasonal employment, lowered occupational status, and reduced wages (appendix table 1).

Unable to Work in a Particular Community

This classification, although relatively unimportant among the other causes of economic distress, is nevertheless significant in that it isolates a special migration problem. The heads of the families included in this group had been definitely eliminated from the labor market in the community where they had been settled, but they were partially or wholly employable in other communities. The greater part of this group consisted of persons who had developed occupational diseases which prevented further work at their usual occupation—of copper miners, for example, who had left Butte because they had developed lung trouble and had been advised by their doctors to try to find lighter work in a warmer climate. A few families included in this category left because the bad name of some member had made it impossible for any of the family to find work (appendix table 1).

Farming Failure

Farm owners and tenants who had been displaced from the land did not comprise a large part of the migrant families studied. As against the 40 percent who reported unemployment, only 8 percent reported displacement from the land as the basic reason for leaving settled residence.

Only slightly more than one-tenth of the families primarily in economic distress were farming failures. More than half of these families were drought refugees. A very small number left farms which had been ruined by floods. The remainder, constituting more than a third of the families reporting farming failure, was made up largely of evicted tenants; all the agricultural regions contributed to this group in about equal proportions (appendix table 1).

Other Economic Difficulties

Another group—slightly larger than the group reporting farming failure as their basic reason for leaving settled residence—migrated because of special problems growing out of all the economic difficulties that have been discussed (appendix table 1). These families were separately recorded because of the fact that their unemployment, failure as farmers, etc., would not have caused migration had it not been for the added difficulties. The largest classification in this group contained those families which reported that they either could not get relief at all or were unable to live on the relief they received (see history 9, pp. 23–24). A somewhat smaller group left settled residence to avoid the embarrassment of being on relief in a community in which they were well known. The rest of this miscellaneous group was made up of families evicted from their homes (see history 6, p. 23), those which had become too heavy a burden upon their relatives (see history 7, p. 23), and a few which left because of such reasons as pressing debts and the high cost of living.

Ill-Health

The psychological, case-work "solution" to the problem of aiding needy nonresidents, as well as the more realistic approach in terms of economic readjustment, both overlook one extremely important cause of the migration of destitute families. As table 1 shows, the second largest single reason for leaving settled residence was ill-health. Approximately one-tenth of the families began migration primarily because of the illness of some member of the family.

It is significant that so many health seekers participated in this depression migration. As recovery began and as the numbers displaced by unemployment declined, the proportion of health seekers—whose distress is only indirectly related to depression—would be expected to increase. Future efforts toward the solution of the transient problem must take this important cause of mobility into full account.

Only about one-eighth of the families reporting ill-health as the primary cause of migration left settled residence to seek medical care in another community. By far the greater part of these families moved because of the climate in the place where they had been settled (appendix table 1). Many families, containing tubercular patients, had been advised to leave damp climates or areas in which there had been severe dust storms. Frequently reported, also, were persons who had to leave high altitudes because of heart trouble, persons with asthma, persons who could not stand severe winters, and families in which members were suffering from malaria.

Domestic Trouble

Domestic trouble was the basic reason for the migration of a relatively small group of families, comprising 6 percent of the total. The majority of these families migrated because of trouble between husband and wife; of these, separations and divorces accounted for nearly all, while desertion was a relatively insignificant cause. Among the rest of this group quarrels between a family and its relatives and the death of husband, wife, or parents were reported with about equal frequency (appendix table 1).

Disliked Separation From Relatives or Friends

Approximately 1 family in each 25 reported that it left its settled residence because of personal distress growing out of separation from its relatives. Often the wife was homesick and wanted to be near her parents. Other families had received word that their relatives were destitute or were ill, and they had left settled residence to rejoin their relatives and to help them.

Other Personal Difficulties

A few families left settled residence for other personal reasons. Some reported that they had been either directly compelled to leave (see history 11, p. 24) or had been made so uncomfortable that they wanted to leave. Another group, comprising 2 percent of all families, reported that they personally disliked the climate, the foreigners, or some other feature of the community. A handful of families reported such other miscellaneous reasons as fear of earthquakes and flight from the Cuban revolution and from vigilante terror in East Arkansas.

REASONS FOR SELECTING DESTINATION

The fact that such a preponderant number of migrant families left their settled residence in distress provides but half the explanation of their migration. It is necessary to turn at this point to the second and equally important half of that explanation contained in the reported reasons for the selection of a particular destination.

Families With No Destination

Actually, the families were seldom literally driven from their homes by adversity. Their migration rarely resulted from a simple choice between either leaving settled residence or facing utter disaster. Despite the hardships which the families reported, only a very few left settled residence without a particular destination in mind. Of the families which began migration from a community in which they had been settled and self-supporting, 92 percent intended to proceed to a specific place (table 2). Only 8 percent set out with no destinations at all or with such vague destinations as "the West," "eastern Colorado," or "the cotton fields" in mind.

Table 2.—Migrant Families With and Without Specific Destination and Reason for No Destination

Destination	Migrant families
Total_____	4, 328
	Percent distribution
Total_____	100
Specific destination_____	92
No specific destination_____	8
Seeking work_____	4
Migratory occupation_____	2
Other_____	1
Not ascertainable_____	1

As table 2 shows, one-half of the families without destinations set out to travel from community to community in search of work (see history 5, p. 22). A smaller group left settled residence to follow migratory work, such as cotton picking, sugar-beet work, or carnival and circus work. A third group—made up of health seekers without specific destination, those trying to find relatives, and those who simply set out to wander with no particular purpose in mind—comprised only 1 percent of the families.

Type of Contact at Destination

Those families which did intend that their migrations should end in a specific, predetermined place very rarely reported a capricious and unreasoning choice of their destination.[7] Migrations based upon a long and desperate gamble that conditions might be improved were decidedly not the rule though they were sometimes reported. The families studied showed a clear tendency to migrate only when the probability of an improved status appeared to be reasonably high (table 3).

Table 3.—Type of Contact Migrant Families Had at Destination

Type of contact at destination	Migrant families
Total	3,899
	Percent distribution
Total	100
Definite contact	80
Former residence of family or members of family	12
Residence of relatives or close friends	43
Particular skill of family head in demand at destination	2
Other definite contact [1]	23
No definite contact	20
Heard rumors that locality had advantages	16
Attracted by advertising	1
Chance selection of destination [2]	3

[1] Includes such contacts as letters of recommendation, job transfers, physicians' referral of health cases, purchase or trade of homes or farms, etc.
[2] Includes families which happened to get a ride, which were driven to nearest place of refuge, etc.

NOTE.—429 families, whose type of contact at destination or reason for selecting destination was not ascertainable, which had no destination, or whose place of destination was not ascertainable, are not included.

That the family migrations were essentially cautious rather than quixotic is indicated in table 3, which shows the types of contact that attracted the families to the destination they chose. Slightly more than half of the families chose a destination in which there were close personal friends or relatives who were more or less obligated to assist them (table 3). Friends or relatives lived at the destination of 43 percent of the families, and an additional 12 percent, returning to a place in which they had formerly resided, probably had even more valuable and numerous contacts at their destination.

[7] Several families driven out by dust storms reported that they had selected particular places on the Pacific coast as their destinations because they wanted to live at the greatest possible distance from the Dust Bowl. Such explanations were very infrequently reported.

During the depression it was a common occurrence for the groups most seriously affected by reduced earnings to double-up within one household. Pooled resources increased the security of all, and the crowding together of many people under one roof reduced the total cost of rent and heat. The large proportion of migrant families moving to places where they had relatives or close friends suggests that the same expedient played a substantial part in setting into motion the families studied. The principal difference between this particular group of migrant families and the nonmigrants who pooled their resources was that the migrants had to cross a State boundary in the process.

In addition to the families which returned to a former residence and those which moved to a community in which relatives or friends resided, a third large group of families also had a definite contact at their destination. This group, comprising 23 percent of the families with destinations, was made up of families which chose their destinations because of such specific entrees as letters of recommendation to employers, the sight-unseen purchase of farms or homes, satisfactory reports of employment opportunity through correspondence, and employment office direction.

Finally, a small group of families with none of the three types of specific contacts discussed had destinations in a community where the special skills of the economic head would in all probability have been in demand. This group included such people as foundry and rolling mill workers who migrated from one steel town to another, textile workers moving to another cotton mill town, and meatcutters moving to Kansas City.

The total number of families with definite contacts at their destination comprised nearly four-fifths of the families. It is thus clear that the families were generally neither foolhardy nor particularly adventurous in undertaking the migration which involved assistance from transient bureaus. Least of all were they intent upon seeing the country at the Government's expense. Instead, they were, in general, distressed groups which saw a reasonable solution to their problems through migration to another community. The essence of the migration studied is contained in this fact.

A minority of the families, comprising about one-fifth of the total group, were an exception to this generalization. As table 3 shows, 20 percent of the families selected a destination with which they had no definite links of any sort. The greater part of these families were attracted by vague rumors that times were good or that the climate was healthful at the place of destination. A few of them were attracted by advertised economic advantages. There were frequent instances of migration to submarginal land that had been incorrectly advertised to be rich, productive soil from which a good living could be made.[8] After making a down payment on the land, the families discovered that it was either worthless or that the cost of improving it was beyond their means; and at the time the families were interviewed, all had abandoned the farms to which advertising had attracted them. Finally, there was a residual group whose definite destinations had been selected through sheer chance. These were families which "happened to get a ride" to a particular place (see history 6, p. 23), those whose destinations were determined by special bus rates, and those which selected their destinations for "no particular reason."

Objectives Sought at Destination

What the families hoped for at their destination was a solution to the basic problems which had confronted them at their settled residence. Accordingly the particular advantages they sought were generally the obverse of the kind of distress they reported as their reason for leaving settled residence. The relative importance of the different objectives reported by the families is shown in table 4.

Economic Betterment

Approximately four-fifths of the families selected their destination primarily in hope of economic betterment. The greater part of these—and indeed the majority of all the families—were seeking employment. Second in importance was a destitute group made up of a substantial number of unemployables (see ch. VI, p. 111) who migrated to the homes of relatives or friends in the expectation that they would be taken in and helped until they were able to support themselves again. These families, together with those seeking employment, made up almost the entire group which reported that they sought economic betterment at their destination.

All other kinds of economic betterment sought are conspicuously small. Only 5 percent of the families intended to take up land as either owners or tenants. About half that number planned to open a small business establishment of their own. Although 4 percent of the families left settled residence primarily because of distress related specifically to relief, only 1 percent of the families had relief as their basic objective at their destination. A handful of families selected their destination in order to be in a place where living costs would be cheaper, in order to look after property, to prospect for gold, or to trap (see footnote 1, table 4).

---

[8] For instance advertising circulars described submarginal land in the two poorest agricultural counties in the State of Washington in this way: "Soil sub-irrigated, black, silt, and sand loam; abundant water supply; numberless trout streams * * *. A farmer can start with small capital and work into a beautiful farmhome with all modern advantages close at hand." A letter in the files of the Works Progress Administration Division of Social Research tells of one farmer "remarking grimly that a certain lumber company [which advertised its cut-over properties as productive farm land] was responsible for more bankrupt farmers in eastern Washington and northern Idaho than the depression itself."

Table 4.—Objectives Sought by Migrant Families at Destination

Objectives sought at destination	Migrant families
Total_____	4,005
	Percent distribution
Total_____	100
Economic betterment_____	79
Employment_____	57
Promise of work_____	14
Hoped to find work_____	43
Farm_____	5
Had arranged to secure farm_____	1
Hoped to secure farm_____	4
Business_____	3
Had arranged to open business_____	1
Hoped to open business_____	2
Help from relatives or friends_____	11
Relief_____	1
Cheaper cost of living_____	1
Miscellaneous economic objectives [1]_____	1
Personal objectives_____	21
Healthful climate or medical care_____	10
To rejoin relatives_____	8
Sentiment_____	1
Miscellaneous personal objectives [2]_____	2

[1] Include such reasons as: to take advantage of special bus rate, to collect debts, to look after property, to buy fruit to peddle, to bet on horse races, to prospect for gold, to trap fur-bearing animals, etc.
[2] Include such reasons as: to seek safety from vigilante mobs, to take a vacation, happened to get a ride, to follow the voice of God, to march in the bonus army, to seek revenge, to put children in school, etc.

NOTE.—323 families, whose place of destination or reason for selecting destination was not ascertainable and which had no destination, are not included.

However cautious the families may have been, the specific economic betterment which they sought was more often hoped for than promised. Table 4 shows how many families left settled residence with the positive assurance that they would find employment, farms, and businesses, and how many were only more or less vaguely hopeful of securing them. While 43 percent of the families *hoped* to find work at their destination, only 14 percent had been promised work; 3 percent hoped to secure a farm, as against 1 percent which had already rented or bought a farm before reaching their destination; and 2 percent *hoped* to open a business, as against 1 percent which had definitely arranged to open a business before moving.

Although this general view of the families' economic prospects shows that few had a definite promise of work when migration began, it must be remembered that the majority of the families had contacts which appeared to promise them a measure of security at their destination. It is significant, moreover, that the families whose prospects for work were least definite tended to migrate most readily to a destination at which they had close personal ties. A separate tabulation showed that well over one-half of the families which merely hoped for work, but only about one-fifth of those promised work, migrated to a former residence or to the residence of relatives.

Personal Objectives

The chief objectives of 21 percent of the families were of a personal nature. Nearly half of these families were health seekers who had been advised by their physicians to move to a specific place for hospitalization or for a particular kind of climate. The only other important group, comprising 8 percent of the total, consisted of families which wished to rejoin their relatives for personal reasons—because of homesickness and loneliness, to nurse relatives who were ill, to be with dying relatives, or to attend the funeral of a relative who had died.

Sentimental reasons occupied an insignificant place among the reasons for selecting a particular destination. Such explanations as "the North always represented freedom and equality to us," or "we always wanted to live in Detroit," or "we always wanted to see the West" were reported, but not frequently. Such reasons were the principal motivation of only 1 percent of the families. Approximately the same number of families reported the usual remarkable assortment of non-classifiable reasons for selecting destination: to take a vacation, to follow the voice of God, to seek revenge, etc. (table 4, footnote 2).

REASONS FOR MIGRATION, BY STATE

The same pattern of causes which governed the migration of the families as a whole was also operative in each of the individual regions of the United States. Except in a few States where obviously peculiar conditions existed, families emigrating from widely dissimilar States reported the same reasons, distributed in much the same proportion. The reasons for selecting destinations, while somewhat more varied, also tended toward similarity in different parts of the United States. The amount of variation in the reported reasons for migration to and from the different States [9] is shown in figures 2, 3, and 4.

Reasons for Leaving Settled Residence, by State

Economic Reasons

Unemployment, the reason for leaving settled residence which was most frequently reported by the families as a whole, was also the most frequently reported reason in 29 of the 30 States and groups of States shown in figure 2. Its importance as the basic unsettling force was generally uniform, even among States with altogether dissimilar economic and social characteristics. For example, in 14 of the 30 groups unemployment accounted for 38 to 43 percent of the emigrating families. Among these 14 groups were such widely diverse

---

[9] Because of the small number of families moving to and from several States, two or more contiguous States were sometimes combined in figs. 2, 3, and 4. The same combinations used here are also used in ch. II, figs. 5–10.

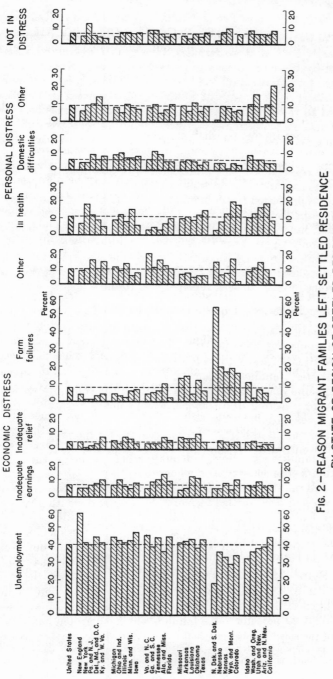

FIG. 2—REASON MIGRANT FAMILIES LEFT SETTLED RESIDENCE
BY STATE OR REGION OF SETTLED RESIDENCE

Note: Dotted lines represent average for United States.

Source: Appendix table 2.

AF–2851, WPA

sections as New York, and Pennsylvania and New Jersey; Kentucky and West Virginia; Georgia and South Carolina; Oklahoma, Arkansas, and Utah and Nevada; and Arizona and New Mexico (fig. 2 and appendix table 2).

The importance of unemployment as a displacing force was consistently below the average in the States of the central and northern Plains—Nebraska, Kansas, Colorado, Wyoming and Montana, and, above all, North Dakota and South Dakota—where farming failures were reported more frequently than elsewhere.

Inadequate earnings as a reason for leaving a settled residence were also reported in a generally uniform proportion throughout the country. Only one consistent regional variation may be observed in figure 2; families leaving the Southern States—Tennessee, Alabama and Mississippi, Florida, Louisiana, and Oklahoma—reported inadequate earnings in slightly higher proportions than families emigrating from other regions. In Alabama and Mississippi, where this cause was most important, however, it accounted for only 13 percent of the families leaving as against an average of 7 percent for the country as a whole.

Regardless of how much relief standards may have differed throughout the United States, inadequate relief [10] displaced about the same proportion of families in each of the 30 State groups. Such variations as occurred had only a slight consistency by sections. In a number of Southern States, for example, inadequate relief displaced a proportion of families slightly above the average; the proportion was highest in Oklahoma and was above the average in Kentucky and West Virginia, Florida, Louisiana, Arkansas, and Alabama and Mississippi. Yet in other Southern States where in all probability the same resident relief policies existed—in Georgia and South Carolina, in Tennessee, Virginia and North Carolina, and in Texas—the proportion of families reporting inadequate relief was below the average proportion in the country as a whole.

Farming failure displaced slightly more than half the migrant families which had been settled in North Dakota and South Dakota. In these two States the immediate cause of farming failures was in nearly every instance a long record of agricultural depression climaxed by total crop failure in the 1934 drought. It is significant, however, that the drought dominated the movement from the Dakotas alone. In no other State or region did the proportion displaced from the land exceed one-fifth of the total number of emigrants. In five Plains States—Nebraska, Kansas, Colorado, Wyoming, and Montana—between 15 and 20 percent of the families which emigrated had failed

---

[10] In fig. 2 inadequate relief included the few families which were unwilling to apply for relief in their home communities.

to earn a living on farms. But in Oklahoma the proportion of farm failures was only 12 percent, and in Texas it was only 6 percent.

Other States which contain agricultural subregions lost an insignificant number of families because of farming failure. In Michigan, Minnesota, and Wisconsin, in which the Lake States Cut-Over region lies, the proportion of migrant families which were displaced from the land was well below the national average. In both Arkansas and Missouri farming failure accounted for only one-seventh of all emigrating families. And in the Cotton States the proportion of farming failures varied from 4 percent in Virginia and North Carolina to a high of only 10 percent in Alabama and Mississippi.

Other economic distress, as shown on figure 2, included business failures, inability to work in a particular community, evictions, and other forms of economic distress which were shown separately in table 1. Accordingly, the rather wide variations which appear in this column of figure 2 are the result of several unrelated forces. In Virginia, Kentucky, and West Virginia the proportion of families reporting other economic distress was increased by the emigration of coal miners whose ill-health prohibited any future work in the mines. In Montana there was a similar emigration of many copper miners. The other economic distress in North Dakota and South Dakota consisted chiefly in the bankruptcy of small shopkeepers ruined by the drought. In Pennsylvania and New Jersey the bankruptcy of small merchants, as in lunchrooms or delicatessens, and the high cost of commutation from settled residence to a job once held were the principal forms of other economic explosive forces.

Personal Reasons

In the East ill-health was not a frequently reported cause of migration except in New York, and Pennsylvania and New Jersey, where tuberculosis necessitated a change of climate for many families. It is particularly significant that all Southeastern States except Florida reported a proportion far below the national average.

In the West ill-health was much more important as a reason for leaving settled residence. It caused the migration of 20 percent of the families leaving Wyoming and Montana, where ill-health resulting from severe winters was the chief complaint. The high proportion of health seekers leaving Minnesota also resulted from the cold winters. Health-resort States generally had a high proportion of emigrants reporting ill-health. Nearly one-fifth of the families leaving Arizona and New Mexico were motivated by ill-health, and approximately the same proportion left Colorado, where the high altitude caused heart ailments. The health seekers who left Texas were chiefly families from the urban areas or from the Panhandle which migrated because of tuberculosis.

Domestic trouble was infrequently reported in all States. It displaced 10 percent or less of the families from every geographical division except Georgia and South Carolina, where a high incidence of broken families raised the proportion to 11 percent. Other personal difficulties, including a number of such separate categories as absence of relatives, personal dislike of community, and community disapproval, were about uniformly reported in the different sections of the country.

Reasons for Selecting Destination, by State

Contacts at Destination, by State

In all the States combined, more than one-half the migrant families selected as their destination a community in which they had close personal contacts, and in addition about one-fourth were attracted by some other definite entree. Less than one-fourth had no definite contact at their destination. Against this average, one broad regional variation may be noted (fig. 3 and appendix table 3). Migrant families with destinations in the States east of the Mississippi River showed a more-than-average tendency to select as their destination a community in which they had formerly resided, or in which they had

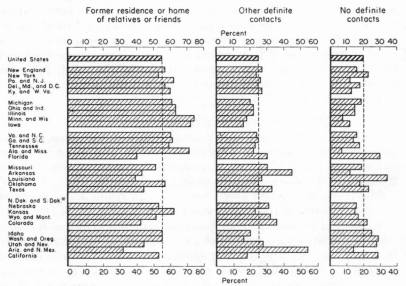

FIG. 3 – TYPE OF CONTACT OF MIGRANT FAMILIES AT DESTINATION BY STATE OR REGION OF DESTINATION

* Base too small for calculation.

Note: Dotted lines represent average for United States.

Source: Appendix table 3.

AF-2852, WPA

relatives or close personal friends. Conversely, the importance of rumor—indicated in the third column of figure 3—in attracting migrant families was most marked in the West and played a very small part in determining the movement of the families whose destinations were in the East.

As a result of special circumstances a few individual States had their own peculiar variations of this pattern. In Florida and Louisiana the proportion of families migrating to the place in which they had close personal contacts was far below average and the proportion attracted by rumor was very large. In Arkansas and Texas, with a high proportion of families migrating to the oil and cotton fields where seasonal work had been promised, the proportion reporting other definite entree was far above average. Other contact was also important for the families with destinations in Colorado, and Arizona and New Mexico, where the most frequently reported entree was a physician's referral.

Of the families with California destinations, the proportion moving to a community in which they had close personal contacts was 54 percent, approximately equal to the national average. The family movement into California, rather than being unique, thus appears to have been attracted by essentially the same general forces which dominated migrant family movement in the rest of the United States. Idaho, and Washington and Oregon, like California, reported about the average proportion of families attracted to places where they had relatives or close personal friends. It should be noted, however, that in three of these States somewhat more than the average proportion of families were attracted by rumor.

Objectives at Destination, by State

Just as unemployment was the chief reason for migrant families leaving settled residence in nearly every State, so a search for work was almost uniformly the most frequently reported objective of the families at their destination (fig. 4 and appendix table 4). In 27 of the 30 States and State groupings shown in figure 4, employment was the objective of the majority of the families.

Several States containing submarginal agricultural regions reported more than the average proportion of families whose objective was to secure a farm. In New England and Kentucky most of these families came from urban centers hoping to secure a farm to tide them through the depression. In the Mississippi Valley, on the other hand, these families were sharecroppers (as in Missouri and Arkansas) or tenants (as in Oklahoma and Nebraska) who were seeking to improve their status as farmers. The families intending to secure a farm in Idaho, and Washington and Oregon were made up of a heterogeneous group which took up submarginal farms on logged-off land.

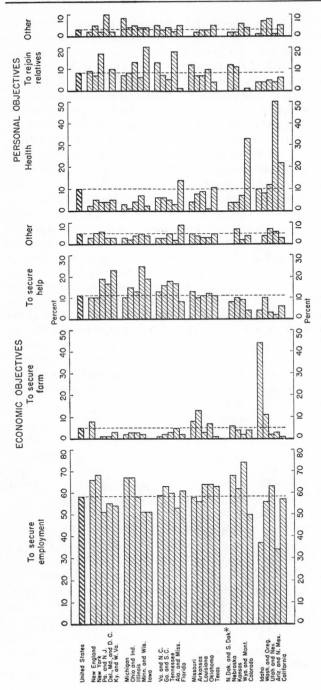

FIG. 4 – OBJECTIVES SOUGHT BY MIGRANT FAMILIES AT DESTINATION
BY STATE OR REGION OF DESTINATION

* Base too small for calculation.

Note: Dotted lines represent average for United States.

Source: Appendix table 4.

4F-2853, WPA

In any case, however, the proportion of families seeking a farm was generally very small. Only three of the geographical groupings shown in figure 4 had more than 10 percent of the families reporting the object of securing a farm at their destination, and only in Idaho [11] was the proportion above 15 percent. The preponderance of families seeking employment and the relative insignificance of those hoping to secure farms reflect the essentially urban-industrial perspective of the families which received assistance from FERA transient bureaus.

The proportion of families migrating to secure help from their relatives was far greater in the East than in the West. In the Southeastern States these were principally broken families, and the large proportion shown in figure 4 reflects the high incidence of domestic trouble reported in the Southern States (fig. 2). In the Midwestern States, on the other hand, the proportion of broken families was very small, and the large representation of those seeking help from relatives resulted from the doubling-up of complete families.

The destinations of health seekers made a simple and obvious pattern. Although the need for hospitalization attracted a few families into nearly every State, only six States and State groupings received more than the average proportion of these families. In the East Florida stood out, and in the West almost all States from Texas to California were above average. The highest proportion of all was reported for Arizona and New Mexico, where exactly half the families were health seekers. The next largest proportion was reported by Colorado, with 33 percent. California was third, with 22 percent of the families reporting that they had selected that destination hoping that the climate would improve their health.

FAMILY HISTORIES

1. THE SLADE FAMILY [12] settled in Dalhart, Tex., in 1932. A friend had opened a coalyard there and had invited Mr. Slade to come and manage the business for him. The job promised to be permanent. After a year had passed, however, the owner's destitute nephew arrived in Dalhart, and the owner felt obliged to give him Mr. Slade's job. A long search for another job in Dalhart was without success. The Slades decided that it would be utterly impossible to find work there. Accordingly, they packed their furniture and moved to Denver, where they had formerly lived. Mr. Slade found occasional odd jobs in Denver but could not support his wife and small son on his earnings.

[11] In Idaho the sample study was made only in Boise and Sand Point. Practically every transient bureau family under care at Sand Point had come to the community to take up logged-off land. For that reason, Idaho is represented as having a larger proportion of families which hoped to secure a farm at their destination than would have been shown had the migrant families in every Idaho transient center been included in this study.

[12] The names throughout this section are fictitious, and many of the places have been changed to conceal the identity of the families whose histories are described.

When their savings were all spent, they came to the transient bureau for help.

2. JIM KOVICH went to work as a rough carpenter in the Youngstown, Ohio, steel mills in 1925. He had steady work until he was caught in a general layoff in the spring of 1930. After that, his family lived on short-time jobs and savings for 4 years. Finally, in 1934 they had to go on relief. Mr. Kovich was very restless on relief, and when he heard from a friend that he might get work in Flint, Mich., he left his family in Youngstown and went to investigate the rumor. Within a month he found a job, and in March 1935 he sent for his wife and three children. In August he was laid off again. He had been unable to save any money on the job. In September the Koviches came to the transient bureau for help.

3. ROY HARRIS had been a West Virginia coal miner for 30 years. In the summer of 1934 the mine at which he had been working closed down. He was too old to get a job in another mine, and there was no hope of other work. The Harrises applied for resident relief but were unable to live on the allowance they received. Mr. Harris had a brother living in St. Louis. In the spring of 1935 Mr. and Mrs. Harris and the two children moved to St. Louis to try to locate the brother, who they thought could help them find work. When they found Mr. Harris's brother, he was unable to help them, and the family applied for transient relief.

4. HARRY LARSON worked out of Devils Lake, N. Dak., as a brakeman on the Great Northern. He lost his job in 1933. Since Devils Lake is principally a railroad town, there was no chance of finding other work there. Mrs. Larson had formerly lived on a farm in the northern Minnesota cut-over region. The couple believed that the best solution of their problem would be to return to Minnesota and take up a plot of land. This experiment soon failed. The frost ruined their first crop and left the couple stranded. The Larsons then moved to Duluth and went on transient relief.

5. GEORGE PASTOR, 40 years old, had been a cotton-mill worker in the Piedmont for 25 years. In 1928 he found a job in Greenville, S. C., where he remained for 7 years. In January 1935 the mill in which he worked began to lay off workers. Mr. Pastor was first reduced to 3 days' work a week, then to 2. Because there was no prospect that the mill would run full time soon, the Pastors and their two children set out to make the rounds of all the textile mills in the South to try to find work. When they arrived in New Orleans, Mr. Pastor was promised a job in a cotton mill as soon as it reopened a month later. Afraid to risk losing the chance to work, Mr. Pastor would not leave New Orleans. When they ran out of money, they came to the transient bureau for help until the mill reopened.

6. WILLIAM KRUGER had been working as a house painter in Chicago for 10 years. Work became harder and harder to find, and after September 1933 there was none at all. In the summer of 1934 the couple applied for relief, but while waiting for relief to be granted they were evicted from their home. On the same day, learning that a friend was preparing to drive to San Antonio, the couple persuaded him to let them go along. Mr. Kruger was unable to find work in San Antonio and the couple registered at the transient bureau. After 6 weeks they moved to Shreveport, La., where Mr. Kruger found a job driving a caravan of automobiles to Los Angeles. When they registered at the Los Angeles transient bureau, they were promptly returned to Chicago for resident relief. The Krugers were by now completely dissatisfied with Chicago. In June 1935, after 2 months in Chicago, Mr. Kruger found another job driving a caravan to San Francisco. They had been in the San Francisco transient bureau for 3 weeks when interviewed and insisted that they would not return to Chicago. Mr. Kruger had been promised a job as painter, and the couple proposed to settle down in California.

7. MR. AND MRS. ROBERTS were both over 70. Since 1929 they had been living in Kansas City on their small savings, on Mr. Roberts' earnings from light carpentry work, and on the contributions of their son. In 1932 they moved to Council Bluffs, Iowa, to help their son build a house. They lived in Council Bluffs for 3 years. In 1935 the son lost his job and in order not to be a burden Mr. and Mrs. Roberts moved back to Kansas City, where they owned a house that could not be rented. Meanwhile, they had lost their legal settlement status in Missouri, and when they needed relief they had to go to the transient bureau.

8. THE JOHNSON FAMILY raised cattle in Clark County, Kans. The dust storms of 1935 turned the farm into a waste of sand dunes. Moreover, Mr. Johnson and two of the children contracted "dust pneumonia." In desperation they wrote to a Spokane real estate office to inquire whether they could secure a plot of land there with little money. When they were informed that Washington had "good, cheap land and a pleasant climate," they decided to leave for Spokane immediately. The very next day they sold all the livestock for whatever it would bring, paid the grocery bill, piled their furniture in the the old Ford truck, and set out for Spokane. When they arrived there in June, their money had run out. They were unable to get any land and were forced to register at the transient bureau within a week after their arrival.

9. THE MOSHER FAMILY, consisting of Mr. and Mrs. Mosher and their eight children, were Negro farm owners in Russell County, Ala. Many of their friends and relatives had moved to Chicago in 1917

and 1918, and the Moshers had long wanted to move North also. After the depression they had an increasingly difficult time managing their farm. By 1933, after they could no longer support themselves on the earnings, they applied for relief. The relief offered them was inadequate. In November 1934 Mrs. Mosher's brother died in Chicago, and she and two of the children were given a ride North to attend the funeral. When they arrived in the North they found it much to their liking. They sent word back to Alabama for the rest of the family to follow them. The Mosher children started North one by one, and by September 1935 six of them had arrived. In August 1935 the family had to apply for transient relief. Chicago social workers were not successful in persuading them to return to Alabama, and the family was to be dropped from the rolls on October 1. Their plans were to try not only to stay in Chicago but also to bring the rest of the family North to join them.

10. "DR." HUNT and his wife had been constantly on the road since they were married in 1930. Dr. Hunt, a quack, had devised a cure for all human ailments. He had been making a living by peddling his nostrums from city to city, and by 1935 he had visited every State with his cures. Feeling an urge at that time to settle down, he stopped off in Pittsburgh. He planned to open a "foot clinic" in Pittsburgh and to establish permanent quarters in which to manufacture his cure for varicose veins. Meanwhile, he applied for relief at the transient bureau.

11. JACK CARSON lost his job as switchman in Nashville in 1931. He and his wife then went into the bootlegging business. In 1933 they were caught by the police and were given a prison sentence, suspended on the condition that they leave the State. In compliance the couple set out on a freight for the Southwest, where they understood they could find work picking cotton. Since 1933 they had been traveling about from place to place as migratory-casual workers picking cotton in Texas and New Mexico and picking berries in Arkansas. They had become extremely dissatisfied with this work, and when they were interviewed in Milwaukee, they declared that they intended to remain there if they had to go to jail.

12. HAZEL SMITH had married Ed Smith in 1932, soon after he arrived in Sand Point, Idaho, looking for a place to farm. The couple moved out to a plot of logged-off land near Sand Point. For 2 years they struggled to make the farm pay, but in 1935 they lost it. The couple and their small child had no place to go except to Mr. Smith's parents in San Diego. Upon arrival in San Diego they found that Mr. Smith's parents were on relief and unable to help. The family then proceeded to San Francisco, where they hoped to find work. There they registered at the transient bureau. Mr. Smith looked for

a job for a month, then suddenly he disappeared. After 3 months he had not been heard from.

13. JOE WATKINS had been a plumber in Tulsa, Okla. In 1934 his wife developed tuberculosis. The family physician told her that she would have to have a change of climate immediately and arranged for her to receive medical care in Phoenix, Ariz. Since Mrs. Watkins was too ill to travel alone, Mr. Watkins quit his job in Tulsa to accompany her. When the couple reached Albuquerque, Mrs. Watkins had a severe hemorrhage and was not able to proceed to Phoenix. After 6 months in Albuquerque their savings were gone, and they had to apply at the transient bureau for relief.

14. THE CAMPBELLS had been living with Mrs. Campbell's parents in Fort Smith, Ark., ever since they were married in 1933. The old folks became more and more insistent that they leave. In February 1935 Mr. Campbell received word from his brother that there were good chances for work in Los Angeles. Accordingly, the couple set out with their baby for Los Angeles. When they arrived they found work as farm laborers near San Bernardino, but when this work was ended, they had to apply for transient relief. The couple insisted that they be permitted to remain in California, which they greatly preferred to Arkansas.

15. THE BISHOPS felt that they had never been settled since they were married. Mr. Bishop had been a hotel clerk in New York, but he lost this job 1 week after his marriage. The Bishops then set out for Jacksonville, Fla., to visit an aunt. After a month in Jacksonville they started toward the Pacific coast. When they were interviewed in the El Paso transient bureau, they stated that they were on their way to California because they had always wanted to see the West.

Chapter II

ORIGINS AND MOVEMENT

DISTRESS AT the place of origin and reasonable expectation of betterment at the place of destination were shown in the preceding chapter to have been the motivation for the depression migration of most of the families studied. The geographical movements produced by the action of these forces are traced in this chapter, and the general trends are described.[1] These trends are then compared with the trends revealed in the record of internal American migration prior to 1930 in order to show the relationship between this distress migration and "normal" predepression population mobility.

Fortunately, there is available a record of the geographical mobility of all migrant families under care by transient bureaus in the United States, as well as those included in the representative sample on which this report is based. The origins and movement of the 29,885 interstate migrant families which were registered in FERA transient bureaus on June 30, 1935, are presented in figures 5–10.[2]

---

[1] It should be noted that the States in which the families were registered in transient bureaus were not necessarily the same States to which the *destination* discussed in the preceding chapter refers. A family's *destination* was the place to which it intended to migrate at the time of leaving a settled residence. The correspondence between the State of destination and the State of transient bureau registration was nevertheless large.

[2] Every 3 months beginning September 30, 1934, each State transient director reported the State of origin of all unattached and family transients under care on the last day of the quarter (FERA Form 304). The Quarterly Census report for June 30, 1935, rather than the sample on which this study is based, was used in drawing the origin and place-of-registration maps (figs. 5–10), the trend maps (figs. 11 and 12), and the rate-of-immigration and emigration maps (figs. 13 and 16). Although tests showed that the origin and place-of-registration data derived from the sample were almost identical with the data derived from the Quarterly Census, in the sample the absolute number of families migrating to and from certain States was so small as to make graphic illustration difficult.

The maps on the left side of these figures show the movement of migrant families out of the several States or regions represented. The corresponding maps on the right side of the page show the movement of migrant families into the State or region represented.[3]

MOVEMENT BETWEEN STATES

Geographical Scatter

At first glance, these maps appear to show a chaotic geographical scattering of families. The families leaving many States spread broadcast across the map, and many States attracted families from all parts of the country. This tendency is clearest on the maps showing the movement to and from the Northeastern and Midwestern States and is especially marked on the Illinois, Iowa, and Michigan maps.

To a lesser degree the same tendency characterized the movement to and from all other areas. Families from nearly all States found their way into a majority of the other States. On the average, the migrant families in each State on June 30, 1935, included families from 32 different States. At one extreme, families in New York, Illinois, and California transient bureaus came from all the other States. In the New Mexico transient bureaus, filled largely with health seekers, there were families from all States except New Hampshire and Delaware. At the other extreme, the transient bureaus of Maine had only 12 families under care, representing in all 7 States but including families from as far as Oklahoma and Nevada.

Also represented in the broad geographical scatter were such movements as from North Dakota to Virginia, from Montana to New Hampshire, Washington to Maryland, Rhode Island to Idaho. Inasmuch as about 30,000 families were involved, however, some long-distance migrations would be expected. The important fact, as the next section will show, is that long-distance migrations represent the extreme rather than the typical case of family migration.

Distance Traveled

Most of the migrations were confined within the general vicinity of the State in which they originated (figs. 5–10). On the maps this tendency is revealed by the clustering of the largest circles about the particular State represented. It is especially noticeable on the maps showing migration to and from the Eastern, Midwestern, and Southern States.

---

[3] Because space does not allow all States to be individually represented on the maps, two or more States are sometimes grouped on one map. When such combinations are made, the interchange of families between the States within the group is shown in the lower left corner of the map, as "Interstate, intraregional movement."

Fig.5–STATE OR REGION OF ORIGIN AND OF TRANSIENT BUREAU REGISTRATION OF MIGRANT FAMILIES

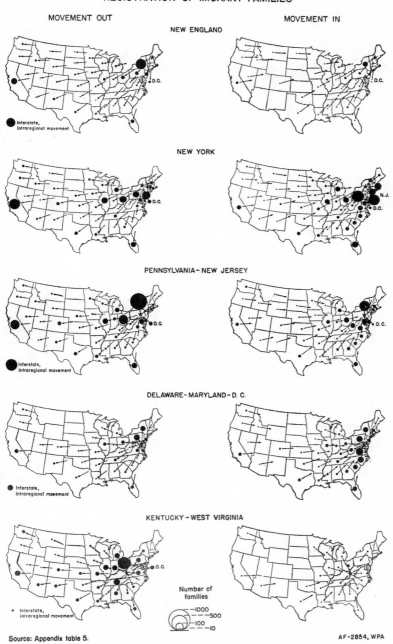

MOVEMENT OUT

MOVEMENT IN

NEW ENGLAND

NEW YORK

PENNSYLVANIA–NEW JERSEY

DELAWARE–MARYLAND–D. C.

KENTUCKY–WEST VIRGINIA

Number of families

Source: Appendix table 5.

AF-2854, WPA

FIG. 6-STATE OR REGION OF ORIGIN AND OF TRANSIENT BUREAU REGISTRATION OF MIGRANT FAMILIES

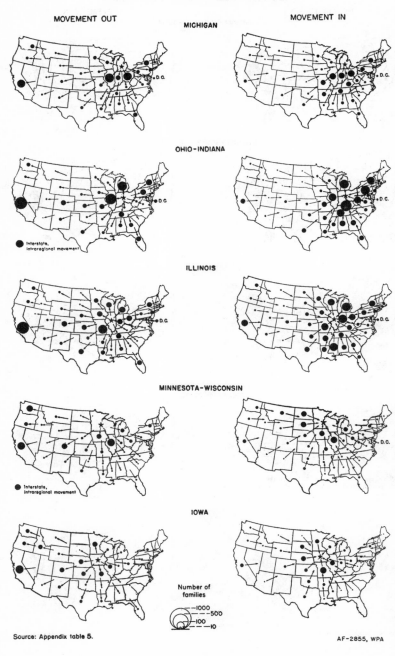

Source: Appendix table 5.

AF-2855, WPA

FIG.7–STATE OR REGION OF ORIGIN AND OF TRANSIENT BUREAU REGISTRATION OF MIGRANT FAMILIES

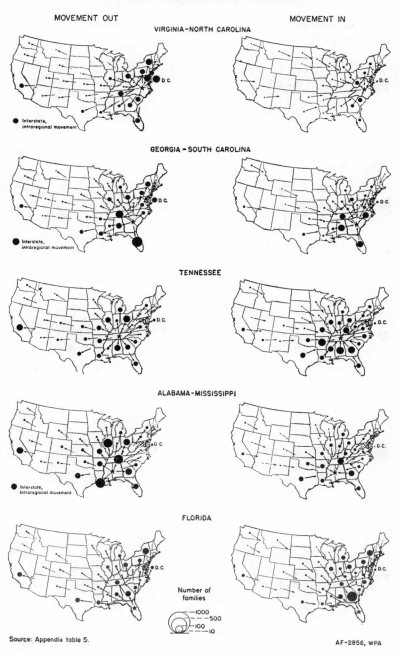

MOVEMENT OUT

MOVEMENT IN

VIRGINIA–NORTH CAROLINA

GEORGIA – SOUTH CAROLINA

TENNESSEE

ALABAMA–MISSISSIPPI

FLORIDA

Number of families

Interstate, intraregional movement

Source: Appendix table 5.

AF-2856, WPA

Fig.8–STATE OR REGION OF ORIGIN AND OF TRANSIENT BUREAU REGISTRATION OF MIGRANT FAMILIES

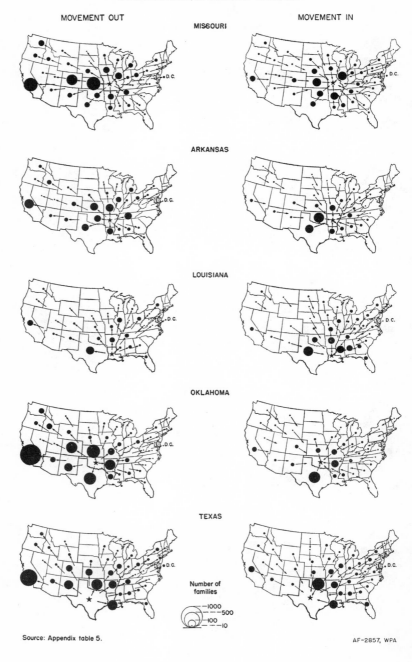

MOVEMENT OUT

MOVEMENT IN

MISSOURI

ARKANSAS

LOUISIANA

OKLAHOMA

TEXAS

Number of families

—1000
—500
—100
—10

Source: Appendix table 5.

AF-2857, WPA

FIG.9-STATE OR REGION OF ORIGIN AND OF TRANSIENT BUREAU REGISTRATION OF MIGRANT FAMILIES

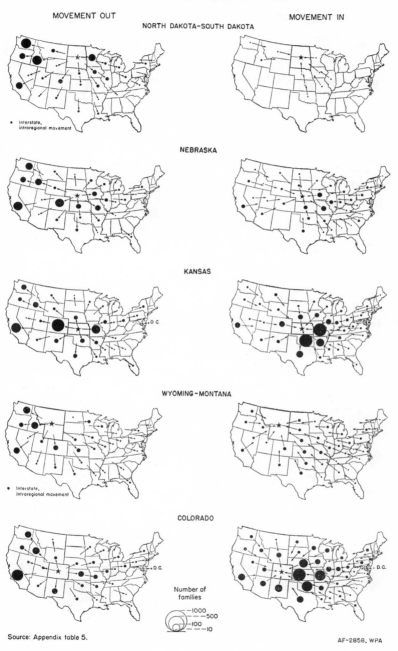

MOVEMENT OUT

MOVEMENT IN

NORTH DAKOTA-SOUTH DAKOTA

• Interstate, intraregional movement

NEBRASKA

KANSAS

WYOMING-MONTANA

• Interstate, intraregional movement

COLORADO

Number of families

—1000
—500
—100
—10

Source: Appendix table 5.

AF-2858, WPA

FIG.10-STATE OR REGION OF ORIGIN AND OF TRANSIENT BUREAU
REGISTRATION OF MIGRANT FAMILIES

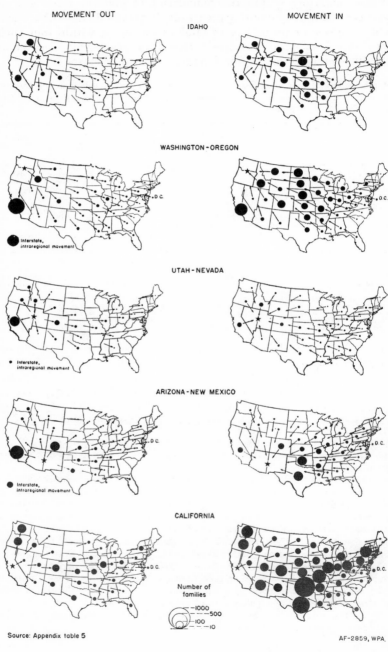

MOVEMENT OUT   MOVEMENT IN

IDAHO

WASHINGTON-OREGON

UTAH-NEVADA

ARIZONA-NEW MEXICO

CALIFORNIA

Number of
families

−1000
−−−500
−100
−−−10

Source: Appendix table 5   AF-2859, WPA.

Statistically this tendency may be measured by a count of the families migrating within the boundaries of uniform zones set up about each State, representing progressively greater distances traveled. Table 5 shows the proportion of families migrating within four such zones, based upon the distance between the geographical center of each State and the geographical center of all other States.[4]

Table 5.—Distance [1] Between State of Origin and State of Enumeration of Migrant Families [2] and of Persons in the General Population 1930 [3] Residing in a State Other Than State of Birth

Distance	Migrant families	General population, 1930
Total	29, 885	25, 388, 100
	Percent distribution	
Total	100	100
Zone 1 (to States 400 miles or less from center of State of origin)	38	53
Zone 2 (to States 401 to 1,500 miles from center of State of origin)	40	31
Zone 3 (to States 1,501 to 2,100 miles from center of State of origin)	19	13
Zone 4 (to States more than 2,100 miles from State of origin)	3	3

[1] Distance is measured in terms of straight line distance from the geographical center of the State of origin (or State of birth for the general population) to the geographical center of the State in which families were registered in transient bureaus (or State of 1930 residence for the general population), Geological Survey, "The Geographic Centers of the Continental United States and of the Several States," mimeographed release No. 22164, U. S. Department of the Interior, Washington, D. C., 1938.
[2] Division of Transient Activities, *Quarterly Census of Transients Under Care,* June 30, 1935, mimeographed report, Federal Emergency Relief Administration, Washington, D. C., 1935. 419 families from U. S. possessions or from foreign countries are not included.
[3] Bureau of the Census, *Fifteenth Census of the United States: 1930,* Population Vol. II, U. S. Department of Commerce, Washington, D. C., 1933, ch. 4, tables 32–34.

The first zone includes all the families migrating to a State whose geographical center is within a 400-mile radius of the center of the State in which they originated. Measuring from South Dakota, for example, this zone includes the States of North Dakota, Minnesota, Iowa, Nebraska, and Wyoming, but it does not include Montana.[5] On the average seven neighboring States are included within the 400-mile

[4] The United States Geological Survey's calculations of the center of each State's area were used as the basis for measuring the distance between centers of States.

Distance-traveled tables based upon the distance from State centers were the most practicable of the several that were tried. Zones based upon contiguity of States were abandoned because of the extremely wide divergence in the size of the areas covered. States contiguous to Maine, for example, comprise an area only one-seventieth as great as the area of States contiguous to Oklahoma.

It is interesting to note, however, that the Fifteenth Census classifies birth-residence data according to whether those moving were living in States adjacent to State of birth or living in other States. Of the 25,388,100 persons who, in 1930, were living in a State other than their State of birth, 48 percent were in adjacent States. For migrant families, on the other hand, only 40 percent were registered in States adjacent to States of origin.

[5] When the geographical center of a State comes within a particular zone, the entire State is included in that zone.

radius around any given State. For the next zone, where the radius is 1,150 miles, on the average 23 States are added to those in zone 1. Measuring from South Dakota again, the radius of 1,150 miles includes Virginia on the east, Texas on the south, and California on the west. The third zone includes families migrating within a radius of from 1,151 to 2,100 miles, and adds, on an average, the next 15 States in order of distance. Finally, the most distant zone includes the States whose geographical centers are more than 2,100 miles from a given State, and comprises an average of the three most distant States from a given State.

Each decennial census of population records the number of persons who are residing on the census date in a State other than their State of birth. Although obviously not strictly comparable with the data on migrant families, the census data do reveal the long-time mobile behavior of the American population. Using the census data as a basis for rough comparison, it may be seen that migrant families traveled somewhat greater distances than the persons in the United States population of 1930 who were residing in a State other than their State of birth (table 5). The distance between the State of origin and the State of transient bureau registration was less than 400 miles for 38 percent of migrant families; but the distance between State of birth and of residence was less than 400 miles for 53 percent of the mobile United States population. On the other hand the same proportion (3 percent) of migrant families and of the mobile United States population traveled more than 2,100 miles.

The numerical differences in the two sets of figures, however, should not obscure a general similarity between the mobility of migrant families during the depression and the mobility of the population as a whole. According to the census data short-distance moves greatly outweighted long-distance moves in the birth-residence movement of the total population up to 1930.[6] The same kind of movement, though to a somewhat less extent, was characteristic of migrant families.

The migrant families' tendency to move relatively short distances reflects the fact that a large proportion of families, despite the desperate predicament in which they found themselves at the time of moving, did not venture far beyond the region with which they were familiar. The preponderance of short-distance moves places the

---

[6] It is impossible to reproduce here for comparison a series of maps parallel with those in figs. 5–10, representing the movement of the total population as recorded in the birth-residence data of the 1930 Census. See Galpin, C. J. and Manny, T. B., *Interstate Migrations Among the Native White as Indicated by Differences between State of Birth and State of Residence*, U. S. Department of Agriculture, Bureau of Agricultural Economics, Washington, D. C., 1934. Galpin's and Manny's technique for depicting mobility has been incorporated into the maps in figs. 5–10.

much-discussed depression movement to the West coast in a new perspective. Although the transcontinental migrations of families were by far the most spectacular, they were actually much less important numerically than the short migrations. Moreover, the tendency of migrant families to remain within the region with which they were immediately familiar shows the error of the frequently-repeated statement that they were chiefly unstable wanderers.

Trends and Reciprocated Movement

The reasons for migration which were reported by the families themselves usually implied no consistent direction of migration. With the exception of the drought, the forces which displaced families from settled residence were generally prevalent everywhere. Although its intensity varied, unemployment—the principal reason for leaving settled residence—was serious in all States; and ill-health and domestic difficulties, among the other reasons, have little relation to geography.

The forces which attracted families were even less localized. Only the migrations of families seeking cheap land and a healthful climate implied migration to particular States to the exclusion of others. Migrations to localities where work had been promised involved many geographically meaningless cross currents of mobility. The large number of families which chose as their destination a community where there were relatives or friends would obviously scatter widely over the country.

As a result, a considerable amount of migrant family mobility consisted of a balanced interchange between the States (figs. 5–10). Very rarely was there a large movement from any given State to another without a substantial counter movement. For example, New York gained 283 migrant families from New Jersey and in return lost 148 migrant families to New Jersey; gained 81 from Florida and lost 57; gained 71 from Ohio and lost 110 (appendix table 5). There was much of this kind of reciprocated geographical mobility, with the result that net population displacement was only a fraction of the population movement.

East of the Mississippi the reciprocated movement of families formed the greater part of all movement. Except for a pronounced net emigration from Kentucky, North Carolina, Mississippi, and West Virginia, the movements in and out of the Eastern and Southern States tended to balance each other. Figures 5, 6, and 7 do reveal two trends of migration in the region east of the Mississippi—one flowing from the South to the industrial North, the other from the Northeastern States westward—but these trends made up a small part of the total movement of the region. West of the Mississippi (figs. 8, 9, and 10) the movement in and out of each State was less evenly balanced. The movement out of the Great Plains States, for example, greatly exceeded the movement in; and the family gains of the Pacific Coast States were far in excess of their losses.

For all the States combined the number of families which were involved in reciprocated migration between States was much greater than the number whose migration resulted in a net population displacement. On June 30, 1935, the number of families in FERA transient bureaus was about 30,000. The population displacement resulting from the movement of these families amounted to 10,524 families, representing the net gain of 16 States and the District of Columbia from the other 32 States. In other words, about two-thirds of all movement resulted in the balance of losses and gains within each of the States and, in terms of net population displacement, was canceled. The remaining one-third of the movement was net displacement (table 6 and appendix table 6).

Table 6.—Net Population Displacement and Reciprocated Movement Resulting From the Movement of Migrant Families [1] and of Persons in the General Population 1930 [2] Residing in a State Other Than State of Birth

Type of movement	Migrant families	General population, 1930
Total	29,885	25,388,100
	Percent distribution	
Total	100	100
Net displacement [3]	35	29
Reciprocated movement [4]	65	71

[1] Division of Transient Activities, *Quarterly Census of Transients Under Care*, June 30, 1935, mimeographed report, Federal Emergency Relief Administration, Washington, D. C., 1935. 419 families from U. S. possessions or foreign countries are not included.
[2] Bureau of the Census, *Fifteenth Census of the United States: 1930*, Population Vol. II, U. S. Department of Commerce, Washington, D. C., 1933, ch. 4, tables 32–34.
[3] Net displacement is the sum of the net gains of States gaining population (or net losses of States losing population). See appendix table 6.
[4] Reciprocated movement is derived by summing (1) the number of movers to all the net-loss States and (2) the number of movers from all the net-gain States. See appendix table 6.

The Significance of Reciprocated Movement

The high proportion of reciprocated movement had an important bearing upon the question of public responsibility for transient relief. Local communities are usually well aware of newly arrived migrants in need of relief, while those distress migrants who depart from the same community are likely to be forgotten. Accordingly, local relief officials are commonly inclined to believe that transiency is a one-way movement in which all other communities are contributors and their own community is recipient. This belief is frequently put forward in defending a policy of extending no aid to nonresidents. Actually, however, the influx of needy migrant families into a majority of the States was either roughly balanced by the movement out or was substantially less than the movement out. A large overbalance of immigration was recorded only for six far Western States and Louisiana, New York, Ohio, and the District of Columbia.

In a limited sense the reciprocated movement is a symptom of mistaken purpose lying behind the mobility of many of the families which eventually turned to transient bureaus for assistance. In the belief that they were moving toward regions of greater opportunity, many of the families actually moved into communities from which families like themselves were at the same time departing because of a lack of opportunity. Thus, it would appear that a large part of the movement studied dissipated itself in "waste" motion. Such a conclusion is not without value in demonstrating the disparity between desirable social goals and the realities of uncontrolled social behavior. Yet, in terms of the concrete realities facing the families in 1934 and 1935, this conclusion is somewhat academic. As figures on relief turnover and duration of unemployment show, it would be difficult to maintain that, by and large, the families would have been wiser had they never undertaken to relocate where conditions seemed better (see chs. IV and VI).

The proportion of net and reciprocated mobility shown in table 6 overemphasizes the confusion of the movement. It does not take rural-urban mobility into account. Moreover, if the trends for each State were measured in terms of interchange with each other *individual* State, rather than in terms of interchange with all States *combined*, the proportion of net movement would be shown to be greatly increased. For a particular State a small net gain or loss may conceal large net gains from certain States and large net losses to others. Thus, Illinois had a net gain, from all States combined, of 251 families. But the sum of its net gains from interchange with Mississippi, Alabama, Indiana, New York, and other individual Eastern and Southern States was 665 families; and from interchange with Missouri, Kansas, Colorado, California, and other Western States, it lost a net of 414 families. In table 6 the eastward net gains and the westward net losses of Illinois are not included and only the difference between the two (251 families net gain) is represented.[7] Because of a general tendency for each of the chain of States from east to west to gain families from its eastern neighbors and to lose families to its neighbors on the west, the method used in table 6 for calculating net geographical change somewhat understates the net geographical displacement of the migrant family population.

In any case it is significant that the rate of net geographical displacement for families registered with transient bureaus was slightly

_____

[7] In fig. 11 the net gains and losses are shown on the basis of each State's interchange with each other State individually.

higher than that for persons in the general population who were living outside their State of birth. In so far as this comparison is valid it suggests that, small as the net trends in migrant family movement were, they were nevertheless more pronounced than the trends in the movement of the total population up to 1930. In other words, the migrant families moved more consistently northward and westward than did the total population.

Direction of Movement

The reasons for migration reported by the families rarely showed any awareness of the broad geographical significance of their moves. The many families which told in detail why they had migrated seldom gave explanations that went beyond the immediate reason for the move. Most of the families simply left a community in which they could no longer earn a living and proceeded to another community because of the rumor or hope—usually based upon the presence of relatives and friends—that they would be less insecure. One effect of the unguided action of these families was the seeming geographical confusion which manifested itself in the extent of the scattering of some of the families and in the relative importance of the reciprocated movement of families among the States. When the balanced interchange is canceled and the remaining net movement is traced upon the map a somewhat different picture is revealed. Despite the chaos that might naturally have been expected from the independent and unguided action of the 30,000 families, there were consistent trends of net population displacement (fig. 11).

The flow maps that have been developed after eliminating reciprocated migration show, first of all, that the net movement of migrant families was predominantly westward.[8] The westward flow of families into California, Colorado, Washington, Kansas, Idaho, Oregon, and New Mexico far exceeded all other net movement; and the general direction of the net movement for the entire United States with the exception of the southeastern region was toward the west. Although there was some eastward movement from the Great Plains into Minnesota and Iowa on the north and into Arkansas and Louisiana on the south, by far the greater part of the emigrants from the Great Plains moved westward. Even within the region north of the Ohio River and east of the Mississippi, the States tended to gain from eastern neighbors and lose to western neighbors.

---

[8] The trends shown record the net gain or loss of every State from every other *individual* State, rather than from all States *combined*.

In order to avoid a confusing maze of small lines, all net gains and losses of less than 15 families are excluded. This adjustment eliminated approximately one-fifth of the net movement. Although some of the rejected moves ran counter to the chief lines shown in fig. 11, the majority of them were also net northward and westward moves.

FIG. II— NET DISPLACEMENT OF MIGRANT FAMILIES*
June 30, 1935

NORTH-SOUTH DISPLACEMENT

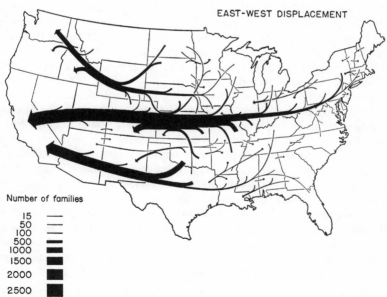

EAST-WEST DISPLACEMENT

Number of families

15	—
50	—
100	—
500	—
1000	■
1500	■
2000	■
2500	■

*Net interchange of fewer than 15 families
between States excluded.

Source: Division of Transient Activities,
Quarterly Census of Transients Under Care,
June 30, 1935, Federal Emergency Relief
Administration, Washington, D.C.

AF-2882, WPA

Only the families in the Southeastern States failed to follow the prevailing westward tendency (fig. 11). The contribution of the entire South to the Pacific Coast States was insignificant. Within the southern region itself, there was a slight movement from Georgia, Alabama, and Mississippi into Louisiana. But the greater part of the net loss of the Southern States moved northward into four industrial States—New York, Illinois, Ohio, and Michigan.[9]

This movement, in which Negroes played an important part (appendix B), flowed north along four parallel lines: the first moved up the Atlantic seaboard to the District of Columbia, Maryland, and New York; the second moved from Mississippi, Tennessee, and Kentucky to Ohio and Michigan; the third moved from Mississippi, Alabama, and Georgia to Illinois; and the fourth, starting from Arkansas, culminated in Illinois and Chicago. Within the South, only the movement toward Florida ran counter to the general northward trend.

Figure 11 also shows that the greater part of the net displacement flow of migrant families not only *culminated* west of the Mississippi River but also *originated* there. The excess of outflow over inflow for Oklahoma alone was nearly as large as the total excess that moved westward across the Mississippi River from all States to the east of it. Moreover, the net loss of Texas, Missouri, Kansas, and South Dakota each exceeded the net loss of any State east of the Mississippi. The greatest single net movement was westward from the two tiers of States immediately west of the Mississippi.

This fact emphasizes an essential difference between the mobility of the migrant families originating on the two sides of the Mississippi River. In the first place, families in the West moved very much more readily than those in the East. Although the region east of the Mississippi contains 70 percent of the total population, it contributed, out of the approximately 30,000 families registered in transient bureaus on June 30, 1935, only about 13,000 families, while about 17,000 originated in the States to the west. Moreover, the net population displacement in the West was, as figure 11 shows, even more disproportionate. In other words, the movement of the eastern sections, despite the flow out of the Northeast to California and out of the Cotton States into the industrial East, consisted in the balanced interchange of families among the States to a much greater extent than did the movement in the West, where special conditions produced an exodus into Colorado and the Pacific Coast States.

The Direction of Movement   Migrant Families Compared With the General Population, 1920–1930

A comparison between the displacement flow of migrant families and the flow of the general United States population in the decade

---

[9] There was practically no interchange between Pennsylvania and the Southern States.

from 1920–1930 reveals a striking general similarity.[10] The chief feature of both movements was the predominating westward drift, and the chief destination for both was California. The movement northward out of the Cotton States follows the same general routes in both instances; in both, this movement is distinctly less important than the westward movement. In both, there is a net movement out of the less industrialized Eastern States into the more highly industrialized States: from Arkansas into Missouri and Michigan; from Kentucky into Indiana, Michigan, and Ohio; and from West Virginia into Ohio and Pennsylvania. Other similarities—such as the net movement from Georgia to Florida, from Pennsylvania and New England to New York, and the movement down the coast from the Pacific Northwest into California—might be traced at length.

Within the general pattern of similarity, several important differences between the movement in the twenties and the movement of migrant families appear. The distress movement of migrant families from the Great Plains States was much more pronounced than the general population movement out of these States during the 1920's. In particular, the migration from the southern Plains States to California formed a greater part of the net displacement of migrant families than of the movement of the general population; and two entirely new movements, (1) off the northern Plains into Washington, Idaho, and Oregon, and (2) off the southeastern Plains into Colorado, New Mexico, and Arizona, assumed an important place in the depression migration of families. Moreover, instead of the normal westward infiltration into the Plains States, many migrant families left these States, especially the Dakotas and Oklahoma, and moved eastward, reversing the trend of the 1920's.

In the northeastern industrial States other differences appeared. The migration of the 1920's into Michigan, following the automobile boom, reversed itself for the families studied; and Michigan lost families to both Illinois and Ohio, though it continues to gain from the States south of the Ohio River. Between 1920 and 1930 Illinois gained large numbers of migrants from Iowa and Missouri, probably through rural to urban migrations. For the families studied, however, this trend disappeared.

---

[10] Thornthwaite, C. W., *Internal Migration in the United States*, Bulletin 1, Philadelphia: University of Pennsylvania Press, 1934, Plate V–A, Plate VI–A (D), and Plate III–A.

The trends in the movement of migrant families (fig. 11) includes the movement of both white and Negro families.   Thornthwaite's trend map for 1920–1930 [Plate VI–A (D)] shows the net movement of the native-white population only. The size and direction of the migration of all Negroes born in the South and living in the North in 1930 are shown in Thornthwaite's Plate V–A; and the growth of this migration during each decade beginning with 1890–1900 is shown in Plate III–A

In the South two States show marked differences. Tennessee lost population to many States in the 1920's and gained from none; but from the interchange of migrant families it gained from Texas, Arkansas, North Carolina, Georgia, Alabama, Mississippi, and Kentucky. North Carolina, on the other hand, gained population in the 1920's from Georgia and South Carolina; but the trend in the movement of migrant families was away from North Carolina to not only Georgia and South Carolina but also to Tennessee, Florida, and Virginia.

Though these differences are important, they should not obscure the close parallels between the displacement of the families studied and the displacement of the general population in the 1920's. The most significant tendency shown in figure 11 is the similarity of migrant family movement to the recent drift of the general population.

Rate of Emigration

The foregoing discussion has considered the interstate movement of migrant families in terms of the absolute number of families moving to and from each State. In order to determine the regions from which the families emigrated most readily, these absolute numbers must be considered in terms of the number of families residing in each State and therefore theoretically likely to migrate.

On June 30, 1935, throughout the United States as a whole, 1 interstate migrant family was under care in FERA transient bureaus for each 910 families in the total population, or 1.08 migrants per 1,000 resident families.[11] Because of the wide variety of social and economic conditions in the various regions of the country, in many States the ratio of families leaving the State to families living in the State fell exceedingly far above and below this national average.

To cite the high and low extremes in the rate of emigration, Nevada and Arizona, which contributed to other States 1 migrant family for each 160 to 200 families in their populations (6.41 and 5.07 families contributed respectively per 1,000 population families) had by far the highest rates (appendix table 7). At the other extreme were New Hampshire and Massachusetts, which contributed only 1 migrant family out of each 5,500 to 3,500 population families (.18 and .30 families contributed respectively per 1,000 population families).

The geographical distribution of the States with high and low migrant family contributions per 1,000 population families is shown in figure 12. This map reveals that the States from which migrant families were most likely to leave were practically all Western States

---

[11] The population data refer to multiperson families as reported in the Bureau of the Census, *Fifteenth Census of the United States: 1930*, Population Vol. VI, U. S. Department of Commerce, Washington, D. C., 1933, p. 36.

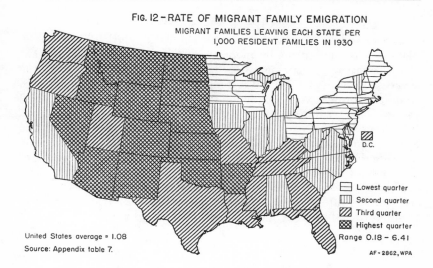

FIG. 12 – RATE OF MIGRANT FAMILY EMIGRATION
MIGRANT FAMILIES LEAVING EACH STATE PER
1,000 RESIDENT FAMILIES IN 1930

D.C.

Lowest quarter
Second quarter
Third quarter
Highest quarter
Range 0.18 – 6.41

United States average = 1.08
Source: Appendix table 7.

AF - 2862, WPA

and that, excepting only California, the entire western United States from the Great Plains to the Pacific Coast States contributed migrant families at a rate above the United States average. All the States with exceptionally high rates were in this region.[12]

Migrant families also tended to emigrate from several States in the South at a rate somewhat above the United States average. This tendency was most marked in the States on the fringes of the South, especially in Arkansas and Florida. In the deep South the rate of emigration was either slightly below the United States average (as in Alabama and the Carolinas) or only very slightly above (as in Louisiana, Mississippi, and Tennessee).[13]

Migrant families emigrated least readily from the densely populated northeastern and north central regions of the United States. All the Midwestern States from Minnesota and Iowa to Ohio were well below the average, and the industrial East from Pennsylvania to Maine contributed fewer migrant families in proportion to its resident population than any other section of the United States.

[12] Appendix table 7 presents the rate of migrant family emigration from the various States in terms of the number of families contributed by each State per 1,000 resident families. The table also shows the rank of each State beginning with the highest: Nevada first, Arizona second, and so on through the entire list of States to New Hampshire, the State with the lowest rate.

In fig. 13 the "highest one-fourth" represents the States with rankings from 1st to 12th, the "second highest one-fourth" represents those from 13th to 25th, etc.

[13] Against the national average of 1.1 migrants contributed per 1,000 population families, the rate for Arkansas was 2.8; for Mississippi, 1.4; for Georgia and Alabama, 1.1. The rate for five Western States, on the other hand, was above 4.0. See appendix table 7.

Emigration and Relief Intensity

The preceding chapter emphasized the basic relationship between distress and migrant family mobility, and it would be supposed that the varying rates of emigration reflect regional differences in the severity of the depression. But if one compares the rate of emigration from the States with the highest percent of unemployed gainful workers—such as Michigan or Pennsylvania—with the rate of migration from the less severely stricken States, the inadequacy of this explanation is quickly revealed. A given degree of adverse economic pressure did not produce the same rate of emigration in all sections of the United States.

Figure 13 shows how the severity of the depression, as measured by the average intensity of general relief during 1934 (excluding rural rehabilitation and other special programs), varied among the States.[14]

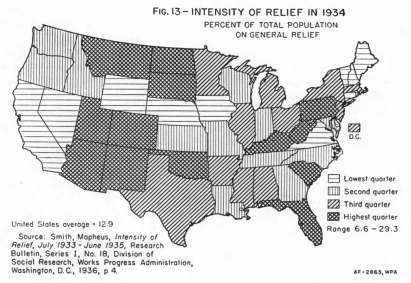

FIG. 13 – INTENSITY OF RELIEF IN 1934
PERCENT OF TOTAL POPULATION
ON GENERAL RELIEF

D.C.

☐ Lowest quarter
▥ Second quarter
▨ Third quarter
▧ Highest quarter

United States average = 12.9

Range 6.6 – 29.3

Source: Smith, Mapheus, *Intensity of Relief, July 1933 - June 1935*, Research Bulletin, Series I, No. 18, Division of Social Research, Works Progress Administration, Washington, D. C., 1936, p. 4.

AF-2863, WPA

Despite obvious limitations these data do after a fashion provide an index of the varying extent of destitution throughout the United States. It is recognized that the intensity of relief is affected not only by the extent of need but also by the availability of funds for relief and by local policies in the administration of relief. The low intensity of relief in the South, for example, is doubtless an inaccurate representation of the actual extent of destitution in that region, and the data for the Southern States must be considered in the light of that

[14] See Smith, Mapheus, *Intensity of Relief July 1933–June 1935*, Research Bulletin Series I, No. 18, Division of Social Research, Works Progress Administration, Washington, D. C., March 25, 1936.

qualification. For most of the United States, however, the index used is reasonably trustworthy. If it be assumed that the intensity-of-relief data represent the varying force of economic pressure in each State, a comparison of figures 12 and 13 will reveal the responsiveness to that pressure among the States.

It will be observed from a comparison between figures 12 and 13 that there was no consistent Nation-wide relationship between relief intensity and the rate of family emigration. It is true that several States with a high relief intensity also had high family emigration rates. Montana, North Dakota, Oklahoma, and South Dakota, for example, fell into the highest quarter-group in both figure 12 and figure 13. Likewise, Connecticut and Maine appear in the lowest quarter-group on both maps. But Nebraska, Wyoming, and Nevada, for example, had extremely high family emigration rates and a very low relief intensity. Pennsylvania, Ohio, and Minnesota were well above average in relief intensity, but all had very low family emigration rates.[15]

The Western States in general had high emigration rates regardless of varying intensity of relief. The Midwestern and Northeastern States, in contrast, contributed in relation to their population few migrant families to other States, even though the intensity of relief was frequently very high. Within the South, also, there appeared to be no consistent relationship between the variations in relief intensity and the rates of family emigration.

Rate of Emigration: Migrant Families Compared With the General Population

Figure 14 shows the rate at which the general population born in the various States had emigrated to other States, according to the birth-residence data of the 1930 Census.[16] A comparison of each State's rank in figure 14 with its rank in figure 12 shows that migrant families tended to emigrate most readily from those States which had normally been contributing the greatest proportion of their native population to other States.

It has been pointed out that the West contained the States with the highest rates of migrant family emigration. The West also con-

---

[15] The coefficient of rank correlation between intensity of relief and family emigration rate was ($\rho = .334$).

[16] Bureau of the Census, *Fifteenth Census of the United States: 1930*, Population Vol. II, U. S. Department of Commerce, Washington, D. C., 1933, ch. 4, tables 32–34.

In fig. 14 the States are divided according to the magnitude of their emigration rates into 4 groups of 12 States each. Those 12 States which had the highest percent of their native population living in other States are represented as the "highest one-fourth" of the States; the 12 States with the next highest percent of natives living elsewhere are represented as the "second highest one-fourth" of the States, etc.

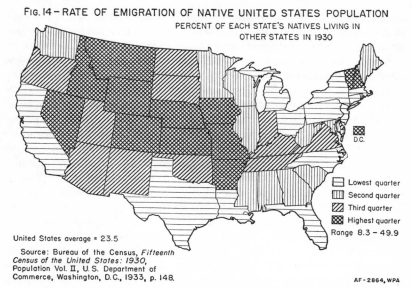

Fig. 14 – RATE OF EMIGRATION OF NATIVE UNITED STATES POPULATION
PERCENT OF EACH STATE'S NATIVES LIVING IN
OTHER STATES IN 1930

Lowest quarter
Second quarter
Third quarter
Highest quarter
Range 8.3 – 49.9

United States average = 23.5

Source: Bureau of the Census, *Fifteenth
Census of the United States: 1930,*
Population Vol. II, U. S. Department of
Commerce, Washington, D.C., 1933, p. 148.

AF-2864, WPA

tained most of the States which had contributed the highest proportion of their natives to other States before 1930. Nine of these States
had the same high quarter-group ranking on both maps. In all
States in which the quarter-group ranking was not identical the family
emigration rank was consistently higher than the emigration rank
derived for the general population. Thus, emigration from the
Western States, normally very high in comparison with the other
sections, became relatively higher among families studied.

In North Dakota and South Dakota, and to a lesser extent in Nebraska, the increase in the relative importance of migrant family
emigration resulted from the agricultural depression and the 1934
drought. In all other Western States, however, the direct effect of
these two forces was small, inasmuch as the migrants came largely
from the urban unemployed.[17] The increased importance of the
emigration of migrant families in other Western States appears to
have resulted more from the greater susceptibility of newcomers—
who form a large part of the population of these States [18]—to unsettling
forces intensified by the depression than from the action of any one
particular localized force.

In the Midwestern and Northeastern States the relationship between
migrant family and general population emigration ranks is the oppo-

[17] See ch. I, fig. 2. Farming failure was an important cause of emigration only
for the families leaving the Dakotas. Only 12 percent of all the migrant families
from Oklahoma and only 6 percent of those from Texas were farmers who had
failed.

[18] See fig. 16, which shows the rate of immigration of the native-born population
into these States as recorded in the 1930 Census.

site of that found in the Western States. The Midwest and Northeast as shown in figure 14 have contributed a relatively slight proportion of their native population to other States before 1930; and, as figure 12 indicates, this region also contained most of the States with the lowest rates of migrant family emigration. Eight of these twenty-one States had identically low quarter-group rankings on both maps. In only one State, Michigan, the migrant family emigration rank was higher than the general population emigration rank by one quarter-group, reflecting in all probability the depressed state of the automobile industry after 1930. The rank of each of the remaining States and the District of Columbia was consistently lower in terms of its relative rate of migrant family emigration than in terms of the contribution of its native population to other States before 1930. In other words, the Midwestern and Northeastern States, most of which normally have low emigration rates, were by comparison with the other sections of the country even less important as the source of migrant families.

Chief among the Midwestern and Northeastern States in which the rank in terms of migrant family emigration was lower than the rank of native population emigration were Maine, New Hampshire, Vermont, Minnesota, Wisconsin, Iowa, and Missouri. The low intensity of relief in the New England States offers a possible explanation for the low rate of family emigration by reflecting the lesser pressure of adverse economic conditions. In the Midwest the normal movement to the Great Plains was cut short by the agricultural depression; and Iowa, like the New England States, was less affected by the depression, as its low intensity of relief shows (fig. 13).

A substantial movement of the general population from the States on the fringe of the South was a normal occurrence up to 1930. The relative position of these States in terms of migrant family emigration was much the same as in the emigration of the general population. The relative importance of emigration from Arkansas increased slightly and that from Virginia decreased slightly; while Kentucky and Tennessee maintained the same quarter-group rank on both maps. In the lower South, on the other hand, the rate of emigration of the general population before 1930 was small in comparison with the other States. In all the States from Louisiana to North Carolina, and including Florida, the general population was comparatively immobile notwithstanding the high birth rate of the region, or, indeed, the northward migration of Negroes between 1910 and 1930. These same States became relatively much more important as contributors of migrant families. The rank of Mississippi, Georgia, and North Carolina was raised by one quarter-group and the rank of Louisiana and Florida was raised by two quarter-groups. Although these changes are in part a reflection of a relative decrease in emigration from the Northeast and Midwest during the depression, they nevertheless suggest a growing tendency toward mobility within the lower South. The increase in mobility is particularly noticeable in Florida, where the high rate of migrant family emigration doubtless represents the backwash of the Florida boom.

Rate of Immigration

The constant westward movement of migrant families brought large numbers into California, Colorado, Idaho, and Washington; and a somewhat less marked northward immigration flowed into New York, Ohio, and Illinois. The total number of migrant families in transient bureaus was by no means uniformly distributed in absolute numbers throughout the various States. In terms of relative numbers expressing the transient bureau case load of each State as a proportion of its family population, the variation among the different States becomes even greater.

Appendix table 8 shows the number of migrant families in each State on June 30, 1935, per 1,000 resident families in the State. The table reveals an even wider gap between the State with the highest and the State with the lowest rate of immigration than was discovered to exist between the two extremes in the rate of emigration. Idaho, the State whose rate of immigration was highest, had 1 migrant family for each 100 families residing in Idaho; [19] whereas South Dakota at the other extreme had less than 1 migrant family for each 10,000 resident families (.03 families received per 1,000 resident families).

Inasmuch as the rate of immigration relates the number of destitute, newly arrived families to the size of the resident family population, it provides a rough measure of the varying seriousness of the migrant family relief problem from the point of view of the residents in each State. It is interesting to observe that in June 1935 the problem was most serious in Idaho, followed, as appendix table 8 shows, by New Mexico and Colorado. California, with less than half as many families under care per 1,000 population families as Idaho, only ranked as the fourth highest State. Appearing in order slightly below California were Washington, Wyoming, and the District of Columbia.

Figure 15 shows the migrant family immigration rank of each of the States. In brief, the map reveals that most of the States with the highest rates of immigration and more than half of those in the second highest quarter-group were located west of the Mississippi River. In the East only the District of Columbia and Florida had immigration rates in the highest quarter-group, and 19 of the 26 States [20] had immigration rates in the lowest or second lowest quarter-groups.

---

[19] The migrant family case load of Idaho transient bureaus was not reported in the Quarterly Census of June 30, 1935. Accordingly, the figure reported in the *Midmonthly Census of Transient Activities* of June 15, 1935, was used.

[20] Including the District of Columbia but excluding Vermont which had no transient program.

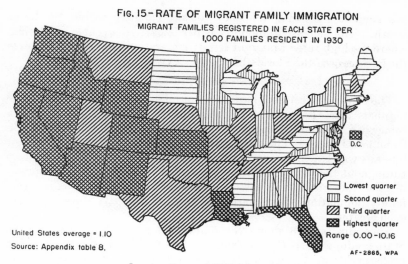

FIG. 15 – RATE OF MIGRANT FAMILY IMMIGRATION
MIGRANT FAMILIES REGISTERED IN EACH STATE PER
1,000 FAMILIES RESIDENT IN 1930

Lowest quarter
Second quarter
Third quarter
Highest quarter
Range 0.00 – 10.16

United States average = 1.10

Source: Appendix table 8.

D.C.

AF-2865, WPA

Immigration and Relief Intensity

A comparison between the rate of immigration map (fig. 15) and the intensity-of-relief map (fig. 13) reveals that there was no consistent relationship between migrant family immigration and relief intensity. Five States had very high relief rates together with very low rates of migrant family immigration; these States were North Dakota and South Dakota, to the west of the Mississippi River, and Pennsylvania, West Virginia, and Kentucky, to the east. At the same time, four other States with very high relief rates—Florida, Colorado, New Mexico, and Arizona—also had very high rates of migrant family immigration. Moreover, some of the States with the lowest intensity of relief had low rates of immigration (for example, Maine, Maryland, and Iowa), while some had high rates (for example, Wyoming, New Hampshire, and Delaware). Clearly there was no general connection whatever between these two factors.[21]

Rate of Immigration: Migrant Families Compared With the General Population

Migrant families did, however, show an extremely great tendency to seek out those States into which the population had largely been flowing during the lifetime of the persons enumerated in the 1930 Census. Figure 16 shows for 1930 the proportion of the residents of each State who were born in other States, in terms of quarter-group rankings. A comparison between figures 15 and 16 reveals very little change in the relative positions of the States.

---

[21] The coefficient of rank correlation between intensity of relief and family immigration rates was ($\rho = .086$).

FIG. 16–RATE OF IMMIGRATION OF NATIVE UNITED STATES POPULATION
PERCENT OF RESIDENTS IN EACH STATE IN 1930
BORN IN OTHER STATES

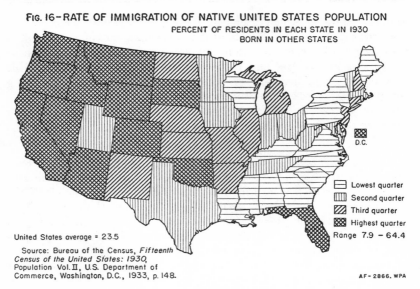

United States average = 23.5

Lowest quarter
Second quarter
Third quarter
Highest quarter
Range 7.9 – 64.4

Source: Bureau of the Census, *Fifteenth Census of the United States: 1930*, Population Vol. II, U.S. Department of Commerce, Washington, D.C., 1933, p. 148.

AF- 2866. WPA

In the West the only marked differences on the two maps are for North Dakota and South Dakota. The 1930 population of these two States contained a relatively high proportion of the natives of other States because of the comparative newness of their development as States and the normally high population turnover in the Plains States. Migrant families, on the other hand, avoided these two States, doubtless because of the drought.

In the Midwest and Northeast the majority of the States had the same low quarter-group rank on both maps. The principal changes are the increased relative importance of Illinois, Ohio, and New York (the States in which the movement of white and Negro migrant families from the South terminated) and the decreased relative importance of Michigan and of the satellite States close to New York.

In the South the States whose 1930 population contained the highest proportion of natives born in other States were Florida and Arkansas. The rate of migrant family immigration into these States remained high, and Tennessee and Louisiana were added to them. In Alabama, Georgia, and South Carolina the proportion of 1930 residents born in other States was extremely low, but the migrant family immigration rates in these States were somewhat higher. This change suggests an increase in the mobility of the southern population during the depression.

RURAL-URBAN MIGRATION

The Quarterly Census of Transient Activities, which permitted the foregoing analysis of the movement of families between the States, recorded for each family only the State from which migration began and the State in which transient bureau registration occurred. It does not supply information about the intervening movement; nor does it distinguish between the families which were at their destination at the time of registration and those which were still en route to their destination. Furthermore, no information was supplied concerning the rural-urban mobility of migrant families. In order to fill in these gaps, it is necessary to turn again to the migrant family interviews upon which the other chapters of this study are based.

An Urban Migration

The origins and destinations [22] of migrant families were both predominantly urban. By and large, the families moved from city to city, rather than from the farm to the city or from the city back to the farm. Urban places, that is, places of more than 2,500 population, were the origin of 70 percent of the migrant families with settled residence; and villages and farms were the origin of 30 percent of the families. [23] Upon leaving settled residence, 76 percent of the families had urban destinations, 17 percent had farm and village destinations, and 7 percent set out with no destination in mind (see table 7).

Table 7.—Rural-Urban Origins and Destinations of Migrant Families

Rural-urban interchange	Migrant families immigrating
Total	4,084
	Percent distribution
Total	100
To city [1]	76
From city	56
From villages and farms [2]	20
To villages and farms	17
From city	9
From villages and farms	8
To no destination	7
From city	5
From villages and farms	2

[1] Places of 2,500 or more population.
[2] Places of less than 2,500 population.

NOTE.—244 families, for which size of place of destination or settled residence was not ascertainable, are not included.

[22] It is necessary to distinguish between the *place of destination*, recorded only for the families interviewed, and the *place of registration*, recorded both for the families interviewed and in the Quarterly Census.

[23] As against this 70 percent urban composition, 58 percent of all multiperson families in the United States as a whole lived in urban places in 1930 and 42 percent lived in rural places. See Bureau of the Census, *Fifteenth Census of the United States: 1930*, Population Vol. VI, U. S. Department of Commerce, Washington, D. C., 1933, pp. 13–15.

A majority of the families moved *from* city *to* city. As table 7 shows, 56 percent of all families had both origins and destinations in urban places and only 8 percent of the families had both origins and destinations on farms or in villages. For 29 percent of the families the first moves from settled residence involved an interchange between urban and rural places. These were composed of 20 percent which left farms and villages for cities and of 9 percent which moved from cities back to villages and farms.

The Back-to-the-Land Movement

The growth and decline of the back-to-the-land movement among migrant families are shown in figure 17. A total of 9 percent of the

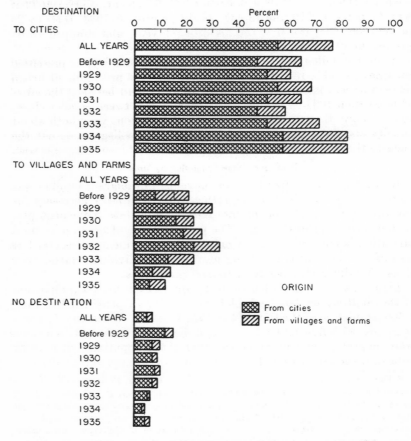

FIG. 17 – RURAL-URBAN MOVEMENT OF MIGRANT FAMILIES
BY YEAR OF MOVE

Source: Appendix table 10.

AF-2626, WPA

first moves from settled residence were from cities to farms and villages. Of the families which left their last settled residence before 1929, only 8 percent moved back to the land. As the depression grew worse, this movement increased until in 1932, 23 percent of the families leaving settled residence moved from cities to farms and villages. Thereafter, as recovery began, it declined rapidly; and in 1935 only 6 percent of the urban families leaving settled residence moved back to the land.

The movement from farms and villages into the cities showed exactly the opposite trend. An average of 20 percent of the moves were from rural to urban areas. Before 1929 the movement was slightly below average size, comprising 17 percent of all moves from settled residence. In 1929 it declined to 9 percent, and in 1932 it was 11 percent. It rose rapidly to 20 percent in 1933, then to 25 percent in 1934, the first serious drought year, and dropped to 24 percent in 1935.[24]

A more detailed classification of rural-urban mobility is presented in appendix table 10. This table shows that the predominant urban movement was itself made up chiefly of movement between the cities of more than 100,000 population, rather than between smaller cities. It also shows that the rural origins and destinations were both about equally distributed between open country and village and that the back-to-the-land movement was thus a movement into villages as well.

Rural and Urban Emigration by State

Recognition of the fact that the movement of migrant families was largely one of city dwellers migrating to other cities is necessary for the proper interpretation of the data on interstate movement presented earlier in this chapter. The predominance of urban over rural migration is characteristic not only of the movement in general but also of the movement involving most of the individual States, even those containing chronically distressed rural areas.

Figure 18 shows for each State by quarter-groups the proportion of the multiperson families which were living in places of less than 2,500 population at the time of the 1930 Census. When this figure is compared with figure 19, which shows the proportion of the migrants who emigrated from places of less than 2,500 population, it may be seen that the proportion of rural families was almost universally low.

---

[24] The rural-urban interchange shown in table 7 and fig. 17 applies only to the moves from settled residence to destination. Accordingly, it includes only one move for each family. But many migrant families changed residence after this first move, and the one-fifth of the families which had no "settled residence" nevertheless changed their "residence." A tabulation of the rural-urban interchange involved in *all* these moves shows practically the same characteristics of those described in fig. 17, except that the back-to-the-land movement constituted 15 percent of *all* moves, as against 9 percent of the moves from settled residence.

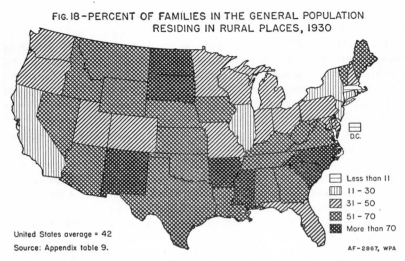

FIG. 18 – PERCENT OF FAMILIES IN THE GENERAL POPULATION
RESIDING IN RURAL PLACES, 1930

D.C.

Less than 11
11 - 30
31 - 50
51 - 70
More than 70

United States average = 42

Source: Appendix table 9.

AF-2867, WPA

Practically all States contributed a smaller proportion of rural migrants than the rural composition of their population would have warranted. In several States the discrepancy is particularly apparent. In most of the Southern States, including Texas and Oklahoma, there was an exceedingly high proportion of the population living in rural places, yet the proportion of rural emigrants from these States was relatively low. Despite the acuteness of the rural problem in this entire area, the families which did leave States within this region tended to come mainly from urban, rather than rural, places. Only in two Southern border States, Kentucky and Arkansas, did the proportion

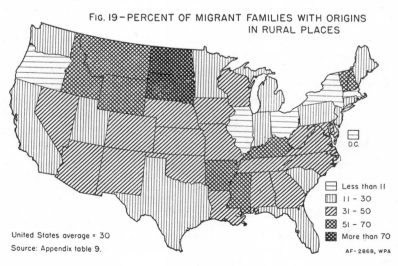

FIG. 19 – PERCENT OF MIGRANT FAMILIES WITH ORIGINS
IN RURAL PLACES

D.C.

Less than 11
11 - 30
31 - 50
51 - 70
More than 70

United States average = 30

Source: Appendix table 9.

AF-2868, WPA

of rural family emigrants approximate the proportion of rural families in the population.

The northern Plains from Kansas to Montana formed the only regional group in which the proportion of migrant families leaving rural places was consistently high. It is significant, however, that even within this region, despite the drought and the long-established tradition of rural mobility within the region, in South Dakota alone were the families leaving rural places overrepresented in terms of the rural-urban composition of the State population (appendix table 9).

Rural and Urban Immigration by State

Figure 20 shows for each State the proportion of the families whose destinations were in rural places. It is obvious from this figure that the proportion of families going to rural places was far less than the proportion leaving rural places. In nearly three-fourths of the States the proportion of families with rural destinations was less than 30 percent of all the families migrating to the State (appendix table 9). Family movement was predominantly urban, not only into industrial States, such as New York, Pennsylvania, and Illinois, but also into many basically agricultural States, such as Kansas, Nebraska, New Mexico, and most of the Southern States. In eight States the *proportion* of families with rural destinations was from 30 to 50 percent of the incoming families. The only States in this group which had a large *number* of incoming families were Arkansas, Oklahoma, and Montana. In only five States did the proportion of families with rural destinations exceed 50 percent; of these, Idaho and Mississippi were the only numerically important States of destination for migrant families.

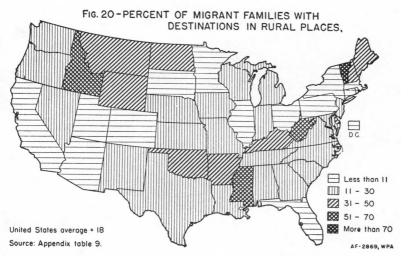

Fig. 20 – PERCENT OF MIGRANT FAMILIES WITH DESTINATIONS IN RURAL PLACES.

Less than 11
11 – 30
31 – 50
51 – 70
More than 70

United States average = 18

Source: Appendix table 9.

AF-2869, WPA

Movement Beyond Destinations

It is important to bear in mind that figure 20 is based upon the State of destination of the families rather than upon the States in which families were registered in transient bureaus. Figure 20 thus records only the proportion of the families which intended, when they left settled residence, to take up residence in rural areas in the States specified. By the time these families were interviewed, practically all of them (86 percent) had moved on [25] from their new rural residences and were registered in transient bureaus in urban places. Two-thirds of them were registered in transient bureaus in a State other than the State of destination (appendix table 11).

In contrast, the families which had reached destinations in urban places tended to remain at their destinations. At the time the families were interviewed, 61 percent of those with urban destinations were still in the city to which they had originally set out, and an additional 8 percent were still within the State of their destination. Only one-third of the families with urban destinations were registered in transient bureaus outside their State of destination.

---

[25] Most of this group had arrived at their destinations in rural places and subsequently departed. Of all the families which set out for definite destinations only 8 percent had not yet reached their destination by the time they were interviewed in September 1935.

Chapter III

THE BACKGROUND OF MIGRATION

IN ANALYZING depression mobility from the point of view of public relief policy, a distinction between wandering and migration is necessary. In so far as public assistance furthers permanent economic adjustment at the same time that it relieves immediate needs, it works toward a solution of the problems growing out of distress migration. Plainly, this end is more easily achieved in assisting migrants than in assisting chronic wanderers.

The essence of the distinction between migration and wandering is the difference in the value that the individual on the road attaches to mobility. At one extreme there is the aimless, "just to be moving" kind of mobility characteristic of persons and families to whom stability has become either impossible or unattractive. Migration, at the other extreme, is the purposeful and socially necessary type of mobility that has stability as its immediate object.

Determining the degree of mobility characteristic of the families studied requires a thorough analysis of the background of the families which turned to transient bureaus for assistance. If the families had developed a long established habit of frequent change of community, or of travel so constant that a residence [1] was seldom established in any community, the evidence would point to the purposeless transiency sometimes observed among nonfamily persons.[2] Con-

[1] The term *residence* is used throughout this chapter to mean a stay for at least 30 days in one community without receipt of transient relief. As used here, residence has none of the special and technical connotations that the term frequently has in statutes and legal writings; e. g., legal residence, voting residence, or relief residence. Nor is residence used as a synonym for *domicile;* i. e., a permanent home. For this later purpose, the term *settled residence* has been adopted to represent the particular residence that the family regarded as its last place of settled abode.

[2] See Webb, John N., *The Transient Unemployed*, Research Monograph III, Division of Social Research, Works Progress Administration, Washington, D. C., 1935, pp. 64–74.

versely, if the families had only recently been dislodged from a community where they had maintained a settled, self-supporting existence for a considerable period of time there would be a strong presumption that their mobility was of the nature of purposeful migration.

In order to derive this distinction, the history of these families during the 6 years preceding this study is divided into two periods. One of these periods includes the time between each family's first application for relief at a transient bureau and the date of interview. The mobility of the families during this period is discussed in chapter IV. But family mobility began before that period; otherwise, the families would have been assisted by the resident rather than the transient relief program. Examination of the history of the families during this earlier period will provide information about the mobility of the families during the years preceding their first stay at the transient bureaus. It is the purpose of this chapter to examine this earlier background period. The period under examination begins on January 1, 1929, for all families formed before that date, and it extends forward to the date when the families left the last place of residence prior to their first application for transient relief. For families formed since January 1, 1929, the date of marriage is substituted for the arbitrary predepression date in 1929.[3]

SETTLED AND UNSETTLED FAMILIES

When classified according to their background prior to the period of transient relief the 5,489 families observed in this study disclosed a range from unbroken residence at one extreme to unbroken mobility at the other extreme. By far the larger number of families, however, had few or no changes of residence prior to their transient relief history. A small number had a record of frequent changes of residence, and a few had never had a residence for even as long as 1 month in one locality. Between these two extremes there was a marginal group whose longest stay in one community was less than a year. The proportions of stable, unstable, and marginal families have first been measured in terms of the length of residence in a community; and, second, these proportions have been compared with a report of families' opinions as to whether they had ever maintained a "permanent" settled residence.

Length of Residence

Families Without Residence

To facilitate a detailed examination of the background of migrant families, they were divided into two groups on the basis of whether or not they had, at any time since January 1, 1929, a *residence* as

---

[3] The relationship between year of family formation and degree of mobility is discussed on pp. 68–70.

defined in this study; i. e., a continuous stay in one community for a period of 1 month or more without relief from a transient bureau.

While the existence of a residence according to this definition reveals little about stability, the *absence* of any residence obviously indicates instability. The classification adopted thus separates from the total group these families which were most highly mobile prior to their transient relief history. The distribution of the families according to whether they had ever had a residence is presented in table 8. Only 4 percent of the families had never maintained a residence of as long as 1 month. The remaining 96 percent had one or more residences of durations that represent a wide range of mobility.

Table 8.—Residence Status of Migrant Families

Residence status	Migrant families
Total_ _	5, 489
	Percent distribution
Total_ _	100
Residence of 1 month or longer since 1929 or since formation if subsequent to that date_ _ _ _ _ _ _	96
No residence of 1 month or longer since 1929 or since formation if subsequent to that date_ _ _ _	4

Although the small group with no residence appears to have been almost completely adrift, consideration must be given to the length of time during which it was possible for them to have had residences.

Table 9.—Year of Formation of Migrant Families Having No Residence of 1 Month or Longer Since January 1, 1929 [1]

Year of formation	Migrant families having no residence of 1 month or longer
Total_ _	240
	Percent distribution
Total_ _	100
Prior to 1929_ _	9
1929_ _	1
1930_ _	1
1931_ _	2
1932_ _	2
1933_ _	5
1934_ _	24
1935_ _	56

[1] For families formed since January 1, 1929, the period under consideration begins with date of marriage.

NOTE.—2 families, whose year of formation was not ascertainable, are not included.

About one-tenth of the families with no residence since January 1, 1929, were formed prior to 1929. A closer approach to absolute instability than that represented by these cases is difficult to imagine. But more than one-half of the families with no residence were formed sometime during the 9 months between January 1935 and the date of interview, and an additional one-fourth were formed during 1934 (table 9). Thus, while the existence of families without residence histories implied the presence of a habitually unstable group, their habits in a majority of cases had not been formed over a long period of time.

Families With Residence

When the duration of residences is examined, it is found that between January 1, 1929, and September 1935 over half (56 percent) of the families included among their residences a stay of at least 3 years in one community (table 10). An additional one-fourth (26 percent) had remained in one locality from 1 to 3 years. In judging this evidence, it is necessary to consider that nearly half of all the family groups were formed since January 1, 1929, and that 1 to 3 years would account for all of the time since marriage for many of these families.

In addition to the fact that 82 percent of the families had lived in one place for at least 1 year since the depression began, it should be noted that over 20 percent of all residences other than the longest also lasted at least 1 year. These residences were necessarily maintained by families among the 82 percent whose longest residence was of equal or greater duration.

Table 10.—Duration of Residences of Migrant Families Since January 1, 1929 [1]

Duration of residence of 1 month or longer	Residences	
	Longest residence [2]	Other than longest residences [3]
Total	5,181	11,216
	Percent distribution	
Total	100	100
Less than 1 year	18	79
1–2.9 months	3	28
3–5.9 months	5	27
6–11.9 months	10	24
1–2.9 years	26	19
3 years or more	56	2

[1] For families formed since January 1, 1929, the period under consideration begins with date of marriage.
[2] 308 families, which had no residence of 1 month or longer since January 1, 1929, or since formation if subsequent to that date, and those for whom the duration of longest residence was not ascertainable, are not included.
[3] 208 residences, for which duration was not ascertainable, are not included.

There remains, however, a minority group of families (18 percent) whose longest residence lasted less than 1 year. These families were clearly marginal as to stability. About half of these families had never remained in one locality longer than 6 months and must be considered more mobile than stable. Some of these families, however, were formed during the year the study was made.

It is now possible, in the light of the data that have been given, to establish tentatively the proportions of families having backgrounds of stability. The families clearly unstable do not constitute a large group. They are represented by the families which had no residences at all, plus those whose longest residence was of very short duration.[4] These two groups, comprising one-fifth of all families, were actually unstable or marginal as to stability. But the other four-fifths had a stable background of a residence lasting from 1 to 3 or more years since 1929.

Stability Measured in Terms of Family Opinion

The arbitrary basis upon which the characteristics of stability and instability were measured was realized at the time the study was planned, and a means of verifying or rejecting length of residence as a measure of stability was included. In addition to an account of the duration of their residences, all families were asked whether they had ever had a residence which they considered to be a permanent settlement[5] for the family group. The distinction between length of stay in a community and the families' attitudes toward the permanence of their stay is clearly illustrated in the history of the Allen family:

The Allens lived in Boston, Mass., from 1924 to 1930 where Mr. Allen was steadily employed as a machinist. In 1930 slack work and reduced earnings caused Mr. Allen to take a job as a traveling representative for a mill machinery company. The Boston home was abandoned and the family traveled with the head. After a year the job failed and left the Allens stranded in Memphis.

For 2½ years Mr. Allen supported his family in Memphis by working as a painter. But the Allen family did not consider their stay in Tennessee to be a settled residence because Mr. Allen could not get work at his real trade. The Allens left Memphis at the first opportunity.

Because of situations similar to the one just described, it would be unwise to attempt final judgment about family stability without considering whether or not the families felt that a stay in a particular community represented settlement. To a certain degree, attitudes toward settled residence are independent of time and provide a check upon tentative conclusions based upon length of residence.

[4] The high mobility of the group is qualified in so far as some of the families were so recently formed that a "longest residence" of less than a year would include most of their residence history periods.

[5] *Settled residence* is used to convey the idea of seeming permanence in contrast with the more or less temporary nature of a *residence*. See footnote 1, p. 59.

In the discussion of the reasons for leaving settled residence (see ch. I), it was noted that about four-fifths of all the families interviewed had, according to their individual standards of judgment, *thought of themselves as permanent residents* of some community at some time since 1929. The remaining one-fifth of the families, which considered that they had not been settled since 1929 (or since the date of marriage if the family was formed after that date), were excluded from the tabulations of reasons for migration.[6] According to the opinions of the families themselves, four-fifths thus had a residence that they considered a settlement and one-fifth lacked this evidence of prior stability.

In order to collate this subjective test of stability with the test based upon length-of-residence records, a comparable time-period must be established. The table below provides the basis of comparison by showing when the families which had once considered themselves settled in a given community had left that community.

Table 11.—Year Migrant Families Left Settled Residence

Year of leaving settled residence	Migrant families
Total	5,479
	Percent distribution
Total	100
No settled residence	21
With settled residence	79
Left prior to 1929	3
Left in 1929	3
Left in 1930	3
Left in 1931	3
Left in 1932	5
Left in 1933	9
Left in 1934	26
Left in 1935	27

NOTE.—10 families, for which date of leaving settled residence was not ascertainable, are not included.

Accepting as a measure of stability the existence of a settlement considered by the family to have been permanent, it may seem at first that the results here are almost identical with those obtained from the data on length of residence. There it was found that 82 percent of the families had lived in one place for 1 year or longer since 1929; but further considerations show that before direct comparison can be made, two adjustments are necessary. In the first place not all of the families which had at one time had a settlement were stable by habit. It seems logical to exclude in table 11 the 3 percent of all families whose last settlement had terminated before 1929, inasmuch

[6] See p. 1, footnote 1.

as the lapse of time indicates the rootless type of existence found among chronic wanderers. In addition the 3 percent who left their last settled residence during 1929 should also be excluded in the interest of comparability since few of these families would have maintained a residence for as long as 1 year since January 1, 1929.

If this 6 percent is deducted from the proportion of families which had a settled residence, the original 79 percent (table 11) is reduced to 73 percent; and it is this proportion that may be used to check the earlier provisional estimate of the size of the stable group (82 percent) based upon length of residence. The difference (9 percent) in stability as determined by these two measures is logical. Length of residence as a measure requires that families be considered as stable if they remained in a community for 1 year or more, even though they establish no permanent ties; at the same time, families' opinions as to last place of settlement requires inclusion of those which intended to remain but had no means of establishing lasting ties.

The important point to be noted is not so much the difference as the agreement between the results determined by the two measures of stability. Over half of the families left their last place of settlement in 1934 and 1935 (table 11), and about the same proportion (table 10) had a residence of 3 years or more between 1929 and 1935. It seems possible to conclude from the two sets of data that about three-quarters of the families in the study of transient bureau cases had the characteristics of stable, self-supporting families prior to their transient relief history.

MOBILITY BEFORE TRANSIENT RELIEF

In deriving measures of stability from the residence history prior to application for transient relief, family mobility has been implied as the complement of stability, but has not been fully described. It is worth while to consider the backgrounds of migrant families from the point of view of moves rather than, as heretofore, from the point of view of residences.

To distinguish periods of mobility from periods of immobility, use will again be made of the arbitrary definition of a residence as a stay of 30 days or more in one community. The application of this definition immediately classified 4 percent of the families as extremely mobile, since it has been shown (table 8) that this proportion of families had no residence since January 1, 1929. Nothing is to be gained from further analysis of this small group, and they will be excluded with the warning that their high mobility is in part attributable to recency of formation. The degrees of mobility represented by the remaining 96 percent of the families will be determined by indicating (1) the continuity of residence and (2) the number of residence changes.

Continuity of Residence

An unbroken sequence of residences, even though there are changes of community over a period of years, may reflect no more than the occasional move that is a commonplace in American life. A break in the sequence, however, specifically indicates periods during which no residence was maintained and consequently reflects some degree of instability. For the purpose of the present discussion, a *continuous* residence history is defined as one in which the time elapsing between terminating a residence (of 1 month or more) in one community and establishing a new residence (of 1 month or more) in another community did not exceed 30 days. A *noncontinuous* residence history is one in which there is a period (or periods) of 30 days or longer between quitting a residence in one locality and establishing it in another.[7]

The results of applying this definition of residence continuity to all families which had a residence history are presented in table 12. Nearly four-fifths of these families had continuous residence histories for upwards of 6 years between January 1, 1929, and the date of quitting their last residence prior to application for transient relief. A break of 30 days or more in the residence histories of the remaining one-fifth indicates the existence of one period or more of protracted mobility.

Table 12.—Nature of Residence Histories of Migrant Families Since 1929 [1]

Nature of residence histories	Migrant families
Total	5, 247
	Percent distribution
Total	100
Continuous	79
Noncontinuous	21

[1] For families formed since January 1, 1929, the period under consideration begins with date of marriage.

NOTE.—242 families, which had no residence of 1 month or longer since January 1, 1929, or since formation if subsequent to that date, are not included.

It must be noted, however, that the distinction between families on the basis of the continuity of their residence histories is incomplete as a measure of mobility. The families with continuous residence histories which had moved from one locality to another several times were obviously less stable than those whose changes of residence were few. Likewise, varying degrees of mobility would be represented among families with noncontinuous residence histories. The fore-

---

[7] The same distinction applies to families whose formation occurred after January 1, 1929. In such cases a lapse of 30 days or more between marriage and first residence constituted a break in residence continuity

going information, therefore, must be supplemented by data on the number of residence changes made by families with continuous and with noncontinuous histories.

Number of Residence Changes

Approximately half of the families had either not changed their community [8] of residence at all or no more than once prior to the migration that led to transient relief (table 13). An additional 18 percent changed their place of residence twice only during the same interval. Thus, according to this measure, the mobility of a large majority of families was clearly restricted during the period examined. Actually, only the very few families which had changed their community of residence five or more times could be considered to have been highly mobile.

Table 13.—Residence Changes of Migrant Families Between January 1, 1929,[1] and First Transient Bureau Registration

Residence changes	Migrant families
Total	5,218
	Percent distribution
Total	100
No change	21
1 change	30
2 changes	18
3 changes	11
4 changes	6
5 changes or more	14

[1] For families formed since January 1, 1929, the period under consideration begins with date of marriage.

NOTE.—271 families, which had no residence of 1 month or longer since January 1, 1929, or since formation if subsequent to that date and those for which the number of residence changes was not ascertainable, are not included.

The analysis of the number of community changes leads to the same conclusion about the mobility of migrant families during the residence history period that was indicated by the previous examination of the length of residence within a community and by the families' opinion as to whether they had a settled residence.

However, some of the families which had changed their residence no more than one or two times also had noncontinuous residence histories. Since a noncontinuous residence history indicates that the process of changing communities involved periods of mobility lasting at least as long as a month, and perhaps much longer, these families were actually more mobile than the tabulation of number of com-

[8] Changes *within* a community are not included among changes of residence.

munity changes shows. The presence of such families does not, however, materially alter the conclusions suggested in table 13. Only 10 percent of the families changed residence no more than twice but had a noncontinuous residence history. This group is more than balanced by 20 percent of the families which moved three times or more and still had continuous residence histories (table 14).

Table 14.—Type of Residence History and Residence Changes of Migrant Families Since January 1, 1929 [1]

Residence changes and type of residence history	Migrant families
Total	5, 218
Continuous history	4, 145
Noncontinuous history	1, 073
	Percent distribution
Total	100
Continuous history	79
No change	19
1 change	26
2 changes	14
3 changes	8
4 changes	4
5 changes or more	8
Noncontinuous history	21
No change	2
1 change	4
2 changes	4
3 changes	3
4 changes	2
5 changes or more	6

[1] For families formed since January 1, 1929, the period under consideration begins with date of marriage.

NOTE.—271 families, which had no residence of 1 month or longer since January 1, 1929, or since formation if subsequent to that date, are not included.

MOBILITY AND YEAR OF FORMATION

Throughout the preceding discussion there have been frequent reminders that nearly half of the families included in this study were formed after January 1, 1929, the date selected for the beginning of the residence histories. The fact that so large a proportion of the families was exposed to the forces causing mobility for less than the full period under examination raises a question as to the validity of number of residence changes in measuring mobility. It may well be asked, for example, whether the large proportion of families—69 percent—which changed community of residence no more than twice indicates a low degree of mobility or simply a short period of existence as families.

The conclusion that at least a substantial majority of the families had a background of stability can carry little weight until the time factor has been examined. It becomes important, therefore, to discover the relationship between mobility and year of formation. The families with residence histories were distributed by year of formation as shown in table 15.

Table 15.—Year of Migrant Family Formation

Year of formation	Migrant families
Total	5,196
	Percent distribution
Total	100
Prior to 1929	57
1929	6
1930	6
1931	6
1932	6
1933	8
1934	8
1935	3

NOTE.—293 families, which had no residence of 1 month or longer since January 1, 1929, or since formation if subsequent to that date, and those whose year of formation was not ascertainable, are not included.

The next step is to examine the number of moves made by families formed in each of the years to discover the source of the large proportion of families with no more than two changes of residence between 1929 and 1935. The results of this examination are presented in table 16.

Table 16.—Year of Formation and Residence Changes of Migrant Families

Year of formation	Total		Residence changes					
	Number	Percent	None	1	2	3	4	5 or more
Total	5,167	100	21	30	18	11	7	13
Prior to 1929	2,928	100	15	31	20	12	7	15
1929	315	100	13	26	17	15	9	20
1930	330	100	15	20	21	15	8	21
1931	304	100	18	29	20	13	9	11
1932	319	100	19	33	17	10	10	11
1933	388	100	29	34	19	8	4	6
1934	423	100	47	37	10	3	1	2
1935	160	100	79	18	3	—	—	—

NOTE.—322 families, which had no residence of 1 month or longer since January 1, 1929, or since formation if subsequent to that date, and those whose year of formation or the number of residence changes was not ascertainable, are not included.

It may be seen that both the number and percent distributions of moves made by families formed in the years 1929, 1930, 1931, and 1932 were much the same. More important, the percent distribution of moves made by families formed in these years was closely parallel to that for all families formed prior to 1929. Referring again to table 15, it will be noted that families formed in years up to and including 1932 comprised more than four-fifths of all the families studied.

Families formed in 1933, 1934, and 1935 did, of course, make fewer moves than families formed in earlier years (table 16). But the difference becomes pronounced only among families formed in 1934 and 1935; and these families make up too small a proportion of all families to bias the results unduly. It follows, then, that the conclusion concerning relatively low mobility of all families is not invalidated by the presence of families so newly formed that they have not yet had time to make more than one or two moves.

Mobility Rate of Recently Formed Families

Table 16 suggests that families formed after 1929 were relatively more mobile than families formed prior to 1929, inasmuch as the percent distribution of moves was about the same, while the time of exposure to mobility was less. In order to measure this increasing tendency to mobility, the moves made by families formed in each of the several years must be adjusted to take into account for the period of exposure. Families formed prior to 1929 can be excluded because they existed during the full period, and the particular year of formation prior to 1929 is not reported. Likewise, the families formed in 1935 must be excluded because they were interviewed before the end of the year (September).

When the mean number of moves made since formation for each year-of-formation group is adjusted for length of exposure—by dividing by the average number of years since formation [9]—a significant trend in mobility is disclosed (table 17).

Table 17.—Average [1] Number of Residence Changes Made per Year by Migrant Families, by Year of Formation

Year of formation	Average number of residence changes since formation	Average number of years since formation to 1935	Average number of residence changes per year
1929	2.85	6.25	0.46
1930	3.08	5.25	0.59
1931	2.28	4.25	0.54
1932	2.08	3.25	0.64
1933	1.47	2.25	0.65
1934	0.83	1.25	0.66

[1] Arithmetic mean.

The more recently a family was formed, the more mobile it was in relation to the length of time it had been formed. The trend disclosed indicates that family mobility tended to be greatest soon after marriage and before the families could gain a foothold in a community.[10]

---

[9] The average number of years since family formation was computed with consideration to: (1) the fact that families formed *during* a given year had an average exposure of half of that year, and (2) the year of interview was three-quarters completed when this study was made.

[10] The coefficient of rank correlation between mean number of moves and year of formation is ($\rho = .94$) a significant value.

MOBILITY OF SETTLED AND UNSETTLED FAMILIES

When changes in community of residence are reduced to annual rates of change,[11] it is found that the rate for all the families as a group increased progressively from 1929 to 1934 (table 18). However, the 1929–1934 trend in the annual rate of change differed significantly according to the families' background during the years preceding their application for transient relief.

Table 18.—Yearly Rate of Residence Change of Migrant Families by Family Settlement Status and by Year of Change

Year of residence change	Migrant families		
	Total	With settled residence	With no settled residence
Total	5,036	4,210	826
Yearly rate of residence change per 100 families			
1929	30	25	87
1930	35	29	96
1931	35	29	94
1932	38	31	93
1933	49	42	98
1934	63	57	94

NOTE.—453 families, which had no residence of 1 month or longer since January 1, 1929, or since formation if subsequent to that date, those formed in 1935, and those whose year of formation, year of residence change, or number of residence changes was not ascertainable, are not included.

The yearly rate of residence change was calculated according to:

$$r = \frac{A}{B + \frac{1}{2}C} \times 100, \text{ in which}$$

A = the number of residence changes made in a given year.
B = the number of families formed prior to that year.
C = the number of families formed during that year. This value is divided by 2 because the average exposure of these families was for ½ of the year in which they were formed.

It will be recalled that when the families' opinion as to whether they had maintained a settled residence was used to measure stability,[12] the families were divided into two groups of unequal size: four-fifths had a residence they considered as settled and one-fifth had no such residence between January 1, 1929, and the receipt of transient relief. Among the first group, families having had a settled residence, the rate of community change was 25 per 100 families in 1929; it rose to 31 per 100 in 1932; and reached 57 per 100 families in 1934 (table 18).

[11] The frequency of the mobility of family groups for any given year was determined by considering the number of community changes made during the year in terms of the number of families in existence that year. It is expressed as an annual rate of community change; that is, as the number of changes during each year per 100 families involved.

The calculation of the yearly rate of residence change is somewhat involved because nearly half of the families were formed during the period under consideration. See note to table 18.

[12] See discussion of Stability Measured in Terms of Family Opinion (pp. 63–65).

Among the families which had no settled residence, the rate showed no such progressive increase. It remained close to 95 for each 100 families and showed little variation throughout the period 1929 to 1934. The comparatively high mobility of the families in this group cannot be explained in terms of the prolongation of the depression, since their rate of residence change was almost as high when the depression began as it was 5 years later.

In part, the consistently high mobility of this group resulted from the nature of the occupations followed by many families. Migratory-casual work, necessitating frequent change of residence as a normal part of the process of earning a living, accounted for many of the families which had never maintained a settled residence.

Doubtless other reasons also played a part in the mobility of this group. Personality defects, alcoholism, and similar conditions, if characteristic of the economic head of a family, affect the ability of a family to maintain itself permanently in a given locality. Many of the families with persistently high rates of residence change presented such problems and could only have been rehabilitated by extremely careful social direction.

By far the larger group of families, however, were displaced by adverse economic pressure. It would seem, therefore, that normal readjustment for such families would require, first of all, the correction of the factor which had been primarily responsible for their migration. Adequate employment would have solved the transient problem presented by the great majority of the families which received assistance from transient bureaus.

The information in this chapter on the background of migrant family mobility leaves little doubt that the majority of the families had been habitually settled and self-supporting in the past. Granted an increase in opportunities for employment, there is no reason for supposing that they would not have shortly resumed their normal way of living.

Chapter IV

MIGRANT FAMILIES AND THE TRANSIENT PROGRAM

FROM THE point of view of the citizens of each community, the out-of-State and out-of-town needy who asked for relief during the depression were not their responsibility. It was soon evident, however, that refusing to assist migrants was of little effect; it neither "prevented" migration nor solved the problem of immediate and pressing need. The fact that the out-of-town applicant may have been the legal responsibility of some other community was of little help, for there were no means by which this responsibility could be invoked. As a result there was a widespread demand that the Federal Government take responsibility for the nonresident in need.

The initiation of a relief program for what came to be known as "transients" was, therefore, a logical development when the Federal Government, through the Federal Emergency Relief Administration, took the leading role in providing direct relief for the unemployed. The FERA first established throughout the United States a uniform requirement of 1 year's State residence for general relief. Then, in cooperation with 47 States and the District of Columbia [1] transient bureaus were established to aid those who could not meet this 1-year requirement. On this basis, the transient program continued in operation from the fall of 1933 until the intake of new cases was closed on September 20, 1935. During this period the transient program assisted approximately 200,000 different families containing some 700,000 individual members,[2] in addition to an even larger number of unattached individuals traveling alone.

[1] Vermont did not operate a transient program.

[2] This estimate is based upon the total family intake during the operation of the FERA transient program (in the neighborhood of 300,000 families), adjusted to account for the families registering more than one time. The mean number of stays per family under care was 1.5 (table 22).

After the close of intake the transient program continued to give assistance for well over a year to thousands of cases under care at the time intake was closed. A limited number of cases, principally former registrants, were admitted to care after the intake of new cases was stopped.

Throughout its life the merit of the transient program was the subject of much dispute. To a considerable extent the controversy was based upon the unavoidable confusion that attended the initiation and operation of a totally new relief program. Although the debate over the merits of the program has not completely died away, the confusion has, and it is now possible on the basis of this study to provide some factual analysis of the transient program in relation to the depression migration of needy families.

THE MIGRATION THAT LED TO TRANSIENT RELIEF

Before turning to the record of migrant family mobility within the transient program itself, it is necessary to examine the mobility of the families immediately prior to their first transient bureau registration. Their last residence could have been terminated only under two conditions:[3] either (1) upon departure from the community or (2) upon application for transient relief in the community of last residence. Table 19 indicates the proportion of families whose last residence was terminated by migration and those terminated by application for transient relief in the community of last residence.

Table 19.—Place of First Transient Bureau Registration of Migrant Families

Place of first transient bureau registration	Migrant families
Total_____	5, 237
	Percent distribution
Total_____	100
Registered in place of last residence_____	39
Registered in place other than last residence_____	61

NOTE.—252 families, which had no residence of 1 month or longer since January 1, 1929, or since formation if subsequent to that date, and whose place of first transient bureau registration was not ascertainable, are not included.

The first transient bureau registration of 61 percent of all families was in a community other than the community of their last residence. For these families registration was immediately preceded by mobility. A variety of circumstances necessitated the first registration of these families. Some had run out of money en route to their original destination. Some had reached and departed from their original destination, and had first registered on their way to a subsequent destination. Others, upon arriving at their original destination or at a subsequent destination, immediately found themselves in acute distress when anticipated help did not materialize.

[3] The definition of a residence specified (a) that the family stay at least 1 month in a community and (b) that it receive no transient relief.

Obviously, an essential function of the transient relief program was to relieve this sort of distress. It would be expected that the families which never had a residence and those which were not at their last place of residence would make up most of the cases to whom transient relief would be necessary. In fact, these two groups combined did comprise a substantial majority of the migrant families. But table 19 reveals the existence of another group whose first stay at a transient bureau was in the place of their last residence of 30 days or longer.

In view of the popular concept of transient relief cases as consisting of needy persons en route, it may seem odd that 39 percent of a representative sample of families under transient bureau care should have obtained assistance in the same community in which they had maintained their last residence. Moreover, very few of these families had traveled to other localities and then returned (table 20). For most of them no mobility whatever intervened between last residence and transient relief.

Since a residence was by definition a stay of 1 month or more within a given community, these families did not register for transient relief until they had already lived for at least 1 month in the community where they applied. Actually, a substantial proportion had lived in the community for 6 months or more. Thus, even though these families had been mobile at some time in the past, they had completed their migration at least temporarily before they applied for transient relief.

Time Elapsed Between Last Residence and First Registration

The intervening period between the last residence and the first transient relief involved a lapse of less than 1 month for 73 percent

Table 20.—Time Elapsed Between Leaving Last Residence and First Transient Bureau Registration of Migrant Families, by Place of First Registration

Time elapsed	Total	Registered in place other than last residence	Registered in place of last residence
Total_____	5,170	2,964	2,206
	Percent distribution		
Total_____	100	100	100
Less than 1.0 month_____	73	56	96
1.0–1.9 months_____	14	22	3
2.0–2.9 months_____	3	6	*
3.0–5.9 months_____	4	7	*
6.0 months or more_____	6	9	1

*Less than 0.5 percent.

NOTE.—319 families, which had no residence of 1 month or longer since January 1, 1929, or since formation if subsequent to that date, and whose place of first transient bureau registration or time elapsed between last residence and first transient bureau registration was not ascertainable, are not included.

of the families (table 20). Practically all of the group which first registered at their place of last residence had done so within a month of the termination of their last residence. Because the last residence of these families ended by definition with their first transient relief, the transition in most cases did not involve any lapse of time whatever. The 4 percent of this group that registered for relief after 1 month had passed represents those who, migrating from their community of last residence to seek employment or help, eventually returned to their last residence and applied for transient relief.

Those families which first registered for transient relief in a different community from their last residence were generally mobile for only a short period of time before applying for relief. Well over half of these families had registered for relief within 1 month, and nearly four-fifths had registered within 2 months of leaving their last residence. On the other hand, 16 percent of these families did not receive assistance at a transient bureau until more than 3 months had passed. Although they may have remained in one locality, or in several, for a short time before moving on to another place, this entire interval must be considered one of wandering, since the stopovers were in no case for as long as 1 month. Inasmuch as these families were ineligible for resident relief and did not seek transient relief, they had other means of support—either reserve funds or, more frequently, migratory work—during this period of wandering.

THE EFFECT OF THE TRANSIENT PROGRAM UPON MOBILITY
"Uncle Sam's Hotels"

The transient program was frequently charged with "encouraging transiency." According to one commonly expressed opinion the transient program subsidized large numbers of undeserving people who were wandering aimlessly about the country. Transient bureaus, it was held, provided free and convenient accommodations for sightseers touring the country. Two editorials illustrate this fairly common point of view:

The *Times* has not cared for the transient bureau idea nationally. It has aggravated, not mitigated the nuisance of wandering, jobless boys, many of them touring the country for the fun of it, and of professional hoboes doing the same. This applies to the families also.[4]

In the past two years, transients have been able to travel in comparative comfort through the aid of "Uncle Sam's hotels" scattered from one end of the nation to the other. Most of the itinerants make no pretension of staying at one place. They blithely skipped from one camp to another, seeing the country while the government footed the bills.[5]

The acceptance of such opinions is not difficult to understand. A small part of the migrant family population did consist of chronic

---

[4] *El Paso Times*, El Paso, Tex., September 16, 1935.
[5] *Pueblo Chieftain*, Pueblo, Colo., November 8, 1935.

wanderers. Although these families were few in number, their seemingly aimless mobility and frequent requests for aid called attention to themselves so forcibly that it was natural, though erroneous, to consider them representative of migrants in general. A small group among the unattached was even more important in creating this impression. An earlier study has pointed out that 7 to 8 percent of the unattached transients receiving aid from the transient program during 1935 reported that a desire for adventure was the reason for their migration.[6] Thus, the extreme case, because of the attention it attracted, was accepted as proof that all needy migrants were irresponsible and undeserving.

Hostility toward all needy migrants was nonetheless the prevailing attitude in most communities. This attitude served to perpetuate or to initiate the "passing on" policy; i. e., overnight care accompanied by an order to leave town the next day, in dealing with these unwanted guests. Indeed, this policy was the only solution, in most communities, that could find support among citizens harassed by the mounting needs of the resident unemployed and the threat of increased taxation to meet these needs. Thus, the attitude of the resident population toward the migrant was in part responsible for the aimless "wandering" that aroused so much criticism.

On the basis of the information obtained in the present sample study, it is possible to test the validity of this criticism.

Turnover Rates

Turnover among migrant families in the transient bureaus can be considered as having two forms. The first consisted of turnover between the different transient bureaus within the national system and is measured by the extent to which families moved about from one bureau to another. The second type of turnover consisted of the process by which the migrant families under care in the entire program were renewed. This type is measured in terms of the rate at which families entered and left the transient program, regardless of moves they may have made from one bureau to another.

The records of the Division of Transient Activities report both types of turnover without distinguishing between them. They report total cases opened, total cases closed, and the number of families under care during a 24-hour period on the 15th day of each month (fig. 21). It is possible to determine from these figures the trends in both types of turnover combined. The migrant family openings rate (the number of cases opened throughout each month as a percent of cases under care on the 15th day of each month) is shown in table 21

---

[6] See Webb, John N., *The Transient Unemployed*, Research Monograph III, Division of Social Research, Works Progress Administration, Washington, D. C., 1935, p. 60 and table 24A.

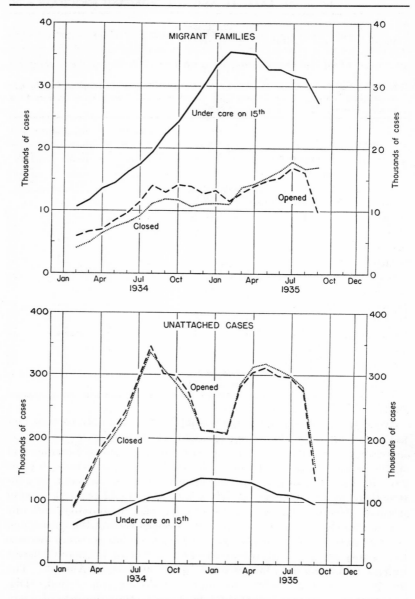

FIG. 21 - NUMBER OF TRANSIENT BUREAU CASES OPENED AND CLOSED
DURING EACH MONTH AND NUMBER OF CASES UNDER
CARE ON THE 15th OF EACH MONTH
February 1934 through September 1935

Source: Appendix table 12.

AF 2870, WPA

for the period February 1934 through September 1935, together with the closings rate (the number of cases closed throughout the month as a percent of the cases under care on the 15th day of each month).

Table 21.—FERA Transient Program Openings and Closings of Migrant Family and Unattached Transient Cases During Each Month per 100 Cases Under Care at Mid-month, February 1934 to September 1935

	Migrant families		Unattached transients	
Year and month	Openings per 100 cases under care	Closings per 100 cases under care	Openings per 100 cases under care	Closings per 100 cases under care
1934				
February	56	38	153	146
March	57	43	193	184
April	51	47	234	227
May	59	52	265	255
June	60	52	279	268
July	65	53	301	296
August	72	58	329	321
September	58	53	280	286
October	58	49	256	246
November	51	39	211	203
December	42	37	156	156
1935				
January	39	34	158	156
February	32	31	154	155
March	37	39	211	214
April	40	40	235	242
May	45	46	258	264
June	46	50	264	273
July	53	56	269	271
August	51	53	262	268
September [1]	36	62	140	162

[1] Intake of new cases closed on September 20, 1935.

Source: Division of Transient Activities, Federal Emergency Relief Administration. See also appendix table 12 of this report.

A little consideration will show that if the result of the transient program had been the encouragement of transiency, a *progressive* increase in mobility would be revealed in the rate of opening and closing cases. This point can be demonstrated by reference to table 21. In 1934 the rate of opening family cases at transient bureaus rose from 59 per 100 cases under care in May to 72 per 100 cases in August. Clearly this is a significant increase in mobility, but one that is explained by the fact that the weather during the spring and summer is favorable to mobility. In 1935 a similar seasonal increase in mobility occurred, but it started at a lower point (45 per 100 cases) in May and reached a lower point (51 per 100 cases) in August. The number of families under care increased during this period. Discounting the seasonal factor there is evidence that the rate of openings for migrant families actually declined, whereas the rate would have risen if the transient program had encouraged irresponsible wandering.

The behavior of the rates at which families applied for assistance (cases opened) should, by themselves, provide sufficient indication that transient relief was not the cause of increased mobility. But additional evidence is available from the rates at which families left transient bureaus. If families wandered about aimlessly, using the bureaus simply as convenient stopover points, the closing rates should have risen as rapidly as opening rates and there would have been no such piling up of cases as is shown by the midmonthly count of cases under care. That this was not the case is shown by the behavior of the closing rate which did not equal or pass the opening rate until April 1935 when the peak of the case load had been passed and a voluntary liquidation of the migrant family population had begun.

It is interesting to compare, in figure 22, the opening and closing rates for migrant families and unattached cases. The higher transient bureau turnover of the unattached person moving about the country without dependents is immediately apparent. Moreover, the rates at which unattached cases were opened and closed increased much more rapidly during the summer than the family rates. From February to August 1934 the opening and closing rates for unattached transients almost doubled. This tremendous increase in mobility is shown by the almost vertical rise of the two curves in figure 22. During the same period of time the opening and closing rates for families rose less than half as much.

For the unattached the marked increase in openings was accompanied by only a slight increase in cases under care on the 15th day of each month (fig. 21). For the families the increase in openings was much less, and the proportionate increase in cases under care by the 15th of each month was much greater. In other words, despite the wide swings in the rates of openings and closings among the unattached transients, the two rates moved together much more closely than the same two rates for family groups.

These comparisons show that there was a decided difference in the transient bureau turnover of the two groups receiving care. The unattached moved more frequently than the family population. It should be noted, however, that the pronounced changes in the mobility of the unattached are associated with the seasons of the year. For neither the unattached nor the family groups is there any evidence that opening and closing rates tended to increase with time; the rate curves did not start at a higher point or reach a higher peak in 1935 than in the preceding year.

The Number of Stays in Transient Bureaus

The use of rates to measure the mobility and turnover of migrant families receiving aid from transient bureaus has the disadvantage of lumping together those who moved within the transient bureau system with those who entered and left the system. Thus, an opening rate and a closing rate of 50 per 100 cases under care could mean that the same 50 families left one bureau and registered at another during

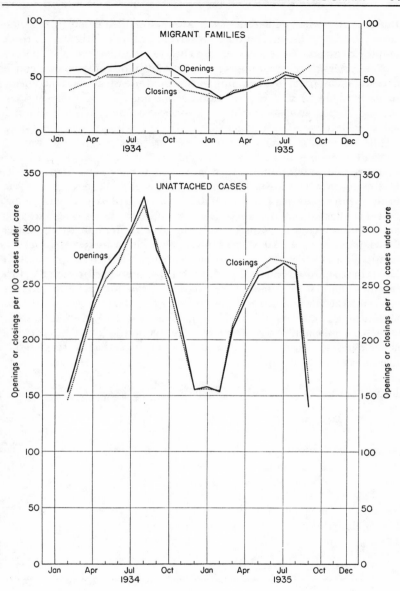

FIG. 22 – RATE OF OPENING AND CLOSING TRANSIENT
BUREAU CASES
February 1934 through September 1935

Source: Table 21.

AF-2871, WPA

the month, or it could mean that 50 new families came to transient relief and 50 different families left transient relief through private employment or some other adjustment.

The inherent shortcoming of rates as an index of mobility can be overcome, in part, by examining the number of stays at transient bureaus made by the migrant families included in the representative sample of this study. The record for 5,489 families is presented in table 22.

The average (mean) number of registrations per family was 1.5; i. e., at the time this study was made each 100 families under care had a record of 50 previous transient bureau registrations in addition to the registration initiating the stay then in progress. Moreover, nearly three-quarters of the families studied had registered for care under the transient program only once, and this stay was still in progress. An additional 16 percent of the families had registered twice. Thus, 9 out of every 10 of the families showed no tendency to use the facilities of the transient program for "seeing the country while the Government footed the bill." Among the remaining 10 percent of the families there were some whose migration was aimless and purposeless; but there were others—the migratory-casual workers—who used the transient bureaus repeatedly in getting to and from areas in which short-time seasonal work was available. For the latter group, transient relief served as a supplement to earnings that were generally inadequate.

Table 22.—Number of Transient Bureau Registrations Made by Migrant Families

Number of transient bureau registrations	Migrant families
Total	5,489
	Percent distribution
Total	100
1 registration	74
2 registrations	16
3 registrations	5
4 or 5 registrations	3
6 or 7 registrations	1
8 registrations or more	1
Average [1] registrations per family	1.5

[1] Arithmetic mean.

An interesting test of the immobilizing effect of transient relief is available from an examination of the stays made by families which had the most unstable backgrounds before the period of transient relief. There were 242 families which had no residence of as long as 30 days in one community from the time of marriage (or January 1,

1929, if formed before that date) until they made the first application for transient relief (ch. III).   Despite this indication of high mobility, nearly two-thirds of these families had stayed in only one transient bureau and were still under care at the time this study was made (table 23).

Table 23.—Number of Transient Bureau Registrations Made by Migrant Families Which Had No Residence of 1 Month or Longer Since January 1, 1929 [1]

Number of transient bureau registrations	Migrant families with no residence
Total	242
	Percent distribution
Total	100
1 registration	64
2 registrations or more	36

[1] For families formed since January 1, 1929, the period under consideration begins with date of marriage.

The stabilization of this group of families is especially significant. The transient relief program provided these families with their first opportunity to get off the road; and the result, as table 23 clearly shows, was for the majority of this particular group the first period of stabilization they had known since their formation into families.

Duration of Stay in Transient Bureaus

Three-fourths of all families had registered only one time for transient relief (table 22).   Over one-half of this group had been under care for 3 months or longer (table 24).   The median length of stay for families which registered only once was 4 months.

Because the sample study on which table 24 is based was conducted toward the close of the transient program, the proportion of families which had been under care for a year or more was greater than could have been possible earlier in the history of the program.   Otherwise, the length-of-stay data may be considered typical of the situation that existed from month to month after the full operation of the program.   It is significant that somewhat over one-third of the families with only one stay in transient bureaus had first registered for transient relief within 2 months of interview.   This fact explains the relatively high turnover (opening and closing rates) discussed earlier. For at least this proportion of the families, transient relief was needed for only a short time to assist in achieving the purpose of the migration.

About one-quarter of the families obtained assistance from transient bureaus two or more times.   The proportion of these families staying

Table 24.—Length of Time Migrant Families Spent at Place of First and Last [1] Transient Bureau Registration

Time spent at transient bureau	Migrant families which registered 1 time only [2]	Migrant families registered 2 or more times	
		At place of first registration [3]	At place of last registration [4]
Total_____	4,008	1,426	1,410
	Percent distribution		
Total_____	100	100	100
Less than 1.0 month_____	22	37	39
1.0–1.9 months_____	12	15	19
2.0–2.9 months_____	10	10	10
3.0–5.9 months_____	18	20	15
6.0–11.9 months_____	27	14	13
12.0 months or more_____	11	4	4
Average [5] (in months)_____	4.0	1.9	1.6

[1] Place of last registration was at place of interview.
[2] 36 families, for which the time spent at transient bureau was not ascertainable, are not included.
[3] 19 families, for which the time spent at transient bureau was not ascertainable, are not included.
[4] 35 families, for which the time spent at transient bureau was not ascertainable, are not included.
[5] Median.

less than 1 month was distinctly higher than among families which had only one contact with transient relief. In part, this difference is the result of families using transient bureaus as stopover points en route to a particular destination, but the group also includes the families whose migrations represented either a regular attachment to migratory-casual work or purposeless wandering.

Table 24 reveals that the last registration of this group of families was of slightly shorter duration than the first stay.[7] This fact does not, however, indicate a progressive increase in mobility between transient bureaus, since the last stay had not yet been terminated at the time this study was made.

The Meaning of the Turnover Rates

With all the evidence in, the effect of the transient program on one aspect of depression mobility may now be seen. The case for the transient program appears clearly in the record of migrant family turnover; i. e., the rates at which families entered and left the transient bureaus.

It has been pointed out that turnover among migrant families was of two kinds. The first consisted in turnover within the national system of transient bureaus or in movement from one bureau to the

[7] In measuring the duration of stays in transient bureaus for families receiving aid more than one time, consideration was given only to the first stay and the stay which was still under way when this study was made, since only about 10 percent of the families had more than two stays.

other. The second form consisted in the process by which the migrant family population as a whole was renewed.

As far as the first form of turnover is concerned, the data on the number and duration of stays in transient bureaus permit a definite judgment. This form of turnover was small and was, in so far as it appeared at all, the result of the presence of a small number—not in excess of 10 percent of the total—of highly mobile families. The transient program did not encourage families "to blithely skip from one camp to another"; on the contrary, the program had a stabilizing effect on families, even on those without a prior residence.

As to the second form of turnover—the renewal process—the pertinent data are those showing the rates at which cases were opened and closed at transient bureaus between February 1934 and September 1935, and the duration of stays in transient bureaus by families with only one transient bureau registration.

Monthly opening and closing rates of 30 to 60 families for each 100 under care could mean, over a period of 20 months, only one of two things: the same families were wandering from bureau to bureau, or the migrant family population was continually in process of rapid renewal. Since the evidence from this study is clear that the amount of bureau-to-bureau wandering was small, it must be concluded that the migrant family population was constantly changing in membership. It has been shown that the average number of transient bureau registrations per family was 1.5. If this figure is used to adjust the total opening and closing rates, it may be seen that roughly 20 to 40 percent of the family case load entered and left the transient relief program each month. In contrast, the monthly closings rate on urban *resident* relief in 1935 was only 5.6 percent.[8]

It is true that some of this turnover resulted from the transfer of family cases from transient relief to resident relief. However, the reports of the Division of Transient Activities show that only 8 percent of the 198,039 family cases closed between July 1934 and September 1935 were transferred to resident relief. Accordingly, allowing adjustment for these cases, and even allowing for the possibility that many other families may have received resident relief later, the turnover of transient relief cases through normal economic adjustment would still appear to be many times higher than the turnover rates on resident relief.

In summary, then, the case for the transient program stands as follows: Transient relief was a stabilizing influence upon families uprooted by the depression. It did not encourage wandering. On the contrary, it prevented aimless wandering by relieving the needs which

---

[8] Unpublished data in the files of the Division of Social Research, Works Progress Administration, Washington, D. C.

are its cause. Stabilization, however, did not imply unlimited dependence upon the transient program for support. Transient relief provided necessary but interim assistance to migrants who in most instances had definite objectives and who were frequently only temporarily in need.

The transient program was set up to fill a gap in the relief system, and its first purpose was to relieve distress. That it also assisted in the relocation of families is beyond doubt. Although the rate of turnover of migrant families from transient relief back into private industry cannot be conclusively determined, it is obvious from the data on number of transient bureau registrations and on total cases opened and closed that the rate must have been very high. Probably it was many times higher than the turnover in the resident relief population. In so far as families were enabled to resettle in an environment more favorable to them than the one they had left, transient relief was beneficial, though this effect was in a sense incidental to the basic purpose of the program. The value of the transient program was that it not only provided immediate relief to a distressed group but also assisted materially in working out a solution of the problems that gave rise to the distress.

LEGAL RESIDENCE REQUIREMENTS FOR GENERAL RELIEF

Finally, in judging the value of the transient program, it is necessary to bear in mind that transient relief took over the no man's land which had been created by the legal residence requirements of the various States.[9] The extent of the responsibility which the transient program thus assumed—and the extent of the needs which would have otherwise been largely unmet—can be inferred from a review of the various legal restrictions governing eligibility for resident relief. The requirements in each of the States and the District of Columbia as of January 1, 1936, are set forth in summary form in table 25. This tabulation presents the situation as it existed at about the time the study was made. Two years later—January 1, 1938—the general picture had changed somewhat and a notation of the changes by States are to be found in table 26.

It should be noted that the provisions shown in tables 25 and 26 have exceptions of two kinds. Some State statutes permit or require temporary aid for the needy nonresident. In practice, however, this type of aid seldom amounts to more than emergency medical care for those in ill-health and overnight care for the able-bodied.

---

[9] Legal settlement is a technical term meaning a residence under circumstances which entitle a person in need to assistance from a political unit. Legal settlement, which is based on State poor laws, must be distinguished from the uniform residence requirement of 1 year in all States established under the FERA and from special State regulations governing eligibility for emergency relief.

Table 25.—Residence Requirements for General Relief, January 1, 1936

State	State requirement	Local requirement
Alabama		6 months in county immediately preceding application.
Arizona		
Arkansas		
California	3 continuous years without receiving relief. Time spent in public institution or on parole not counted.	1 year in county immediately preceding application.
Colorado	1 year immediately preceding application and actual physical presence 350 days. Applicant must be self-supporting or the husband, wife, or minor child of a self-supporting person; otherwise, requirement is 3 years immediately preceding application with actual physical presence for 30 months.	6 months in county immediately preceding becoming chargeable.
Connecticut		4 years in a town or 1 year if owner of $500 worth of real estate. Aliens entitled to relief only by vote of inhabitants or by majority vote of selectmen and justices of the peace and inhabitants. The 4 years must be self-supporting.
Delaware	Legal residence	
Florida [1]	Counties between 9,700 and 10,500, 2 years.	1 year in counties between 9,700 and 10,500 or of 155,000 population.
Georgia		
Idaho	1 year immediately preceding application.	6 months in county immediately preceding application.
Illinois		12 months immediately preceding application.
Indiana		Uninterrupted residence of 1 year in township. If supported by governmental agency during first 6 months, such time is eliminated in computing residence period.
Iowa		1 year continuously in county without receiving support from public funds or care in any charitable institution and without being warned to depart. If warned to depart applicant may be considered resident within 1 year of filing affidavit that he is not a pauper.
Kansas		1 year in county.
Kentucky		
Louisiana		
Maine		5 successive years in town without receiving supplies as a pauper.
Maryland		In Baltimore and Prince Georges Counties applicant must be a resident. In Anne Arundel County 1 year's residence is required.
Massachusetts		5 successive years in a town without receiving public relief
Michigan		1 year in township, city, or county without receiving public relief.
Minnesota	1 year. Time spent in public institution or under commitment to guardianship of State Board of Control, or while receiving relief, is excluded in determining residence.	

[1] No State-wide law in Florida.

Table 25.—Residence Requirements for General Relief, January 1, 1936—Continued

State	State requirement	Local requirement
Mississippi		6 months in county.
Missouri	To receive emergency relief applicant must be citizen of State.	1 year in county next preceding time of any order for relief. County court may in its discretion grant relief to any person without regard to residence.
Montana		1 year in county immediately preceding application.
Nebraska	1 year excluding any period during which person received care or relief.	6 months in county excluding any period during which person received care or relief.
Nevada	3 years	6 months in county.
New Hampshire		5 consecutive years in town. Counties must support any person for whose support no person or town in the State is chargeable.
New Jersey		5 years uninterrupted stay in county or municipality.
New Mexico	1 year	90 days in county.
New York		1 year continuous residence in town or city without receiving public relief. Certain counties in which specified hospitals and veterans' homes are located require 5 years residence for inmates of the specified institutions.
North Carolina	3 years, unless at time of entering State person was able to support himself. Time spent in any institution or on parole therefrom is not counted.	1 year continuously in county.
North Dakota	1 year continuously without receiving public relief. Time spent in charitable, custodial, or correctional institution excluded.	1 year in county or if legal resident of State residence in county in which applicant spent major part of preceding year. Time spent in charitable, custodial, or correctional institution excluded.
Ohio		County, 12 consecutive months town or city, 12 consecutive months in county, 3 consecutive months in town or city without receiving public relief.
Oklahoma		6 months in county.
Oregon	4 years. To receive emergency relief applicant must be citizen of State.	6 months in county without receiving public relief.
Pennsylvania		1 continuous year in poor district with intent to establish permanent abode.
Rhode Island	2 years. For home relief or work relief under State financed and State supervised program ending June 30, 1939. State Unemployment Relief Commission may waive these requirements in special cases.	6 months in town for home relief or work relief under State financed and State supervised program ending June 30, 1939. State Unemployment Relief Commission may waive these requirements in special cases. For local relief 5 years in town without aid; or have estate of inheritance or freehold in town and yearly income of $20 clear for 3 years.
South Carolina		3 successive years in county or city. Person must be citizen of some State and must have maintained self and family during 3-year period.
South Dakota	1 year	90 days in county.
Tennessee		1 year in county (applies to poorhouse care only).
Texas	1 year. Funds derived from the sale of State bonds for emergency relief, used only for aid of a person resident 2 years immediately preceding application.	6 months in county.

Table 25.—Residence Requirements for General Relief, January 1, 1936—Continued

State	State requirement	Local requirement
Utah	1 year (applies only to county permanent poor relief program).	4 months in county; minors 1 year. (Applies only to county permanent poor relief program.)
Vermont	State provides for nonresidents of towns who have resided in State 1 year or more.	3 years in town.
Virginia	3 years unless at time of migration person was able to support self; otherwise, 1 year.	12 consecutive months in county, town, or city without receiving public or private relief.
Washington	--	6 months in county immediately preceding date of application.
West Virginia	3 years unless migrant entered State self-supporting.	1 year continuously in county.
Wisconsin	--	1 year in town, city, or village without being supported as a pauper or employed on a Federal work project, an inmate of any asylum or institution, etc.

Source: See Lowe, Robert C. and Associates, *Digest of Poor Relief Laws of the Several States and Territories as of May 1, 1936*, Division of Social Research, Works Progress Administration, Washington, D. C. Additional material will appear in Lowe, Robert C., *State Public Welfare Legislation*, a forthcoming monograph.

Table 26.—Changes in Residence Requirements for General Relief as of January 1, 1938

State	State requirement	Local requirement
Arizona	3 years immediately preceding application. Temporary absence for a total of 1 year does not affect the right for relief.	6 months in county, immediately preceding application; 12 months immediately preceding application to receive hospitalization or medical care from county board of supervisors, except for emergency cases.
Montana	1 year. Aliens illegally in the United States not eligible.	6 months in county. 1 year's county residence for care at poor farm or workhouse.
New Jersey	1 year without interruption immediately preceding May 4, 1936. 5 years without interruption for persons not qualifying under the preceding provision. Time spent in charitable, custodial, or correctional institution excluded.	1 year in municipality or if legal resident of State, municipality in which applicant spent major part of preceding year. Time spent in charitable, custodial, or correctional institution excluded.
Oklahoma	1 year for State funds.	1 year for State funds. 6 months for county funds.
Pennsylvania	1 year immediately preceding application.	
Washington	--	
West Virginia	1 year when funds are specifically available for that purpose, relief may be granted to those who have not been residents of State 1 year.	Actually residing in county.
Wyoming	1 year without receiving public relief, provided applicant has not been absent from State for a period of 1 year or more immediately preceding application.	1 year in county without receiving public relief, provided applicant has not been absent from county for a period of 1 year or more immediately preceding application.

Source: Lowe, Robert C. and Staff, Division of Social Research, Works Progress Administration, Washington, D. C. Additional material will appear in Lowe, Robert C., *State Public Welfare Legislation*, a forthcoming monograph.

Secondly, by January 1, 1936, about two-thirds of the States had passed special emergency relief legislation which altered, in practice, the poor law provisions listed in tables 25 and 26. The majority of these emergency acts did not contain specific residence requirements, and the requirements of the poor laws were applied in some States but not in others. As a result there has been a vast amount of confusion over the meaning and application of residence requirements, and the provisions set forth in tables 25 and 26 may not represent the actual practice of some of the States. These provisions should, however, convey a fairly clear idea of the difficulties which confronted the nonresident family in need of relief.

The requirement for relief eligibility is often much more stringent than the residence requirement for voting purposes. In a majority of States residence of some specified minimum of time has always been a condition for relief eligibility. Laws prescribing a period of residence either in the State or locality, or in both, as a condition for relief eligibility were on the statute books of 43 States and the District of Columbia on January 1, 1936. In the other five States residence requirements were imposed in actual practice.

In 23 States the laws imposed a local (county, town, or city) residence requirement, and in 18 States they prescribed periods of residence in both State and local units. In the latter case, the required period of State residence was usually greater than the required period of local residence. In general, it may be said that the purpose of dual State residence requirement is to provide State-wide "protection" to the local subdivisions against an influx of indigent interstate migrants, while the purpose of the local residence requirement is to establish the responsibility of communities for persons who meet the State requirements. The less stringent residence requirements of the localities, once State requirements are satisfied, permit some intrastate migration without loss of eligibility for assistance in some specific place in the State.

Several States have two sets of State residence requirements. North Carolina, Virginia, and West Virginia had (on January 1, 1936) State residence requirements of 1 year with this interesting exception: a 3-year State requirement was to be imposed unless at the time of migration to the State the applicant was able to support himself. Texas and Rhode Island make one residence requirement for one relief fund and another requirement for other relief funds. Such requirements are clearly intended to disqualify needy interstate migrants from regular State assistance.

Settlement laws in typical States provided that a migrant would not be eligible for local relief unless he had lived within the State continuously, with intent to establish permanent residence, and without public assistance of any sort for at least 1 year; and in 10 States the residence must have lasted from 2 to 5 years.

Residence statutes as of January 1, 1938, do not, on the whole, reveal much progress toward more consistent and equitable laws than those which were in effect on January 1, 1936, though there have been changes in a few States (table 26). Washington has repealed its residence requirement, while Arizona has enacted a statute which prescribes 3 years' residence in the State. Pennsylvania and West Virginia have repealed their local residence requirement and enacted a 1-year State residence law. Montana, Oklahoma, and Wyoming have added State residence requirements to their already existing local requirements. New Jersey has amended its statutes so as to require a 5-year State residence if an applicant has not lived within the State for 1 year immediately preceding May 4, 1936; the earlier New Jersey statute prescribed a 5-year local residence.

The migrant's legal status was further complicated by statutes in 19 States providing for loss of legal settlement in the State of origin. In most of the States making definite provision, legal settlement was lost (as of January 1936) after 1 year's absence regardless of whether it has been acquired elsewhere or not. In two States it was lost after absence of 30 days. These provisions for the loss of legal settlement often caused migrants to lose residence status in one State before acquiring it in another. An earlier study [10] showed that 40 percent of migrant families in transient bureaus in June 1935 were without legal settlement in any State. It is evident, however, that the large proportion of such cases does not reflect any particular degree of mobility among the families so much as it demonstrates the efficiency with which the settlement laws of the States operate to cancel responsibility for needy migrant groups.

When the 48 States are viewed as a whole the complexity of residence requirements for general relief is immediately evident. Not only is the individual migrant family unaware, in most instances, of these requirements but State relief officials are also constantly confronted with borderline cases where judgment must be exercised, as well as official interpretations of the statutes, and a variety of practices that depart from the letter of the statute. A period of self-supporting residence that in one State makes a family eligible for local assistance is completely inadequate in another State. A family which has resided for 1 year without relief in one State is eligible for assistance; in another State the same family would be a transient family, excluded from local benefits.

[10] Webb, John N. and Bryan, Jack Y., *Legal Settlement Status and Residence History of Transients*, Research Bulletin TR–9, Division of Research, Statistics, and Finance, Federal Emergency Relief Administration, Washington, D. C., 1935.

General relief involves an expenditure that is borne in whole or in part by the community granting aid, and legislators have not been disposed to add to this expense the cost of caring for those who do not "belong" in their community. Whether or not severe residence requirements do protect a State from an influx of needy nonresidents is still a debatable question. But in many cases, the only reasonable solution of distress is emigration. At this point residence requirements and economic forces meet in a head-on collision that can be avoided only by broadening or abolishing the concept that people actually do belong in a particular place regardless of the fact that the place may not provide the means of making a living.

The more rigid requirements for acquisition of settlement status, especially when coupled with provisions making settlement quickly lost (as in California, Kansas, Minnesota, New Jersey, Oregon, and South Dakota, where specifically less time was needed in 1936 to lose settlement status than to acquire it), were clearly designed to send to other States more needy migrants than are received. Obviously, however, since the other States either try to do the same thing or have at least usually protected themselves against those who do try, the gain arising out of the stringency and confusion of the laws is only at the expense of the migrants in need.

Chapter V

PERSONAL CHARACTERISTICS

A DESCRIPTION of the families which received assistance from the transient program has been deferred until their mobility could be fully explored. Having discovered why and where the families migrated and having examined their mobility before and while receiving transient relief, it is important at this point to consider the families in terms of the standard descriptions of population. As part of the search for factors that explain why some distressed families migrated while others did not, it is particularly important to measure the extent to which migrant families were like or unlike families in the general population.

The comparisons to be presented here show that there is a relationship between particular personal characteristics and migration. For example, the comparative age distribution of economic heads of migrant families and of families in the total population reveals a close relationship between youth and mobility; and an examination of the color and nativity of migrant families indicates that native-born white families are more likely to migrate under adverse circumstances than are foreign-born white or Negro families. Data on the personal characteristics [1] of migrant families make it possible to show further that still other characteristics are not necessarily connected with the fact of migration. Domestic discord, for example, or failure to possess such basic social resources as a common school education were characteristic of migrant families to no greater extent than with families which did not migrate under the same economic stress.

[1] An account of the personal characteristics of the heads of migrant families receiving aid from transient bureaus was given in a previous study—Webb, John N., *The Transient Unemployed*, Research Monograph III, Division of Social Research, Works Progress Administration, Washington, D. C., 1935. But because the data there were drawn from a smaller and less representative sample based on 13 cities instead of the 85 cities sampled for this study, this study supersedes the earlier description.

COMPOSITION OF MIGRANT FAMILIES

Migrant families were complete family groups in the great majority of cases. That is, most family groups on the road [2] were identical in membership with the family group before migration. Less than one-tenth of the families had one or more members absent from the relief group, and in only a very small proportion of cases was the economic head [3] of the group among the absentee members (table 27).

Table 27.—Migrant Families Reporting Absence of Members Normally Part of Family Group

Composition	Migrant families
Total	5, 489
	Percent distribution
Total	100
Reporting no absentees	91
Reporting absentees	9
Economic head present	6
Economic head absent	3

Since most of the families left no member behind at the place of last residence, it is suggested that the severance from that community was both complete and final. The small proportion of absentee members is also significant in connection with the families' occupational resources. Because of the fact that nearly all families were complete, their stabilization on a self-supporting basis was dependent upon the human resources of the group at hand.

Not only were most migrant families complete in the sense that all members usually a part of the group were present during migration, but they were also normal [4] family groups. Approximately four-fifths of the migrant families studied consisted of husband and wife (28 percent) or of husband and wife and one or more children (51 percent); and in addition, there was a small proportion (3 percent) of normal families that included some other related or unrelated person (table 28)

[2] Throughout this chapter *migration* refers to the period between leaving the last place of residence lasting 1 month or longer and September 1935.

[3] Because of the presence of incomplete family groups on the road, it is necessary to distinguish between the "economic head" and the "present head" of the group. If the economic head of the family was absent, the present head was some member of the family group other than the person usually responsible for the economic welfare of the group.

[4] Families composed of husband and wife or husband and wife and their children are commonly called "normal families." Families composed of a man and his children or a woman and her children are called "broken families." The terms *normal* and *broken* are used with these specific meanings in this chapter.

Table 28.—Composition of Migrant Families Before and During Migration and Composition of Families in Resident Relief Population, October 1933 [1]

Family composition	Migrant families		Resident relief families Oct. 1933
	During migration	Before migration	
Total	5, 489	5, 489	2, 726, 221
	Percent distribution		
Total	100	100	100
Normal families	82	85	81
Husband and wife	28	26	14
Husband, wife, and children	51	55	60
Normal with others	3	4	7
Broken families	18	15	14
Woman and children	14	11	9
Man and children	2	2	3
Broken with others	2	2	2
Other types	*	*	5

*Less than 0.5 percent.

[1] Division of Research, Statistics, and Finance, *Unemployment Relief Census, October 1933*, Report Number Three, Federal Emergency Relief Administration, Washington, D. C., 1935, p. 35. 1-person families are not included.

It is important to observe from this comparison that the proportion of broken families on the road was only slightly larger than before migration, and that no particular type of broken families showed an appreciable increase. The small increase in the proportion of broken families of the woman-children type (from 11 percent to 13 percent) after migration indicates the extent to which male family heads were absent from the relief group. This reflects the small importance of domestic difficulty as a reason for leaving settled residence (table 1). Moreover, the proportion of migrant families which left their children behind was small, since the proportion of families consisting of only husband and wife increased from 26 percent before to 28 percent during migration. Broken families in which the wife was absent (man-children type) from the relief group did not increase at all.

The composition of migrant families receiving aid from transient bureaus did not differ markedly from that of families in the total resident relief population (table 28). The proportion of "other types" of families, i. e., related and unrelated persons not combinations of husband, wife, or children, but living together as family groups, was negligible among migrant families in comparison with resident relief families. This difference is no indication that persons living in this combination did not migrate; but it does mean that if they did, they did not apply for assistance at transient bureaus as family groups. Because of the youth of the family heads, there was a larger proportion of husband-wife families without children among migrant than among resident relief families; but the over-all proportions of normal and broken families were much the same. Although the proportion of broken families was slightly higher after beginning migration than before migration, the agreement with the proportion in the resident relief population is so close that family composition does not appear to have been a selective factor in determining whether or not a family would migrate.

SIZE

Logically, the presence of children and other dependents should tend to restrict the mobility of families under adverse conditions. And, indeed, a comparison between the size of migrant families and families in the resident relief and general population reveals that size of family was one of the selective factors in depression migration.

Table 29.—Size of Migrant Families, of Families in the Resident Relief Population of 1933,[1] and of families in the General Population of 1930 [2]

| Size of family | Migrant families | | Resident relief families Oct. 1933 | Families in general population 1930 |
	During migration	Before migration		
Total_____	5,489	5,489	2,762,575	27,547,200
	Percent distribution			
Total_____	100	100	100	100
2 persons_____	35	32	20	25
3 persons_____	25	25	20	23
4 persons_____	17	18	19	19
5 persons_____	10	11	14	13
6 persons_____	5	6	10	8
7 persons or more_____	8	8	17	12
Average [3] size_____	3.1	3.2	4.1	3.6

[1] Division of Research, Statistics, and Finance, *Unemployment Relief Census, October 1933*, Report Number Two, Federal Emergency Relief Administration, Washington, D. C., 1934, p. 26. 1-person families are not included.
[2] Bureau of the Census, *Fifteenth Census of the United States: 1930*, Population Vol. VI, U. S. Department of Commerce, Washington, D. C., 1933, p. 36. 1-person families are not included.
[3] Median.

Table 29 and figure 23 show two significant facts: (1) Well over one-half of all the families, both before and after migration, contained only two or three persons, and two-person families occurred more frequently than any other; [5] and (2) migrant families were smaller than families in the general population and were markedly smaller than resident relief families.

In considering size of family as a selective factor in mobility it must be remembered that the families in the study were interstate migrants, and the distance traveled, while generally restricted (see ch. I) was obviously much greater than the distance traveled by intra-

[5] See appendix table 13 for a detailed distribution of migrant families by size and family type.

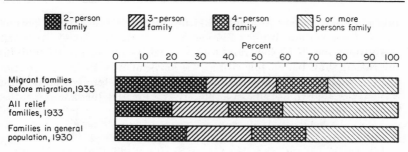

FIG. 23- SIZE OF MIGRANT FAMILIES AND OF FAMILIES
IN RESIDENT RELIEF AND
GENERAL POPULATIONS

Source: Table 29.   AF-2872, WPA

county and intrastate migrants.   The conclusion of this report that
size of family is a selective factor in depression migration is therefore
restricted to the instances of interstate mobility.   A recent report on
the mobility of the families in the general population [6] of Michigan
shows the need for caution in reaching conclusions on the relationship
between size of family and migration in general.

The Michigan report includes a tabulation of the range of moves
during a period of 57 months (April 1930 to January 1935) classified
by the number of dependent children on January 15, 1935.[7]   Despite
its obvious limitations, the Michigan tabulation shows that there is
relatively little relationship between size of family and percent of
moves in intrastate migration, but that there is a definite tendency for
the percent of interstate moves to decline as the number of dependent
children increases.

The comparison of migrant family size first with the size of resident
relief families and second with the Michigan mobility study indicates
that, in this social characteristic at least, migrant families resembled
other mobile groups more than other distressed groups.

AGE

Economic Heads

Youth was a clearly defined characteristic of the economic heads of
migrant families.   Among the family groups included in this study,

---

[6] Webb, John N., Westefeld, Albert, and Huntington, Albert H., Jr., *Mobility
of Labor in Michigan*, Division of Social Research, Works Progress Administration,
Washington, D. C., 1937, pp. 31–33 and particularly table 97.

[7] The lack of comparability between moves made at any time during a period
of 57 months and number of children at the end of the period was recognized.
The purpose of the tabulation was simply to explore the possibilities of the data
by using a small sample of schedules preliminary to the complete tabulation of a
larger sample.   The lack of comparability mentioned above has been minimized
in the larger tabulation which is being made at the present time (October 1938).

approximately one-half of the economic heads were under 35 years of age, and more than three-fourths were under 45 (appendix table 14). In contrast, less than one-third of the heads of resident relief families in 1933 were under 35, and only about three-fifths were under 45.

The contrast in age is still more marked when the economic heads of migrant family groups are compared with the male heads of all families enumerated in the 1930 Census. Forty-five percent of all male family heads in 1930 were 45 years of age or older. This was true, however, of only 22 percent of the male heads of migrant family groups included in this study (fig. 24 and appendix table 14).

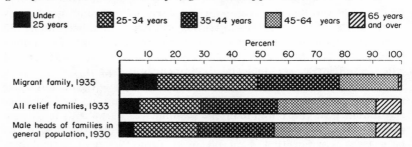

FIG. 24–AGE OF MIGRANT FAMILY HEADS AND OF FAMILY HEADS IN RESIDENT RELIEF AND GENERAL POPULATIONS

Note: Age distribution available only for male family heads in the general population.

Source: Appendix table 14.   AF-2873,WPA

Previous studies have stressed the youth of the depression migrants who received aid from transient bureaus. Unattached transients were found to be even younger than the economic heads of family groups.[8] But youth as a characteristic of migrants is not confined to the depression period or to migrants in need of public assistance. Youth was an important selective factor [9] in the rural-urban migration of the 1920's; and the study of labor mobility in Michigan (1930 to 1935) found "* * * the 20–24 year age group showed a larger proportion of workers moving than any other age group * * * and * * * workers in the most mobile age groups * * * were more likely to have completed * * * longer moves than were those [workers] of other age groups." [10] Accordingly, just as with family size, the age of migrant families was more closely related to the age of other migrants not in distress than of other needy groups that did not migrate.

[8] See Webb, John N., *op. cit.*, p. 24 ff.

[9] Thornthwaite, C. W., *Internal Migration in the United States*, Bulletin I, Philadelphia: University of Pennsylvania Press, 1934, pp. 32–37.

[10] Webb, John N., Westefeld, Albert, and Huntington, Albert H., Jr., *op. cit.*, p. 5.

Age and size of family are related; this relationship qualifies but does not impair the validity of the previous conclusion that size of family, in itself, is a selective factor in migration. The difficulties that stand in the way of distress migration by large families remain regardless of age; and the fact that migrant families are small is in part explained by age and in part by the difficulty of migrating in large groups.

Other Members

In view of the large proportion of young economic heads of migrant families, it is scarcely surprising to find that the age of other principal members of the family groups, mostly wives of economic heads, was even lower. The proportion of other principal members under 35 years of age was 65 percent as compared with 49 percent of economic heads; and the proportion under 45 was 86 percent as compared with 78 percent of economic heads (appendix table 15).

Since over half of all principal members (economic heads and other principal members) were under 35, it follows not only that the number of children per family was likely to be small but also that a large proportion of these sons and daughters would not yet have passed the ages usually associated with common (grade) school attendance. Of the 9,658 individuals apart from economic heads or other principal members of migrant families, nearly one-third were less than 5 years of age and over one-half were between the ages of 5 and 14. Less than one-fifth of all children and other relatives were 15 years of age or older. Thus, not only were the economic heads of migrant families predominantly young but youth was also a characteristic of all members of the family group.

COLOR AND NATIVITY

A comparison of the color and nativity characteristics of migrant families with those of nonmigrant families shows that native-born white families tended to migrate more readily than foreign-born white or Negro families. The proportion of white economic heads was larger among migrant families than among urban resident relief families, although it was about the same as among families in the general population (table 30 and fig. 25).

By comparison with the nativity of the 1930 population, migrant families were composed of a much smaller proportion of foreign-born. Migrant families also included a smaller proportion of foreign-born than the urban relief population.[11] Since a similarly high proportion of native-white persons existed among unattached transients,[12] it is clear that the native-born white, whether families or single indi-

[11] Comparable data in the 1933 FERA Relief Census are not available.
[12] See Webb, John N., *op. cit.*, pp. 33–35.

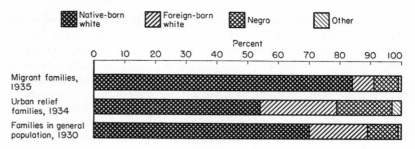

FIG. 25 – COLOR AND NATIVITY OF MIGRANT FAMILY HEADS
AND OF FAMILY HEADS IN URBAN RESIDENT
RELIEF AND GENERAL POPULATION

Source: Table 30.   AF-2874,WPA

viduals, migrated more readily in response to distress than other population groups.

Two forces tended to stabilize the foreign-born population during the depression. During the decades since the period of agricultural expansion, foreign-born white immigrants have settled in large industrial centers and grouped themselves according to racial or national ties. These ties have acted as deterrents to migration, despite the pressures arising from limited economic opportunity and recurring periods of unemployment. In addition, it is probable that local prejudice outside of the highly industrialized States makes the migration of distressed foreign-born persons both more difficult than for the native-born and less likely to provide a solution of their economic problems.

Table 30.—Color and Nativity of Economic Heads of Migrant Families, of Families in Urban Resident Relief Population of May 1934,[1] and in the General Population of 1930 [2]

Color and nativity	Migrant families [3]	Urban resident relief families May 1934	Families in general population 1930
Total	5, 447	201, 994	29, 904, 663
	Percent distribution		
Total	100	100	100
White	91	79	89
Native-born	84	54	70
Foreign-born	7	25	19
Negro	8	18	10
Other	[4] 1	[4] 3	1

[1] Based on preliminary tabulation of schedules used by Palmer, Gladys L. and Wood, Katherine D., in *Urban Workers on Relief,* Research Monograph IV, Division of Social Research, Works Progress Administration, Washington, D. C., 1936.
[2] Bureau of the Census, *Fifteenth Census of the United States: 1930,* Population Vol. VI, U. S. Department of Commerce, Washington, D. C., 1933, p. 11.
[3] 42 family heads, whose color and nativity were not ascertainable, are not included.
[4] Includes Mexicans.

Negroes showed similar characteristics. In comparison with the general family population, Negroes were underrepresented among migrant families but overrepresented among families on urban resident relief. The overrepresentation of Negro families on urban resident relief is evidence that they were less able to withstand the rigors of a depression. Yet, even though subject to greater economic distress, Negro families were much less likely to migrate than white families.

No doubt custom and prejudice operate to restrict the mobility of Negro families just as effectively as they restrict the foreign-born white.[13] Migration without adequate resources, whether by highway or railroad, is much more difficult for Negroes, and particularly so in the South. Moreover, the employment available for Negroes in any locality is restricted by preference for white labor, and the practicability of migration is limited.

Mexican and other race or color groups were proportionately as numerous among migrant families as among families in the general population of 1930. Among migrant families they were chiefly Mexican migratory workers and Indians who were registered principally in the central and southwestern parts of the country.[14]

The fact that foreign-born and Negro families were underrepresented in the transient relief population justifies a supplementary examination into some aspects of the migration of these two minority groups. Information on State of registration, State of origin, and reasons for leaving settled residence and selecting destinations for both foreign-born and Negroes is presented in appendix B.

CITIZENSHIP

Only 2 percent of all heads of migrant families were without full citizenship status, and half of these had received at least first citizenship papers (appendix table 16). Among the foreign-born family heads approximately two-thirds (66 percent) had full citizenship status. An additional one-sixth had first papers, and one-sixth were without any citizenship status. Of the "others" slightly less than three-fourths were full citizens, and the rest were without any citizenship status.

MARITAL STATUS

In view of the predominance of normal migrant families and young family heads, small proportions of single, separated,[15] divorced, and

---

[13] The fact of the northward migration of Negroes during and after the World War does not invalidate this conclusion, since that migration was in response to an abnormal labor demand which nullified the usual difficulties in Negro mobility.

[14] See Webb, John N., *Transients in December*, TR–3, Division of Research, Statistics, and Finance, Federal Emergency Relief Administration, Washington, D. C., March 1935.

[15] "Separation" as used here refers to separation with intent to live permanently apart, rather than temporary separation arising out of the exigencies of migration.

widowed family heads and other principal members may be anticipated (table 31).

Table 31.—Marital Status of Economic Heads and Other Persons 15 Years of Age and Over in Migrant Families and of Heads of Families in the General Population of 1930 [1]

Marital status	Migrant families		Heads of families in general population 1930
	Economic heads	Other members 15 years of age and over	
Total	5, 489	6, 481	29, 490, 174
	Percent distribution		
Total	100	100	100
Single	2	23	5
Married	85	74	79
Separated, widowed, and divorced	13	3	16

[1] Bureau of the Census, *Types of Families in the United States*, special report, U. S. Department of Commerce, Washington, D. C., August 5, 1935, table 1.

The classification of the families' reasons for migration showed that domestic difficulty was a relatively insignificant cause of family mobility. The same fact is reflected in the small incidence of separation, widowhood, and divorce among the family groups. Compared with the returns from the 1930 Census, the proportion of separated, widowed, and divorced heads among migrant families was significantly less than was reported for the total population.

Although the proportion of other persons 15 years of age and over who were married was smaller (74 percent) than among economic heads (85 percent), the actual number was slightly greater. This difference resulted from the presence in a number of family groups of a few married adults other than the spouse of the head. Most of these other married adults were parents or other relatives of economic heads.

SEX

Although migrant and nonmigrant families differed as to age, size of family, and color and nativity, there was little difference in their composition by sex.[16] The economic heads of migrant families

[16] The sex ratio for all members of the migrant family groups included in this study was 97.5 males per 100 females; the ratio for the resident relief population included in the FERA Unemployment Relief Census of 1933 was 103.4; and the ratio for the total population 1930 Census was 102.5. Actually the difference in composition by sex of migrant and resident family groups was less than is indicated by these ratios. Both the FERA Unemployment Relief Census and the United States Census of 1930 included one-person families which were more frequently men than women. Transient bureaus, on the other hand, classified one-person cases as "unattached" or nonfamily persons.

were much more frequently men than women, whereas women were a majority among other principal members. But males and females were about equal in number among all migrants—family heads, other principal members, and children and other relatives (table 32).

Table 32.—Sex and Status in Family of Persons in Migrant Families

Sex	Total	Economic heads	Other principal members	Children and other relatives
Total_____	19,978	5,489	4,813	9,676
	Percent distribution			
Total_____	100	100	100	100
Male_____	49	86	4	51
Female_____	51	14	96	49

The slight excess of females among all persons is partly a result of the presence of more migrant families of the woman-children type than of the man-children type (appendix table 13). In other words, most of the male economic heads were accompanied by a wife, but only a few of the female economic heads were accompanied by a husband.

The fact that about one-half of all members of migrant family groups were females is significant by comparison with the other and larger group of depression migrants—the unattached transients. Among unattached transients the proportion of women did not at any time exceed 3 percent of the total unattached transient relief population.[17] The difficulties of travel were alone sufficient to restrict the number of unattached women, but an additional restriction was imposed by social attitudes which disapproved the wandering of lone women. Obviously social disapproval does not apply to the migration of women as members of family groups, although the difficulty of travel without adequate resources does apply.

EDUCATION

Only a small proportion of the heads of migrant families lacked some formal education, and about three-fifths of them had completed at least the eight grades of common school.

It will be observed in table 33 that the younger heads of families were generally better educated than the older family heads, and that this tendency was consistent throughout except for the age group 16 to 19 years. The lower educational achievement of this group is probably the result of an early assumption of family responsibility.

---

[17] See Webb, John N., *The Transient Unemployed, op. cit.*, pp. 31–32.

Table 33.—Schooling Completed and Age of Economic Heads of Migrant Families

Schooling completed	Total	Age				
		16–19 years	20–24 years	25–34 years	35–44 years	45 years and over
Total_____	5, 437	52	636	2, 000	1, 567	1, 182
		Percent distribution				
Total_____	100	100	100	100	100	100
None_____	3	2	1	2	4	6
Grade school:						
Less than 5 years_____	15	13	8	11	15	21
5–7.9 years_____	23	23	23	23	22	23
8–8.9 years_____	26	27	25	28	27	23
High school (9–12.9 years)_____	28	35	40	32	26	20
College (13–16.9 years)_____	5	—	3	4	6	6
Postgraduate (17 years and over)_____	*	—	*	*	*	1
Average [1] years completed_____	8. 4	8. 4	8. 7	8. 5	8. 3	8. 0

*Less than 0.5 percent.

[1] Median.

NOTE.—52 family heads, whose age or schooling completed was not ascertainable, are not included.

The native-born white heads of migrant families were found to have the highest level of education, followed in order by the foreign-born whites, the Negroes, and the other races (table 34).

Table 34.—Schooling Completed and Color and Nativity of Economic Heads of Migrant Families

Schooling completed	Total	Color and nativity			
		Native-born white	Foreign-born white	Negro	Other [1]
Total_____	5, 405	4, 556	357	415	77
		Percent distribution			
Total_____	100	100	100	100	100
None_____	3	2	7	9	13
Grade school:					
Less than 5 years_____	14	12	20	30	26
5–7.9 years_____	23	23	24	27	32
8–8.9 years_____	26	27	23	15	13
High school (9–12.9 years)_____	29	31	19	14	13
College (13–16.9 years)_____	5	5	5	4	3
Postgraduate (17 years and over)_____	*	*	2	1	—
Average [2] years completed_____	8. 4	8. 5	8. 0	6. 2	6. 0

*Less than 0.5 percent.

[1] Includes Mexicans.

[2] Median.

NOTE.—84 family heads, whose schooling completed or color and nativity were not ascertainable, are not included.

Migrant family heads had a higher level of schooling completed than the heads of either the urban or rural relief population (table 35 and fig. 26).

Table 35.—Schooling Completed by Economic Heads and Other Members 15 Years of Age and Over of Migrant Families and of Heads of Urban [1] and Rural [2] Resident Relief Families

Schooling completed	Migrant families		Heads of resident relief families	
	Economic heads [3]	Other members 15 years of age and over [4]	Urban (Oct. 1935)	Rural (Oct. 1933)
Total	5,441	6,379	6,982	5,333
	Percent distribution			
Total	100	100	100	100
None	4	3	10	8
Grade school:				
Less than 5 years	13	10	22	19
5–7.9 years	23	23	26	27
8–8.9 years	26	27	22	29
High school (9–12.9 years)	29	34	17	15
College (13–16.9 years)	5	3	3	2
Postgraduate (17 years and over)	*	*	*	—
Average [5] years completed	8.4	8.5	7.0	7.6

*Less than 0.5 percent.

[1] Carmichael, F. L. and Payne, Stanley L., *The 1935 Relief Population in 13 Cities: A Cross Section*, Series I, No. 23, Division of Social Research, Works Progress Administration, Washington, D. C., December 31, 1936, p. 9.
[2] McCormick, Thomas C., *Comparative Study of Rural Relief and Non-Relief Households*, Research Monograph II, Division of Social Research, Works Progress Administration, Washington, D. C., 1935, p. 30.
[3] 48 family heads, whose schooling completed was not ascertainable, are not included.
[4] 102 persons 15 years of age and over, whose schooling completed was not ascertainable, are not included.
[5] Median.

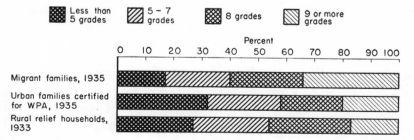

FIG. 26- SCHOOLING COMPLETED BY HEADS OF MIGRANT FAMILIES AND BY HEADS OF URBAN AND RURAL RESIDENT RELIEF FAMILIES

Source: Table 35.

AF-2875, WPA

Some of the difference between the educational attainments of migrant and resident relief families is attributable to the youth of the migrant group and to the underrepresentation of Negroes. In any event, it is obvious that educational attainment was not a selective factor in depression migration.[18]

---

[18] There are no detailed studies of the schooling of the entire population with which the schooling of persons in migrant families may be compared. The Statistical Division of the Office of Education, United States Department of the Interior, in *Biennial Survey of Education, 1932–1934*, p. 14, estimates that 51.5 percent of persons above 21 years of age in 1934 have completed at least the eighth grade, that 13.9 percent have been graduated from high school, and that 2.9 percent have completed college. These figures appear to show that the migrant family heads and the other adult members have had more than average schooling, since 62 percent of the economic heads and 60 percent of the other adult members have completed at least the eighth grade.

Chapter VI

OCCUPATIONAL RESOURCES

A REPRESENTATIVE cross section of the families receiving assistance from transient bureaus necessarily consists largely of families which, at the time of interview, had failed to achieve the purposes of their migration. As soon as migration succeeded, the successful families were no longer a part of the transient relief population and therefore were outside the limits of this study. It is worthy of note, however, that the figures on the turnover among transient families (ch. IV) suggest that migration must have been wholly or partially successful in a large proportion of cases and within a relatively short period of time.

Although this study could not follow migrant families after they left the transient relief population to determine the kind of readjustment that put an end to migration, it is possible to report on three of the most important factors that conditioned the return of migrant families to self-support: (1) employability, (2) usual occupation and industry, and (3) duration of unemployment. For those heads of migrant families who were employable and who, in addition, possessed skills acceptable to industry, it seems reasonable to assume that their return to stability depended chiefly upon an increase in the labor demand of private employment.

EMPLOYABILITY

In this study, employability was determined after a careful consideration of the following factors: (1) interview and case record information regarding the temporary or permanent physical and mental disabilities, temporary or chronic illness, personality and speech difficulties, attitude toward employment, illiteracy, and similar factors bearing on ability and willingness to work; (2) medical examinations, and clinical and hospital reports whenever available; (3) type of work done before migration; (4) age; (5) responsibility for the care of dependent children under 16 years of age; and (6) the interviewers' and case workers' opinions of employability.

107

It was recognized that willingness to work taken in conjunction with an absence of employment handicaps did not assure reemployment by private industry. Any attempt to define employability, or degrees of employability, in terms of probable reabsorption by private industry presumes a knowledge of future developments in economic activity that does not exist. Such factors as age and employment opportunities, to mention only the more obvious, have an important bearing upon the reabsorption of heads of migrant families judged in this study to be employable.

The effect of age on employability has been accounted for, at least in part, by limiting the wholly employable group to economic heads 16 through 50 years of age.[1]   But it is clear that arbitrary limits cannot be applied to such intangible factors as the location of families in relation to opportunity for employment. The intricacies of an employability index which would attempt to measure all factors prohibit its use. On the other hand, the practicability of the simple index—absence of bodily handicaps plus willingness to work—justifies its use. The discussion which follows presents an examination of factors which only affect, but do not necessarily determine, the employability of the economic heads of family groups included in this study.

After these factors had been considered by the interviewers for each case, one of the following classifications was assigned: (1) employable; (2) employable with handicaps; or (3) unemployable. The employable group includes those who were under 51 years of age, were willing to work, and for whom no handicaps were reported. In cases where the economic head was 65 years of age and over, was a woman responsible for the care of dependent children, or was definitely listed as unemployable by the interviewer, the head was judged unemployable. In other cases, the seriousness of handicaps was considered so that a judgment could be made as to whether the economic head was "employable with handicaps" or "unemployable."

Employable Heads

In these terms, somewhat over half (56 percent) of the family heads studied appeared to be unquestionably employable; that is, the head was present in the relief group, had no ascertainable employment handicaps, and was willing to work. The problem represented by this group was thus chiefly of reemployment by private industry at a wage sufficient to insure stability (table 36).

It may be thus said that a majority of the economic heads of migrant families possessed the most important qualification for a resumption of stable, self-supporting lives. They were able to work, willing to

---

[1] By definition, an economic head was a person 16 years of age or older who was responsible for the family group.

work, and were within the preferred age range for private employment. Moreover, the majority had other employable members within the family group.

Table 36.—Employability of Economic Heads of Migrant Families

Employability	Economic heads
Total	5, 426
	Percent distribution
Total	100
Employable	56
Employable with handicaps	33
Unemployable	11

NOTE.—63 family heads, whose employability was not ascertainable, are not included.

Heads Employable With Handicaps

The employability of the economic heads of the remaining families offers a more difficult problem of analysis. Clearly some must be judged totally unemployable by any criterion; and the bodily handicaps of others were such as to restrict the range of gainful occupations in which they might engage. However, there were some whose employment handicaps were probably more apparent than real. For instance, age was considered a partial employment handicap for all economic heads 51 through 64 years and a total handicap for all heads 65 years of age and over. This arbitrary procedure probably does some violence to the facts; but it does less violence than would have resulted from ignoring the well-known tendency of employers in hiring workers to discriminate in favor of younger men.

Approximately one-third of the economic heads of migrant families were neither wholly employable nor wholly unemployable according to the criteria used in this study (table 36). That is, one out of every three of the economic heads was willing to work, but there were one or more reasons [2] for believing that his ability to work was limited by handicaps that would impair his success in the labor market (table 37).

Chronic illness was the employment handicap most frequently reported. Among the more important types of chronic illness were, in order of importance: diseases of the respiratory system; heart, circulatory, and blood diseases; and diseases of the stomach and abdomen.

[2] In a considerable number of cases a person suffered from more than one employment handicap. For instance, an economic head may have lost the fingers of his right hand and he also may have been 55 years of age. In this case there would be both an age and a disability handicap. For purposes of this report only one handicap was tabulated—the one that most directly affected the employment of the individual. In the case cited above, physical disability would be tabulated rather than age.

Table 37.—Employability and Employment Handicaps of Economic Heads of Migrant Families

Employability and employment handicaps	Economic heads
Total_____	5,426
	Percent distribution
Total_____	100
Employable 16–51 years of age_____	56
Employable with handicaps_____	33
Physical disability_____	6
Mental disability_____	1
Chronic illness_____	11
Age (51–64 years)_____	7
Physical injury_____	*
Temporary illness_____	1
Institutionalization_____	*
Women with dependents [1]_____	2
Illiteracy_____	2
Other_____	3
Unemployable_____	11
Age (65 years and over)_____	1
Women with dependents_____	6
All other disabilities_____	4

* Less than 0.5 percent.

[1] Women whose families required only part-time care, who were able and willing to work, and who had work histories.

NOTE.—63 family heads, whose employability was not ascertainable, are not included.

The proportion of family heads handicapped by chronic illness was considerably higher in this than in a previous study [3] of migrant family groups. The difference is partially due to the fact that the earlier study covered continuous monthly registrations [4] which overrepresented the more mobile and presumably the least handicapped portion of the population. The far more complete examination of employability made in the present study also indicates that handicapped migrant family heads tended in the earlier study to overstate their ability to work,[5] either out of pride or the belief that it would improve

[3] See Research Bulletins Nos. TR–1, 2, 3, 6, and 8, December 28, 1934, to August 26,1935, Division of Research, Statistics, and Finance, Federal Emergency Relief Administration, Washington, D. C.

[4] Continuous monthly registrations did not take account of the tendency of family groups to accumulate in areas with healthful climates. Thus, among the *monthly registrations* in Colorado, New Mexico, Arizona, and California, the proportion of family heads suffering from ill-health was probably smaller than the proportion of such persons under care in these States. Since the present study was based principally upon a sample of transient families already under care in transient centers, it may be expected that the proportion of family heads in poor health would be somewhat larger than among family heads currently registered.

[5] The importance of ill-health as a cause of family migration has already been discussed. See pp. 7–8.

their chances of obtaining private employment or employment on the Works Program.

Age was a partially disabling factor for 7 percent of all economic heads and in importance ranked next to chronic illness. Physical disabilities that restricted but did not entirely prevent gainful employment complete the list of the three most important handicaps found among the economic heads of migrant families. These three handicap classifications account for approximately two-thirds of all heads who were considered to be employable with handicaps. Chief among the physical disabilities were: trunk or back injuries; eye injuries; and leg, ankle, or foot injuries. That serious employment handicaps are presented by these physical disabilities under modern hiring procedures is obvious.

Each of the other employment handicaps involved a relatively small number of family heads. Among these other handicaps were the presence of dependent children or invalids who restricted women heads to part-time employment, illiteracy, and other disabilities comprising a wide variety of such circumstances as personality difficulties and unwillingness to work.

In terms of occupational attachment many of the families with heads employable with handicaps were capable of returning to a self-supporting way of life in a new community provided that normal job opportunities were present. Broadly speaking, the usual occupations of these workers (appendix table 17) were such that resettlement would not be unduly difficult in many localities.

It must not be overlooked, however, that many of the families whose economic head was partially handicapped had bunched up in particular localities, where the chances for securing employment adequate to insure a stable self-supporting existence were not promising. For example, many families in which some member was suffering from respiratory disorders migrated to the Southwest, where communities were simply unable to absorb them into private industry. The failure of many of these families to make such an adjustment is evidenced by the large numbers that turned to migratory agricultural work as the only means of remaining in an area believed to be beneficial to the health of the head.

Unemployable Heads

There remain approximately one-ninth of the economic heads who were judged to be totally unemployable (table 37). The most important group among the unemployable heads consisted of women with dependent children requiring their entire time. This group accounted for over half of the totally unemployable heads. Women partially and totally unemployable because of dependent children made up 8 percent of all families and were equal in size to the proportion handicapped and disabled by age.

Next in importance were the family heads who, regardless of age, were so incapacitated by bodily infirmities as to be unfit for gainful employment. Finally, the unemployable group included the economic heads who were 65 years of age and over. Age, however, was the least important of the three factors, accounting for slightly under 1 percent of all economic heads and approximately one-fourteenth of all those classified as unemployable.

It is clear that resettlement of these families on a self-supporting basis was highly improbable. These families contained no members who were either fully or partially employable. In so far as these families were absorbed by communities there was merely a transfer of relief burden from the old to the new place of residence. For many families, particularly the health seekers, such a shift was socially desirable. But the community at their destination is ordinarily reluctant to extend such families aid, and it is seldom that a community of former residence will make any contribution toward defraying the cost of maintaining the family in another locality.

The unemployable family therefore faced the unhappy alternatives of living precariously on what assistance could be obtained in a new community or of returning (or being returned) to a place of former residence where as often as not assistance was no more readily obtained. Though small in number this type of needy nonresident family presents a social problem of great complexity and one that deserves careful and sympathetic consideration on the part of public and private social service agencies. Since the majority of the unemployable heads were mothers who could not work because of the need of caring for young children or invalid dependents, the principal relief problem represented by the unemployable heads was need for aid to dependent children.

USUAL OCCUPATION AND INDUSTRY

About one-ninth of the families lacked an employable economic head, and for this group it seems clear that public assistance was the only means by which stability could be assured. For about nine-tenths of the families, however, employment was necessary for reestablishment. It is worth while, then, to consider their qualifications for employment in terms of the occupation which they usually followed and the industries in which these occupations were customarily pursued.

Because of a pronounced similarity in occupational characteristics between family heads judged to be fully employable and those judged to be employable with handicaps, the two groups have been combined in the discussion which follows. There has been included, however, one summary description of the occupational characteristics of the two groups separately (appendix table 17).

Usual Occupation

In this study the usual occupation was defined as the particular gainful activity at which the economic head of the family had customarily been employed or, in some instances, the activity which the economic head considered his usual occupation by reason of experience or training.[6]

Main Class of Usual Occupation

Broad groups of occupations indicate roughly the general level of skill possessed by workers, and at the same time suggest their economic level. The groupings used in classifying migrant family heads are as follows: (1) white-collar workers, subdivided into professional, proprietary workers (nonagricultural and agricultural), and clerical and salespersons; (2) skilled workers; (3) semiskilled workers; and (4) unskilled workers, who were further divided into laborers (nonagricultural and agricultural) and domestic and personal service workers.

Table 38.—Usual Occupation and Sex of Employable Economic Heads of Migrant Families

Usual occupation	Total	Male	Female
Total	4, 729	4, 527	202
	Percent distribution		
Total	100	100	100
White-collar workers	28	28	28
Professional workers	5	5	6
Proprietary workers (nonagricultural)	4	4	*
Proprietary workers (agricultural)	8	8	*
Clerical and salespersons	11	11	22
Skilled workers	23	24	1
Semiskilled workers	25	25	24
Unskilled workers	24	23	47
Laborers (nonagricultural)	8	8	—
Laborers (agricultural)	7	8	3
Domestic and personal service workers	9	7	44

*Less than 0.5 percent.

NOTE.—760 family heads, who were unemployable, whose usual occupation was not ascertainable, and those who never worked, are not included.

The employable economic heads of migrant families were almost evenly distributed among the white-collar, skilled, semiskilled, and unskilled workers (table 38). It is interesting to compare this distribution with the broad occupational status of the resident unem-

[6] In cases where the economic head had worked at two or more occupations for short periods of time the occupation of his last nonrelief job of 2 weeks, or longer duration was reported as his usual occupation. The number of such cases, however, was small.

ployed in 1935 and of the general population of gainfully employed persons in 1930 (table 39 and fig. 27).

Table 39.—Main Class of Usual Occupation of Employable Economic Heads of Migrant Families, of Resident Relief Families, March 1935,[1] and of Gainful Workers 16–64 Years of Age in the General Population of 1930 [2]

Main class of usual occupation	Employ-able economic heads of migrant families [3]	Economic heads of resident relief families March 1935	Gainful workers 16–64 years of age in general population 1930
Total	4,729	4,037,709	45,913,404
	Percent distribution		
Total	100	100	100
White-collar workers	28	10	42
Skilled workers	23	18	13
Semiskilled workers	25	24	15
Unskilled workers	24	48	30

[1] Hauser, Philip M., *Workers on Relief in the United States in March 1935*, Abridged Edition, Division of Social Research, Works Progress Administration, Washington, D. C., 1937, p. 26.
[2] Bureau of the Census, *Fifteenth Census of the United States: 1930*, Population Vols. IV and V, U. S. Department of Commerce, Washington, D. C., 1933, pp. 44 ff and 352 ff, respectively.
[3] 760 family heads, who were unemployable, whose usual occupation was not ascertainable, and those who never worked, are not included.

Although the economic heads of the two relief groups are not perfectly comparable with all gainful workers 16–64 years of age in the general population, the differences in the distribution shown in table 38 are of such magnitude that significant tendencies are suggested. The occupational status of migrant family heads, in terms of broad occupational groupings, was clearly higher than that of economic heads of resident relief families. A substantially smaller proportion of the migrant family heads was unskilled, and a larger proportion was skilled and white-collar workers.

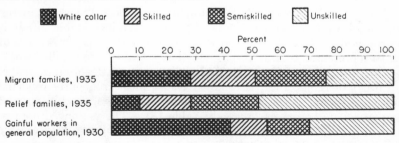

FIG. 27—MAIN CLASS OF USUAL OCCUPATION OF ECONOMIC HEADS OF MIGRANT FAMILIES AND RELIEF FAMILIES IN 1935 AND OF GAINFUL WORKERS 16 THROUGH 64 YEARS OF AGE IN THE GENERAL POPULATION, 1930

Source: Table 39.

AF-2876, WPA

The occupational status of the migrant family heads also compares favorably with that of the gainful workers in the 1930 Census. The general population contained a higher proportion of unskilled workers than the migrant family sample. White-collar workers, however, were greatly underrepresented among migrant family heads. The economic heads of migrant families thus occupied a position intermediate between the resident relief unemployed, in which unskilled workers bulked largest, and the total gainful working population, in which white-collar workers were the largest group.

These broad occupational groups fail to carry over the significant detail associated with individual occupations. In order, then, to get a more specific description of the pursuit followed by the economic heads of migrant families it is necessary to consider some of the more important occupations that make up each of the four broad occupational groups (appendix table 18).

White-Collar Workers

Among the professional and technical workers in migrant groups the most important occuptions were: musicians, technical engineers, clergymen and religious workers, and actors. The importance of actors, musicians, and clergymen reflects to some extent the presence of itinerant showmen and revivalists on the road. The most important occupations included under "proprietors, managers, and officials (nonagricultural)" were retail dealers and managers, peddlers, and building contractors. Clerks in offices, bookkeepers, and telegraph and radio operators accounted for most of the office workers; and salesmen, real estate agents, and canvassers accounted for most of the salesmen and kindred workers (appendix table 18).

Skilled Workers

Because of the relatively high proportion of skilled workers among the employable economic heads of migrant families (table 39) it is of particular interest to examine some of the more important types of skills represented by this group. Well over half of these skilled workers were usually employed in the building and construction industry. In order of importance, the skilled trades most frequently reported were: painters, carpenters, electricians, plumbers, engineers, and structural steel workers (appendix table 18). The prolonged depression of the building industry, together with the fact that a considerable number of building trades workers are accustomed to moving about the country in pursuit of their trades, accounts for the relative over-representation of skilled construction workers among migrant families.

The remaining skilled workers consisted of craftsmen usually attached to manufacturing industries. Mechanics led the list, with machinists, locomotive engineers and firemen, and printing trades workers following in the order named.

Semiskilled Workers

Workers from the building and construction industries were somewhat less important among the semiskilled than among skilled workers. Truck and tractor drivers in building and construction work were, however, more numerous than any other single group among semiskilled workers, and accounted for nearly three-quarters of the semiskilled from the building and construction industry. Machine operators were the principal group among the semiskilled workers from the manufacturing industries. These workers were usually employed in the manufacture of textiles, iron and steel, automobiles, clothing, and food (appendix table 18).

Unskilled Workers

Economic heads of migrant families following unskilled pursuits came in almost equal numbers from manufacturing and allied industries, agriculture, and domestic and personal service. Unskilled workers usually employed on the construction of buildings, roads, and streets and sewers, together with the traditionally mobile laborers in mines and on railroads, made up most of the unskilled group outside of agriculture. Farm hands, including some migratory seasonal workers who regularly follow the crops, account for the fairly large group of unskilled agricultural workers. Among the domestic and personal service workers, cooks in restaurants, construction camps, and hotels, accounted for well over one-third of the group. Barbers, waiters, and domestic servants made up the second most important group of domestic and personal service workers.

Usual Industry

Table 40 presents a summary account of the industrial attachment of the economic heads, and appendix table 19 presents a detailed account of the specific industries.

Table 40.—Usual Industry and Sex of Employable Economic Heads of Migrant Families

Usual industry	Total	Male	Female
Total	4,663	4,466	197
	Percent distribution		
Total	100	100	100
Agriculture, forestry, and fishing	17	17	4
Extraction of minerals	4	5	—
Manufacturing and mechanical industries	37	37	24
Transportation and communication	13	14	2
Trade	13	13	13
Public service	1	1	1
Professional service	6	5	9
Domestic and personal service	9	8	47

NOTE.—826 economic heads, who were unemployable, whose usual industry was not ascertainable, and those who never worked, are not included.

This distribution of family heads did not depart greatly from the industrial distribution of heads of relief families or gainful workers in the general population. Migrant families represented no particular broad industrial classifications to the exclusion of others. Though a few variations appeared, migrant families' industrial attachment was in general a cross-section of the industrial composition of the resident relief and general populations (table 41 and fig. 28).

Table 41.—Usual Industry of Employable Economic Heads of Migrant Families, of Resident Relief Families March 1935,[1] and of Gainful Workers 10 Years of Age and Over in the General Population of 1930 [2]

Usual industry	Employable economic heads of migrant families [3]	Economic heads of resident relief families 1935	Gainful workers 10 years of age and over in general population 1930
Total_____	4,663	3,719,074	47,492,231
	Percent distribution		
Total_____	100	100	100
Agriculture, forestry, and fishing_____	17	22	23
Extraction of minerals_____	4	4	3
Manufacturing and mechanical industries_____	37	39	30
Transportation and communication_____	13	14	9
Trade_____	13	9	16
Public service_____	1	1	2
Professional service_____	6	2	7
Domestic and personal service_____	9	9	10

[1] Hauser, Philip M. and Jenkinson, Bruce, *Workers on Relief in the United States in March 1935*, Vol. II, A Study of Industrial and Educational Backgrounds, Division of Social Research, Works Progress Administration, Washington, D. C. (in preparation).
[2] Bureau of the Census, *Fifteenth Census of the United States: 1930*, Population Vol. V, U. S. Department of Commerce, Washington, D. C., 1933, p. 408 ff.
[3] 826 economic heads, who were unemployable, whose usual industry was not ascertainable, and those who never worked, are not included.

Certain differences in the distributions which appear in table 41 are in part a reflection of other causes than the selective factor of migration. Comparability is biased in particular by (1) the relatively small proportion of female migrant family heads and (2) the comparison of family heads in the relief groups with all gainful workers 10 years and over in the general population.

Other differences between the industrial attachment of migrant family heads and all gainful workers appear to have resulted from variations in the distress mobility of particular industrial groups. Agriculture [7] is clearly underrepresented among migrant family heads. Manufacturing and mechanical industries were overrepresented by comparison with the gainful workers in the general population. As appendix table 19 shows, the particular industries contributing most to this overrepresentation were building and construction, automobile repair shops, and sawmills. Transportation and communication

[7] See ch. II, p. 52 ff.

was likewise overrepresented among migrant family heads, particularly in water transportation, automobile trucking, pipelines, and the construction of streets, roads, etc., industries. The overrepresentation in these particular industries is logical, since most of these industries require a mobile labor supply.

It would seem, then, that industrial characteristics were to some degree a selective factor in the migration of the families studied. The differences revealed in table 41 are not, however, great enough to explain migrant family mobility in terms of industrial attachment. While the pursuits which permitted or required mobility were overrepresented, the overrepresentation in most instances was not great.

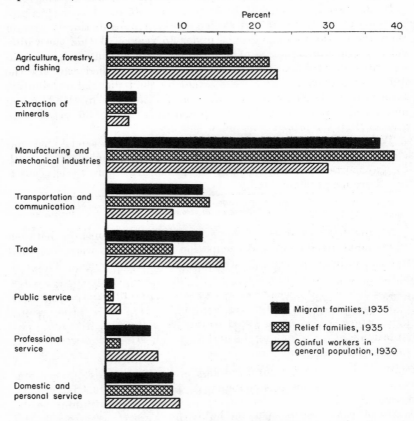

Fɪɢ. 28 – USUAL INDUSTRY OF ECONOMIC HEADS OF MIGRANT
FAMILIES AND RELIEF FAMILIES IN 1935 AND OF
GAINFUL WORKERS I0 YEARS OF AGE AND OVER
IN THE GENERAL POPULATION, 1930

Source: Table 41.   AF-2877, WPA

Supposedly sedentary pursuits—such as in the food industries, the clothing industries, the paper and printing industries, trade, professional service, and domestic and personal service—were represented by large numbers of migrant family heads.

Occupation and Industry by Age

Both age and occupational characteristics appear to have operated as selective factors in the migration of families receiving aid from transient bureaus. It may be of interest, therefore, to compare age with occupational and industrial groupings; this has been done for employable economic family heads in appendix tables 20 and 21.

In the two age groups 35 to 44 years and 45 to 64 years the proportions of white-collar and skilled workers were distinctly greater than among the two age groups under 35 years. Within the white-collar group the older age of proprietors, both agricultural and non-agricultural, explains this difference. Among skilled workers the difference is explained to a large extent by the industrial distribution (appendix table 21) which shows that for workers in the building and construction industries the proportions above 35 years were greater than the proportions below this age.

The greater relative importance of youth in the semiskilled and unskilled groups was the result principally of the attachment of youth to transportation industries and to agriculture where these occupational groups predominated.

Education and Occupation

In an effort to discover some significant relationships between educational attainment and occupation these factors were compared in terms of broad educational and occupational groupings. The comparison suggests nothing that goes beyond common knowledge. The proportion of white-collar workers was about two times as great among economic heads with better than a grade school education than among those who stopped at or failed to complete the first 8 years. This situation is reversed among the unskilled and, to a lesser degree, among the semiskilled. The proportions of skilled workers were about the same for these two educational groups (appendix table 22).

DURATION OF UNEMPLOYMENT

Duration of unemployment for migrant family heads has been measured in two ways: first, in terms of the time elapsed since the family economic head was last employed for at least 1 month at his *usual occupation;* and second, in terms of the time elapsed since his last employment (a) for at least 2 weeks and (b) for at least 1 month at *any* nonrelief job. The totally unemployable family heads have been eliminated from the tabulations which follow in order to permit comparison with the employable urban relief workers and WPA project workers.

Time Since Last Job at Usual Occupation

Long unemployment involves a deterioration of skill which lowers the reemployment opportunity of workers without affecting the distribution of their usual occupations. Accordingly, the information on usual occupations in this chapter is conditioned by the lapse of time since the family heads worked at their usual occupation.

The median time elapsed since the migrant family heads' last employment at their usual occupation was 18.5 months. It was accordingly substantially less than the median duration of 30.3 months for the urban workers [8] on resident relief in May 1934.[9] The distributions for both these groups are shown in table 42.

Nearly three-fifths of the migrant family heads had last worked at their usual occupation within 2 years of the time this study was made; and nearly two-fifths had worked at their usual occupation within 1 year. In contrast, only 43 percent of the urban workers on resident relief reported work at their usual occupation within 2 years, and only one-fourth reported a duration of less than 1 year.

For both groups, the workers displaced from their usual occupation since the depression (less than 5 years) comprised an overwhelming majority of the total. But among the migrant family heads the recently displaced workers by far outnumbered the long-time depression unemployed, while among urban workers on relief recent and long-time depression unemployment occurred in approximately equal proportions (table 42).

It is obvious, then, that by comparison with the resident relief population, the deterioration of skills had made less serious inroads upon the occupational resources of the migrant family heads. The shorter duration of unemployment of migrant family heads since

---

[8] The sample of urban workers on relief represents a resident relief group in May 1934, more than a year earlier than the time of the migrant family study. However, this disparity does not invalidate the comparison made. A survey of WPA workers conducted 7 months after the present study shows an even greater median duration of unemployment than was revealed in the urban workers' sample. The median duration of unemployment for the three groups was as follows:

Migrant Family Heads, September 1935_____ 18. 5 months
Urban Workers on Relief, May 1934_____ 30. 3 months
Economic Heads Employed on WPA, April 1936_____ 40. 6 months

See Shepherd, Susan M. and Bancroft, Gertrude, *Survey of Cases Certified for Works Program Employment in 13 Cities*, Research Bulletin, Series IV, Number 2, Division of Social Research, Works Progress Administration, Washington, D. C., 1937, p. 36.

[9] About seven-eighths of the urban workers' sample consisted of family heads.

their last job at usual occupation thus reinforces the conclusion drawn from the broad occupation comparisons in the preceding section. Not only did migrant families tend to fall into higher occupational classifications than urban relief workers, but their experience in the higher classification was also substantially more recent.

Table 42.—Duration of Unemployment Since Last Job of at Least 1 Month at Usual Occupation of Employable Economic Heads of Migrant Families and of Urban Workers on Relief May 1934 [1]

Duration of unemployment since last job of 1 month at usual occupation	Employable economic heads of migrant families [2]	Urban workers on relief May 1934 [1]
Total_____	4, 468	198, 130
	Percent distribution	
Total_____	100	100
Less than 5 years_____	83	85
Less than 2 years_____	59	43
Less than 3 months_____	11	7
3–5.9 months_____	11	6
6–11.9 months_____	17	13
12–23.9 months_____	20	17
2–4.9 years_____	24	42
Over 5 years_____	17	15
5–9.9 years_____	14	11
10 years or more_____	3	4
Average [3] duration (in months)_____	18. 5	30. 3

[1] Based on Palmer, Gladys L. and Wood, Katherine D., *Urban Workers on Relief*, Part I.—The Occupational Characteristics of Workers on Relief in Urban Areas May 1934, Research Monograph IV, Division of Social Research, Works Progress Administration, Washington, D. C., 1936.
[2] 1,021 family heads, who were unemployable, who never worked, and whose duration of unemployment at usual occupation was not ascertainable, are not included.
[3] Median.

Time Elapsed Since Last Job at Any Occupation

Data on the time elapsed since the last job at any occupation provide a basis for comparing the success of migrant families in finding work at any job, both before and after migration to another labor market, with the success of other needy groups which did not migrate. Comparison between the migrant families and the urban workers on resident relief presents a striking difference. Eliminating short-time jobs and calculating for purpose of comparison on the basis of jobs lasting at least 1 month, the median duration of unemployment was 7.8 months. In contrast, the median duration of unemployment for urban workers on relief in May 1934 was 22.7 months; and for WPA workers [10] in the last quarter of 1935 it was 24.0 months, more than three times as long (table 43).

About two-thirds of the migrant family heads had been unemployed for less than 1 year as compared with only about one-third

[10] Ninety-five percent of the WPA workers were family heads.

of the urban workers on relief. This disproportion between groups became even greater for those unemployed less than 6 months and less than 3 months. Among the urban workers on relief 41 percent had not worked since early in the depression as compared with only 11 percent of the migrant family heads.

It is clearly indicated that migrant family heads had been much more successful in finding work outside their usual occupation than the workers on resident relief (tables 42 and 43 and fig. 29). The median duration of unemployment for migrant families dropped from 18.5 months in terms of usual occupation to 7.8 months in terms of any occupation, while for the resident urban relief workers the decrease was only from 30.3 months to 22.7 months. This striking difference suggests that the shorter duration of unemployment of migrant families was the result of their access, through mobility, to another labor market. And, indeed, as table 44 shows, the low duration of unemployment is traceable principally to the jobs the family heads found after leaving settled residence. It should not be overlooked, however, that the median duration of unemployment among the families which did *not* find work after migration (13.1 months) was substantially lower than the median for resident relief workers.

Table 43.—Duration of Unemployment Since Last Job of at Least 1 Month at Any Occupation of Employable Economic Heads of Migrant Families, of Urban Workers on Relief May 1934,[1] and of Urban Workers on WPA October—December 1935 [2]

Duration of unemployment since last job at any occupation	Employable economic heads of migrant families [3]	Urban workers on relief May 1934	Urban workers on WPA October–December 1935
Total	3,997	206,394	347,802
	Percent distribution		
Total	100	100	100
Less than 5 years	97	92	88
Less than 2 years	86	51	50
Less than 3 months	23	8	5
3–5.9 months	20	8	8
6–11.9 months	23	16	13
12–23.9 months	20	19	24
2–4.9 years	11	41	38
Over 5 years	3	8	12
5–9.9 years	3	6	12
10 years or more	*	2	—
Average [4] duration (in months)	7.8	22.7	24.0

*Less than 0.5 percent.

[1] Based on Palmer, Gladys L. and Wood, Katherine D., *Urban Workers on Relief*, Part I.—The Occupational Characteristics of Workers on Relief in Urban Areas May 1934, Research Monograph IV, Division of Social Research, Works Progress Administration, Washington, D. C., 1936, p. 44.
[2] From unpublished data in the files of the Division of Social Research, Works Progress Administration.
[3] 1,492 family heads, who were unemployable, who worked less than 1 month at last job, whose duration of unemployment or occupation was not ascertainable, and those who never worked, are not included.
[4] Median.

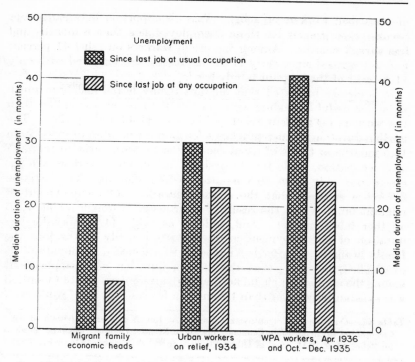

FIG. 29 - UNEMPLOYMENT SINCE LAST JOB AT USUAL OCCUPATION
AND LAST JOB AT ANY OCCUPATION

ECONOMIC HEADS OF MIGRANT FAMILIES
URBAN WORKERS ON RELIEF 1934, AND
WPA WORKERS 1935 AND 1936

Sources: Tables 42, 43 and Footnote 8, Chapter VI.

AF-2879, WPA

The fact that the short duration of unemployment of migrant family heads resulted from (1) jobs secured outside their usual occupation and (2) jobs secured after beginning migration suggests that many families had turned to migratory-casual employment. As an earlier transient study showed, this is what actually took place. Among the family heads studied in *The Transient Unemployed* only 3 to 7 percent had usual occupations as migratory-casual workers; but 23 to 33 percent had migratory-casual work as their first job after beginning migration, and 23 to 38 percent had migratory-casual work as their last job before registering for transient relief.[11] This fact not only implies low earnings but also a lowered occupational status which

---

[11] See Webb, John N., *The Transient Unemployed*, Research Monograph III, Division of Social Research, Works Progress Administration, Washington, D. C., 1935, pp. 54–55 and appendix table 23B.

qualifies to some extent the conclusion to be drawn from the relatively low duration of unemployment of family heads since last job at usual occupation.

Table 44.—Duration of Unemployment Since Last Job of at Least 2 Weeks at Any Occupation of Employable Economic Heads of Migrant Families

Duration of unemployment since last job of at least 2 weeks at any occupation	Economic heads of migrant families		
	Total	Worked since leaving settled residence	Did not work since leaving settled residence
Total	4,098	2,248	1,850
	Percent distribution		
Total	100	100	100
Less than 3 months	23	35	10
3–5.9 months	20	21	16
6–11.9 months	22	23	21
12–23.9 months	20	16	25
More than 2 years	15	5	28
Average [1] duration (in months)	8.0	5.2	13.1

[1] Median.

NOTE.—1,391 family heads, who were unemployable, who had no settled residence, who never worked, or whose duration of unemployment or occupation was not ascertainable, are not included.

Chapter VII

CONCLUSIONS

THIS REPORT has been concerned with a detailed description of the characteristics and behavior of migrant families which received relief from the transient program during the operation of the Federal Emergency Relief Administration. As such, it has dealt with only one group among depression migrants. This fact should not, however, obscure the broader implications of the information presented. These families were one of the few groups which have left a sufficiently complete record to permit detailed analysis of population mobility during the depression.

The record of the families studied is also significant in its own right. "Mobility in trouble" is one of the most immediate problems related to the internal migration of the American population. In the administration of the broad program of public assistance now being developed by several Federal agencies, distressed population mobility is one of the problems still unsolved. For this reason alone the experience of the transient program warrants careful consideration.

THE NORMALITY OF TRANSIENT RELIEF FAMILIES

Relief for the needy migrant was one of several important experiments in public assistance administration during the depression. Because it departed radically from established procedures, the transient relief program was frequently the subject of criticism. A persistent theme of transient relief's critics, still heard today, is the argument that the transient population includes a large criminal element; that transients are lazy and degraded persons disturbing to settled community life, and therefore are "undesirables." Finally, and particularly during the operation of the transient program, transients were criticized as irresponsible and willful wanderers, out to see the country at the expense of those who would give them relief.

The common element in all these criticisms is the belief that transients are abnormal people. This belief is, on the face of it, highly suspect. The two elements of transiency are mobility and need of public assistance, neither of which is exceptional. The tendency toward mobility is one of the basic characteristics of the American population, as the rapid spread of population across the American continent and the birth-residence data of each decennial census amply prove. Nor can need of public assistance be pointed to as abnormal when it is remembered that, coincident with the operation of the transient program, the relief rolls included as many as 27,000,000 persons at one time. The type of criticism cited appears to be a counterpart of the argument that industrial unemployment exists because "some folks just won't work."

The present study of families registered at transient bureaus provides direct evidence on the normality of migrant families' behavior and characteristics. Comparisons of personal characteristics, for example, suggest that the transient families were, if anything, somewhat "above" the average family on relief. The majority of the families studied were young, experienced, and free from handicaps that would retard their reemployment by private industry.

In terms of ability to find work in a crowded labor market the family heads had been more successful than the great majority of relief family heads. The reabsorption of transient relief families proceeded at a much higher rate than the reabsorption of workers on the resident relief rolls. Family mobility could have been called excessive only by supposing that a small number of highly mobile families was typical of the entire group, which was not the case. Finally, when the motivation of these families is considered it becomes clear that cautiousness rather than irresponsibility governed the families' plans to migrate.

An illustration of the difficulty of depression migration will show the lack of realism in the belief that family migration resulted from a lack of responsibility. The following is a case history of a family on the margin of mobility:

In an industrial city of moderate size the head of a family of five had worked for a millwork manufacturer for 11 consecutive years up to January 1932 when the factory closed. During these 11 years weekly earnings varied, according to business conditions, from $20 to $35 a week. With no more than the average run of expenses incident to a growing family, the head had laid aside some $400 in savings and was carrying two insurance policies of modest size.

During the 5 years following the closing of the millwork plant, the head obtained two full-time jobs lasting about a year each. In between times the family lived on their savings, the proceeds obtained by cashing the insurance policies, on odd jobs, and local relief.

At first, the family had no thoughts of leaving the community because of the persistent hope, supported by recurring rumors, that the millwork factory would resume operations. Gradually the head came to realize that this was not likely to happen, and that his only employment asset—skill as a mill hand—was of little value so long as he remained where he was.

Had the family been willing to move in 1932 and, in addition, had known where to go while they had the means to make a self-supporting migration they might have avoided the "dead-end" in which they found themselves in 1937. With a wife and three children, no money, and an accumulation of debts, migration seemed impossible to the head who continued to realize the need for leaving the community but who found, in his own words, "Going is harder than thinking about it."

This summary illustrates the inertia that must be overcome before the migration of a needy family can occur. Bad as it is, the local situation is known; friends, the church, relief officials, the grocer, milkman, coal man, etc., have been as helpful as possible. How can the family live in another community where such assistance will not exist? The risk seems too great as long as any hope remains that work will be found locally. The transient relief program, however, was evidence that the time did come for many families when all of the real or imagined advantages of remaining where they were did not offset the hopelessness of their predicament. The break was made; families did leave their home communities; and when they came to be in need of public assistance, they learned of the legal concepts of residence and discovered that they were transients.

All these pieces of evidence point in the same direction. While none is conclusive in itself, the sum of the evidence directly contradicts the argument that transient families were "unworthy," "undeserving," and "undesirable."

Future efforts toward providing relief to nonresidents should recognize the fundamental normality of needy migrants. The transient relief problem does not call for special techniques of assistance based on the supposition that migrants in need are essentially different from residents in need. Indeed, the principal difference between migrant and resident is created artificially by legal settlement requirements— requirements that are customarily invoked only in the presence of need. Overemphasis upon the surface distinctions between transients and residents has heretofore been a persistent source of error in attempts to provide transient relief.

TRANSIENT RELIEF AND RESTRICTIONS UPON MOBILITY

Public action has frequently set up barriers against internal migration. Witness, for example, the fact that a number of States have long prohibited employment agencies from sending workers to jobs outside their State borders, and the time-honored use of vagrancy laws and legal settlement restrictions as means of penalizing out-of-State workers. After 1930, because of the intrusion of the relief problem, the restrictions put upon the mobility of needy persons became much more stringent and more generally applied. The border-blockades of Florida, Colorado, and California, as illustrations of such restrictions, have established a particularly dangerous precedent for interfering with the free flow of the American population in the future.

A less spectacular but more serious immobilizing force is the administration of general relief. Resident relief, whether work or direct relief, exacts proof of residence before the grant of assistance is made and continues the grant only as long as the applicant remains a resident. In so far as resident relief is the means of assisting the working population of a community to remain where it may again be absorbed by industry, it acts as a brake on wasteful migration. But when resident relief "freezes" the unemployed workers in a community where industry cannot upon revival reabsorb them, it prevents a desirable migration and perpetuates stranded populations.

During the depression the legal residence requirements for relief benefits placed a severe economic penalty upon the migrant in need of assistance outside his State of residence. Theoretically, however, the social necessity of population mobility during both boom and depression had not been reasonably questioned since the beginning of the nineteenth century. The defense of the residence requirements and the return-to-legal residence procedures has always been in terms of practical necessity in administering limited relief funds and never as a sound contribution to population policy.

One of the indirect results of the transient relief program was to neutralize, during the period of its operation, the tendency of the resident relief program toward penalizing migration already under way or accomplished. The transient program alleviated the distress accompanying population readjustment during the depression by providing relief to needy migrants who would otherwise have been ineligible on the grounds of nonresidence status. Accepting the premise that population mobility is desirable, and accepting the evidence that the families were not irresponsible wanderers, this function of the transient program assumes greater importance than is ordinarily recognized.

TRANSIENT RELIEF AND POPULATION REDISTRIBUTION

Obviously, however, the fact that the transient program neutralized some of the restrictions upon internal population mobility does not necessarily argue its usefulness. Migration as an end in itself has no particular virtue; and "the record of unguided migration," as has been demonstrated,[1] is in part a record of needless waste. The important question is whether any gain accrued from the total movement of the families. Did the families assisted by the transient program tend to migrate from the areas of less economic advantage to the areas of greater economic advantage?

To answer this question in generalized terms, it may be said that the greater part of the movement of the families which registered at transient bureaus produced no population displacement whatever because of the balanced give and take among the various States.

---

[1] Goodrich, Carter and Others, *Migration and Economic Opportunity*, Philadelphia: University of Pennsylvania Press, 1936, pp. 503–519.

Over and above this balanced movement, however, there remained an amount of net population displacement which showed clear geographical trends. These trends were predominantly westward, but also included a northward net movement out of the deep South into the industrial centers of the North.

Accordingly, the most significant characteristic of the net movement was a marked similarity to the net movement of the total American population during the prosperous decade from 1920 to 1930. But the similarity between the displacement of population resulting from the movement of transient-bureau families and the net displacement of the American population during the 1920's is not proof that social gains accrued from the transient bureaus' contribution to population redistribution.

The American "problem areas" have been demarked and recommendations have been ventured as to the desired geographical direction that future migrations should take.[2] The net displacement of the migrant families bears only a partial similarity to the ideal pattern of migration that the Study of Population Redistribution has constructed. This similarity consists chiefly in a large net emigration from the Great Plains and also in net emigration from the deep South northward, though this particular trend among migrant families was exceedingly feeble by comparison with the recommendation for a large scale emigration from the South. The remainder of the net migrant family movement bears little relationship to the ideal pattern, and even runs counter to it.

The movement of migrant families thus appears to be another instance in the record of waste involved in unguided migration and another illustration of the need for planned migration. These judgments are doubtless valid in the long view.[3] Under the exigencies of

---

[2] *Ibid.*, pp. 52–53. See also, Beck, P. G. and Forster, M. C., *Six Rural Problem Areas, Relief—Resources—Rehabilitation*, Research Monograph I, Division of Research, Statistics, and Finance, Federal Emergency Relief Administration, Washington, D. C., 1935.

[3] It may be pointed out, however, that the theoretical need for population redistribution is acceptable only when related to a disparity between the geographical concentration of population and resources. One of the recommendations for population redistribution is based upon the observation of "overpopulation" in the South. But the distress of the South results from existing economic relationships rather than a scarcity of resources. As T. J. Woofter, Jr. has pointed out, "Some observers conclude from the fact that the South ranks low in almost every index of wealth and culture that there are too many people in the area. As the economy of the region is at present organized, this is true, but this condition does not necessarily have to continue. More rational land use, more diversification of production and, above all, an increase in the standard of living of the people through the use of home-produced goods can provide for an increased southern rural population at a higher level of living." (See "Southern Population and Social Planning," *Social Forces*, Vol. 14, No. 1, October 1935, pp. 16–22.)

a severe depression, however, the logic of the long view becomes tenuous, and the blue-prints for the future redistribution of the American population must be set aside until the problem of industrial unemployment has been solved. Outlines of the course population distribution should take, even when postulating normal times, are more convincing in describing where the flow should *originate* than in describing what its *destination* should be. And when millions of gainful workers are unemployed, where does economic opportunity lie?

These facts are of special significance in view of the difficulties which recent experimental attempts at planned migration have already encountered and which any future attempts have to face. A planned migration of any considerable numbers from the stranded populations will involve problems of extreme complication and magnitude—problems of an upset labor market at urban destinations and of an agricultural surplus at rural destinations, not to mention the problems of financing a subsidy for a large number of migrants. The inevitable conclusion must be that the problem of population redistribution, difficult at any time, is scarcely possible of solution during a depression.

If no one can trace abstractly the direction in which depression population movement should flow, no one can appraise abstractly the immediate gains and losses of the depression movements which did occur. Nevertheless, it is difficult to question the wisdom of the individuals who took part in the movement of the families studied here. It must be borne in mind that the families aided by the transient program were by and large normal and responsible groups, and that their migration represented a search for more favorable opportunity. Notwithstanding any appraisal of the geographical trends involved, the migration of transient-bureau families did make sense to the migrants. The extremely high turnover rate of transient relief families is itself sufficient evidence that the families were the best judges of whether they should migrate and of where their destination should be.

IMPLICATIONS FOR THE FUTURE

It remains to consider what bearing the findings of this report have upon the continuing problem of need for public assistance arising out of family group migration. As a factual study of families which were assisted by the one national experiment with transient relief the report should be of some help in looking to the future. Taken as a whole the evidence of the report argues against the need for a separate program of transient relief based upon the assumption that needy migrants are somehow inherently different from needy residents. Specific evidence has been presented to show that families receiving aid from the transient program were in no way unusual except for their mobility; that they were young, with employable heads, in most instances; that their migrations were cautious in nature and were undertaken in an attempt to overcome difficulties caused by the depression; that their efforts at relocation, by and large, were successful and therefore made only temporary demands upon the transient relief program.

In view of this evidence of the essential normality of transient relief families and the additional fact that all States contributed and all States received these migrants, it might seem that the solution of the transient relief problem lies in the complete integration of transient with resident relief by modifying the existing relief procedures and requirements that artificially create the separate category of the "transient."

The experience of the past, however, stands in the way of accepting as likely of realization so simple a solution. States become acutely aware of the inflow of needy outsiders because of the public assistance problem that results, while there is little but the occasional request for verification of legal residence to remind the individual States that the outflow of their own citizens creates a similar problem elsewhere. Moreover, the principle of legal residence which has for so many years governed the attitudes of States and their subdivisions toward relief is based upon the belief that every person "belongs" to some community and should expect assistance only in that specific place. And, finally, there is the obvious fact that some few States have a particular attraction for migrants, with the result that these States receive many more migrants than they give. Such States are prone to insist that by giving relief to nonresidents they only increase the inflow. Yet no one has demonstrated that the hardships and uncertainties of migration are undertaken for the sake of transient relief, and border blockades and the refusal to give any form of assistance have been singularly ineffective in stopping the inflow.

The implications of this report, then, are clear, though its conclusions are neither novel nor startling. The transient relief problem does not originate in, nor can it be confined to, any particular region. All States are affected, but in different degrees. It is difficult to see how a total solution is to be achieved unless there is a coordination of efforts from outside the individual States. The problem is national, and the need of the moment is Federal leadership in achieving a solution which would take account both of the needs of the migrant and the interests of the States.

Appendixes

Appendix A

SUPPLEMENTARY TABLES

Table 1.—Reason Migrant Families Left Settled Residence

Reason for leaving settled residence	Migrant families	
	Number	Percent
Total	4,247	100
Economic distress	2,941	69
Unemployment	1,705	40
Layoffs attributed to depression	1,232	29
Completed job of definite duration	109	3
Locality too small	108	3
Drought	60	1
Migration of industry	16	*
Layoffs attributed to other causes [1]	180	4
Inadequate earnings	308	7
Reduced to part-time work	239	6
Forced into lower occupational status	27	1
Seasonal work only	20	*
Reduced wages	22	*
Unable to work in particular community	113	3
Physical disability	80	2
Personal handicaps	33	1
Farming failure	333	8
Dust or drought	196	5
Floods	13	*
Other failures	124	3
Business failure	142	3
Attributed to depression	135	3
Attributed to drought	7	*
Inadequate relief	146	3
Unwilling to be on relief	46	1
Unwilling to apply	26	1
Unwilling to continue	20	*
Evicted from rented or owned domicile	71	2
Relatives unable to continue support	51	1
Miscellaneous economic difficulties [2]	26	1
Personal distress	1,040	25
Ill-health	448	11
Unhealthful climate	388	9
Inadequate medical care	60	2
Domestic difficulties	254	6
Desertion	34	1
Separation and divorce	128	3
Quarrels with relatives	35	1
Death of breadwinner	44	1
Other domestic difficulties [3]	13	*

See footnotes at end of table.

Table 1.—Reason Migrant Families Left Settled Residence—Continued

Reason for leaving settled residence	Migrant families	
	Number	Percent
Personal distress—Continued.		
Disliked separation from relatives or friends	167	4
Community disapproval	42	1
Social handicaps, prison records, etc	14	*
Illegitimate children	4	*
Other community disapproval [4]	24	1
Personal dislike of community	86	2
Climate as personal factor	8	*
Death as personal factor	11	1
Boredom and other repulsions	67	1
Miscellaneous personal difficulties [5]	43	1
Not in distress	266	6
Job required travel	144	3
Left job	73	2
Left farm	14	*
Left business	22	1
Other [6]	13	*

* Less than 0.5 percent.

[1] Most of these families reported that new managers brought their own crews or that they were dismissed to make a job for the manager's relatives (see history 1, pp. 21–22).

[2] Includes families whose pension was discontinued, whose scholarship expired, who wished to avoid high cost of commutation, etc.

[3] Includes families in fear of ex-husband, those attempting to secure support of child, those searching for fiance, etc.

[4] Includes families moving because of unpopularity growing out of political campaigns, because of racial prejudice, etc.

[5] Includes families fleeing from revolution, lack of school facilities, fear of earthquakes, etc.

[6] Includes families leaving to look after personal business, to take vacations, etc.

NOTE.—81 families, whose reason for leaving settled residence was not ascertainable, are not included.

Table 2.—Reason Migrant Families Left Settled Residence, and State or Region of Settled Residence

State or region of settled residence	Total number	Reasons for leaving settled residence									
		Percent distribution									
		Total	Economic distress					Personal distress			Not in distress
			Unemployment	Inadequate earnings	Farm failure	Inadequate relief	Other economic distress	Ill-health	Domestic trouble	Other personal distress	
Total	4,195	100	40	7	8	4	9	11	6	9	6
New England	129	100	58	5	4	4	8	7	4	6	4
New York	210	100	41	5	1	1	9	18	4	9	12
Pennsylvania and New Jersey	237	100	40	7	1	2	14	12	9	10	5
Delaware, Maryland, and District of Columbia	66	100	44	8	3	3	9	9	6	14	4
Kentucky and West Virginia	153	100	41	10	4	7	13	5	8	9	3
Michigan	112	100	44	7	4	5	10	9	9	8	4
Ohio and Indiana	212	100	42	10	3	3	8	12	10	5	7
Illinois	213	100	41	6	2	7	12	8	7	10	7
Minnesota and Wisconsin	113	100	42	5	6	6	5	15	7	8	6
Iowa	84	100	47	8	7	3	7	6	8	7	7
Virginia and North Carolina	141	100	45	5	4	3	18	3	6	8	8
Georgia and South Carolina	115	100	39	9	5	3	10	5	11	10	8
Tennessee	100	100	44	10	6	3	14	3	9	5	6
Alabama and Mississippi	149	100	36	13	10	7	11	7	5	7	4
Florida	108	100	44	9	2	5	9	10	5	10	6
Missouri	266	100	41	4	13	7	6	10	5	9	5
Arkansas	142	100	42	5	14	6	7	11	6	6	3
Louisiana	67	100	43	12	4	6	4	9	5	11	6
Oklahoma	281	100	38	11	12	9	5	12	3	6	4
Texas	235	100	43	6	6	4	5	15	5	9	7
North Dakota and South Dakota	94	100	18	5	54	—	13	3	4	1	2
Nebraska	116	100	36	5	20	5	6	8	4	9	7
Kansas	140	100	33	8	17	4	7	13	1	8	9
Wyoming and Montana	79	100	29	4	19	3	15	20	4	6	—
Colorado	115	100	34	10	16	4	2	18	3	7	6
Idaho	53	100	32	7	11	4	8	11	9	10	8
Washington and Oregon	130	100	36	6	2	5	10	13	6	16	6
Utah and Nevada	47	100	38	9	7	2	13	17	6	2	6
Arizona and New Mexico	78	100	39	6	5	3	9	19	4	10	5
California	210	100	44	7	*	3	4	9	4	21	8

* Less than 0.5 percent.

NOTE.—133 families, whose settled residence was in a foreign country or in U. S. possessions and whose State of settled residence or reason for leaving was not ascertainable, are not included.

Table 3.—Type of Contact Migrant Families Had at Destination, and State or Region of Destination

State or region of destination	Total number	Type of contact							
		Percent distribution							
		Total	Definite contact				No definite contact		
			Former residence	Residence of relatives, etc.	Skill of head in demand	Other	Rumors	Advertisement	Chance
Total	3,869	100	12	43	2	23	16	1	3
New England	118	100	12	45	1	26	14	1	1
New York	226	100	17	36	2	22	21	—	2
Pennsylvania and New Jersey	205	100	7	55	2	24	11	—	1
Delaware, Maryland, and District of Columbia	102	100	9	48	4	21	15	...	3
Kentucky and West Virginia	60	100	3	57	10	17	10	—	3
Michigan	108	100	19	42	2	18	11	2	6
Ohio and Indiana	187	100	14	49	2	20	12	—	3
Illinois	174	100	13	50	3	19	12	—	3
Minnesota and Wisconsin	166	100	25	49	1	17	7	*	1
Iowa	50	100	12	60	2	14	6	—	6
Virginia and North Carolina	75	100	15	45	4	20	12	—	4
Georgia and South Carolina	111	100	10	51	6	19	13	—	1
Tennessee	76	100	9	50	3	20	14	—	4
Alabama and Mississippi	99	100	17	54	3	19	7	—	—
Florida	104	100	11	29	5	25	26	1	3
Missouri	177	100	10	41	3	27	16	*	3
Arkansas	89	100	10	33	2	43	11	—	1
Louisiana	56	100	7	32	—	27	32	—	2
Oklahoma	101	100	7	50	4	21	14	—	4
Texas	193	100	10	34	4	29	21	—	2
North Dakota and South Dakota	13	†	†	†	†	†	†	†	†
Nebraska	49	100	6	47	—	31	16	—	—
Kansas	157	100	10	52	3	20	10	*	5
Wyoming and Montana	43	100	7	44	2	30	12	—	5
Colorado	134	100	11	31	2	34	22	—	—
Idaho	121	100	12	43	1	19	6	17	2
Washington and Oregon	264	100	17	38	*	16	19	4	6
Utah and Nevada	57	100	19	25	2	26	26	—	2
Arizona and New Mexico	135	100	8	24	1	53	13	*	1
California	419	100	9	44	1	17	22	2	5

*Less than 0.5 percent.
† Percent not calculated on a base of fewer than 20.

NOTE.—459 families, which had no destination, whose reason for selecting the State of destination, type of contact at the State of destination, or State of destination was not ascertainable, and whose destination was in a foreign country or in the U. S. possessions, are not included.

Table 4.—Objectives Sought by Migrant Families at Destination, and State or Region of Destination

State or region of destination	Total number	Objectives sought								
		Percent distribution								
		Total	Economic betterment					Personal objectives		
			Hope of job	Promise of job	To secure farm	To secure help	Other	Health	To rejoin relatives, etc.	Other
Total	3,974	100	44	14	5	11	5	10	8	3
New England	119	100	42	24	8	10	3	2	9	2
New York	234	100	52	16	—	10	5	5	7	5
Pennsylvania and New Jersey	208	100	34	17	1	19	6	4	17	2
Delaware, Maryland, and District of Columbia	111	100	41	14	1	17	3	4	10	10
Kentucky and West Virginia	61	100	41	13	3	23	3	5	10	2
Michigan	112	100	53	14	2	10	3	3	7	8
Ohio and Indiana	191	100	46	21	3	15	2	1	8	4
Illinois	179	100	45	13	3	13	4	4	13	5
Minnesota and Wisconsin	171	100	37	14	2	25	5	7	6	4
Iowa	51	100	35	16	—	19	4	2	20	4
Virginia and North Carolina	78	100	48	11	1	13	3	6	13	5
Georgia and South Carolina	114	100	47	16	2	16	3	6	7	3
Tennessee	79	100	49	11	3	18	5	5	5	4
Alabama and Mississippi	101	100	35	18	5	17	2	3	18	2
Florida	105	100	43	18	2	8	9	14	1	5
Missouri	178	100	40	18	8	13	5	4	12	*
Arkansas	90	100	45	11	13	10	4	8	7	2
Louisiana	58	100	54	10	3	11	3	9	7	3
Oklahoma	103	100	48	16	7	12	3	1	10	3
Texas	201	100	48	15	1	11	5	11	4	5
North Dakota and South Dakota	13	†	†	†	†	†	†	†	†	†
Nebraska	50	100	42	26	6	8	—	4	12	2
Kansas	158	100	49	13	4	10	7	4	11	2
Wyoming and Montana	46	100	52	22	2	9	2	7	—	6
Colorado	139	100	40	10	4	4	4	33	1	4
Idaho	122	100	31	6	44	4	—	10	4	1
Washington and Oregon	272	100	48	8	11	10	4	8	4	7
Utah and Nevada	60	100	43	20	2	3	7	12	5	8
Arizona and New Mexico	136	100	24	10	3	2	6	50	4	1
California	434	100	47	10	1	6	3	22	6	5

*Less than 0.5 percent.
† Percent not calculated on a base of fewer than 20.

NOTE.—354 families, which had no destination, whose reason for selecting the State of destination or whose State of destination was not ascertainable, and whose destination was in a foreign country or in the U. S. possessions, are not included.

Table 5.—State of Origin and State of Transient Bureau Registration of Migrant Families, June 30, 1935 [1]

State of origin	Total	State of transient bureau registration								
		Alabama	Arizona	Arkansas	California	Colorado	Connecticut	Delaware	District of Columbia	Florida
Total	30,304	417	225	693	6,044	1,847	27	49	379	717
Alabama	596	—	2	16	29	7	—	—	6	38
Arizona	466	—	—	8	239	65	—	—	1	3
Arkansas	1,161	21	15	—	188	39	—	2	1	7
California	1,193	13	14	16	—	103	2	—	8	18
Colorado	838	—	7	14	279	—	—	—	3	2
Connecticut	207	1	1	—	22	2	—	2	3	9
Delaware	53	—	—	—	1	1	—	—	2	—
District of Columbia	119	3	—	2	18	1	—	1	—	9
Florida	534	25	—	8	34	7	1	1	22	—
Georgia	690	48	1	12	25	3	1	—	17	198
Idaho [2]	327	—	1	2	86	25	—	1	1	—
Illinois	1,264	16	10	19	281	53	1	—	12	35
Indiana	685	12	—	6	119	35	—	—	7	11
Iowa	522	1	2	1	126	47	—	—	—	3
Kansas	1,091	1	7	23	193	335	—	—	2	5
Kentucky	657	16	5	11	40	11	2	—	9	11
Louisiana	504	18	4	47	64	6	1	—	2	11
Maine	78	—	—	—	8	—	—	—	1	1
Maryland	209	1	—	—	13	2	2	14	26	7
Massachusetts	284	1	1	—	34	3	—	—	7	15
Michigan	799	14	4	5	127	14	—	—	4	28
Minnesota	334	—	2	1	69	30	—	—	—	1
Mississippi	609	43	2	25	61	4	—	—	4	7
Missouri	1,818	14	10	65	381	235	—	—	4	3
Montana	264	—	1	—	40	2	—	—	—	3
Nebraska	809	—	1	3	160	151	—	—	—	5
Nevada	120	1	1	—	57	9	—	1	—	—
New Hampshire	19	—	—	—	2	—	—	—	1	—
New Jersey	592	—	—	—	52	6	3	6	6	27
New Mexico	369	1	23	5	136	112	—	—	—	1

New York	1,074	4	5	3	255	14	8	5	27	57
North Carolina	409	9	1	1	18	1	—	—	49	31
North Dakota	318	—	—	1	30	17	—	—	—	—
Ohio	843	14	1	4	196	17	2	—	12	36
Oklahoma	2,633	15	51	213	916	228	—	—	1	4
Oregon	503	—	1	1	233	19	—	12	2	1
Pennsylvania	1,140	5	1	3	138	18	1	—	21	27
Rhode Island	59	—	—	1	6	—	1	—	—	2
South Carolina	299	11	—	4	6	1	—	—	29	15
South Dakota	521	—	2	1	65	12	—	—	—	—
Tennessee	687	63	4	39	68	7	1	—	12	32
Texas	1,971	26	32	130	624	79	—	—	10	17
Utah	239	—	—	—	140	33	—	—	—	—
Vermont	86	—	—	—	4	—	—	—	—	1
Virginia	375	7	4	—	17	1	—	2	51	13
Washington	631	—	1	1	300	14	1	—	2	5
West Virginia	341	12	7	1	15	3	—	2	14	8
Wisconsin	318	1	—	1	45	33	—	—	—	2
Wyoming	227	—	1	—	36	43	—	—	—	—
U. S. possessions	119	—	—	—	16	—	—	—	—	—
Foreign countries	300	—	—	—	32	—	1	—	—	8

See footnotes at end of table.

Table 5.—State of Origin and State of Transient Bureau Registration of Migrant Families, June 30, 1935—Continued

State of origin	State of transient bureau registration										
	Georgia	Idaho[2]	Illinois	Indiana	Iowa	Kansas	Kentucky	Louisiana	Maine	Maryland	Massachusetts
Total	393	973	1,525	316	394	1,372	54	820	12	275	80
Alabama	74	—	41	4	1	6	2	66	—	1	1
Arizona	—	7	6	2	1	10	2	5	—	—	—
Arkansas	4	35	60	9	13	124	2	84	—	1	—
California	7	43	81	13	26	56	2	23	—	11	4
Colorado	1	107	19	3	10	69	—	2	—	1	1
Connecticut	—	—	5	2	—	1	—	2	4	2	5
Delaware	1	—	1	—	—	1	—	1	—	3	—
District of Columbia	4	—	6	1	—	—	—	28	—	10	—
Florida	61	—	18	8	—	4	3	29	—	12	2
Georgia	—	—	32	8	1	1	2	—	—	5	—
Idaho[3]	4	—	2	1	2	7	2	30	—	—	1
Illinois	6	7	—	59	46	45	3	4	—	3	3
Indiana	—	—	154	—	9	17	—	6	—	3	1
Iowa	—	35	30	4	—	32	—	—	—	1	—
Kansas	1	72	22	2	20	—	—	6	—	—	—
Kentucky	6	—	40	45	3	7	—	11	—	2	1
Louisiana	4	—	45	1	2	8	—	—	—	3	—
Maine	—	—	1	—	1	1	—	—	—	—	8
Maryland	1	—	10	1	1	3	—	1	—	6	—
Massachusetts	3	—	11	3	2	2	1	4	2	—	—
Michigan	6	—	158	36	8	8	3	11	—	4	1
Minnesota	—	7	28	4	29	7	1	5	—	—	—
Mississippi	5	—	132	3	4	11	—	116	—	3	1
Missouri	4	28	98	17	73	357	3	37	—	2	2
Montana	—	50	2	1	1	12	—	1	—	—	—
Nebraska	—	100	22	2	37	41	—	1	—	—	—
Nevada	—	7	3	—	1	4	—	—	—	—	—
New Hampshire	—	—	—	—	1	—	—	5	1	—	5
New Jersey	5	7	12	6	1	1	—	2	2	12	5
New Mexico	—	—	1	1	—	15	1	—	1	—	—

New York	10	7	77	5	8	5	3	11	1	24	9
North Carolina	28	—	6	1	—	2	2	3	—	23	—
North Dakota	—	28	6	—	1	—	—	3	—	—	—
Ohio	24	—	83	27	7	13	6	12	—	10	2
Oklahoma	4	64	25	2	15	343	—	56	1	2	1
Oregon	—	28	3	11	5	6	—	2	—	40	1
Pennsylvania	5	—	43	1	1	4	1	10	—	1	6
Rhode Island	1	7	2	—	—	—	—	—	—	15	4
South Carolina	53	—	2	1	—	—	2	4	—	—	—
South Dakota	—	164	10	—	25	5	—	1	—	—	—
Tennessee	43	—	53	10	3	15	4	28	—	4	1
Texas	14	14	41	8	13	93	2	187	—	4	1
Utah	—	21	3	—	—	3	—	—	—	—	—
Vermont	2	—	—	—	1	—	—	—	—	—	6
Virginia	8	—	13	1	—	3	1	8	—	52	—
Washington	3	71	15	1	3	4	1	4	—	1	—
West Virginia	—	—	11	6	1	5	5	4	—	9	—
Wisconsin	—	—	80	5	12	5	1	3	—	2	—
Wyoming	1	57	2	1	4	12	—	—	—	—	—
U.S. possessions	—	7	2	—	1	—	—	1	—	—	—
Foreign countries	—	—	8	1	2	4	—	3	—	3	8

See footnotes at end of table.

Table 5.—State of Origin and State of Transient Bureau Registration of Migrant Families, June 30, 1935—Continued

State of origin	State of transient bureau registration										
	Michigan	Minnesota	Mississippi	Missouri	Montana	Nebraska	Nevada	New Hampshire	New Jersey	New Mexico	New York
Total	679	359	128	1,027	99	289	42	131	538	714	1,746
Alabama	14	2	16	12	—	1	1	1	4	5	8
Arizona	—	—	1	6	—	3	2	—	2	42	2
Arkansas	34	1	16	119	—	9	1	—	1	25	4
California	18	12	1	59	5	30	10	2	6	43	40
Colorado	8	4	1	31	1	10	6	—	3	60	5
Connecticut	—	1	1	3	—	—	—	6	9	2	94
Delaware	—	—	—	—	—	—	—	—	6	—	8
District of Columbia	4	—	—	2	—	—	—	1	3	4	14
Florida	17	2	6	6	—	—	—	—	18	4	81
Georgia	17	—	10	3	1	1	1	1	10	3	24
Idaho ²	1	1	—	3	5	1	2	—	—	3	1
Illinois	77	28	4	161	4	21	1	1	13	13	44
Indiana	81	3	2	21	1	7	—	—	3	5	7
Iowa	4	40	—	36	3	36	—	—	1	13	9
Kansas	1	6	3	149	5	23	1	—	1	30	8
Kentucky	40	2	3	22	1	2	1	—	1	14	9
Louisiana	4	—	8	19	—	2	—	—	1	10	17
Maine	2	—	—	1	1	1	1	22	2	4	10
Maryland	4	—	—	3	—	—	—	—	12	3	24
Massachusetts	5	2	—	—	—	3	—	31	8	1	88
Michigan	13	17	5	16	3	7	—	2	11	7	51
Minnesota	6	—	2	9	2	4	—	—	2	1	5
Mississippi	42	1	—	36	—	2	—	—	2	3	4
Missouri	2	10	3	—	6	42	4	—	2	43	15
Montana		16	—	3	—	4	—	1	1	1	2
Nebraska	6	11	—	50	6	—	—	—	1	9	5
Nevada	1	—	—	2	—	2	—	—	1	4	2
New Hampshire	—	—	—	—	—	—	—	—	1	—	5
New Jersey	6	3	1	1	—	—	—	—	2	2	283
New Mexico	5	1	1	8	2	—	—	—	1	—	2

New York	43	5	—	10	1	5	1	14	148	6	—
North Carolina	3	—	—	5	—	1	—	1	17	2	33
North Dakota	1	47	—	1	10	2	2	1	—	1	2
Ohio	90	8	3	17	1	5	—	1	5	12	71
Oklahoma	4	4	4	79	1	13	2	—	1	136	5
Oregon	3	4	3	2	4	3	1	—	1	7	1
Pennsylvania	29	4	3	7	2	7	—	4	182	11	315
Rhode Island	2	—	1	—	—	—	—	1	4	1	12
South Carolina	4	1	3	3	—	3	—	—	9	1	33
South Dakota	4	62	—	11	10	7	—	—	1	2	4
Tennessee	36	3	8	33	1	—	—	—	1	8	14
Texas	12	7	17	50	3	14	1	1	6	148	20
Utah	—	—	—	4	1	2	2	—	—	2	1
Vermont	1	—	—	—	—	1	—	34	3	4	22
Virginia	5	1	1	4	1	—	—	—	22	2	47
Washington	4	8	—	12	10	2	1	—	4	4	3
West Virginia	13	4	—	2	1	2	—	—	6	1	6
Wisconsin	10	34	1	3	3	4	1	1	1	6	11
Wyoming	—	3	—	2	2	6	—	—	—	5	1
U. S. possessions	—	—	—	—	—	—	—	—	—	—	82
Foreign countries	3	1	—	1	2	1	—	5	1	—	192

See footnotes at end of table.

Table 5.—State of Origin and State of Transient Bureau Registration of Migrant Families, June 30, 1935—Continued

State of origin	State of transient bureau registration										
	North Carolina	North Dakota	Ohio	Oklahoma	Oregon	Pennsylvania	Rhode Island	South Carolina	South Dakota	Tennessee	Texas
Total	48	11	1,480	607	755	594	51	193	5	919	1,073
Alabama	2	—	59	3	4	8	—	14	—	113	28
Arizona	—	—	2	5	12	4	—	—	—	5	20
Arkansas	—	—	23	91	8	4	—	—	—	101	96
California	1	—	31	30	141	13	—	3	—	19	68
Colorado	—	—	10	16	34	3	—	—	—	4	9
Connecticut	—	—	4	1	—	7	8	—	—	—	4
Delaware	—	—	—	—	1	27	—	—	—	—	—
District of Columbia	—	—	7	—	1	5	—	3	—	6	3
Florida	4	—	34	2	1	21	—	16	—	37	35
Georgia	8	—	43	3	—	15	—	40	—	89	19
Idaho [2]	—	3	2	3	42	1	—	—	—	—	4
Illinois	—	1	65	11	20	13	1	2	1	35	34
Indiana	—	—	84	4	7	7	—	1	—	24	14
Iowa	—	—	9	4	22	2	—	—	1	2	12
Kansas	—	1	11	33	24	4	—	—	—	2	25
Kentucky	1	—	217	4	2	7	—	3	—	70	15
Louisiana	—	—	26	17	2	2	—	—	—	30	139
Maine	—	—	3	1	—	1	3	—	—	—	1
Maryland	1	—	13	1	—	38	—	1	—	7	1
Massachusetts	1	—	11	—	2	12	15	1	—	1	—
Michigan	1	—	139	4	10	15	—	2	—	15	13
Minnesota	—	1	5	1	14	4	—	—	—	2	9
Mississippi	—	—	23	15	—	1	—	5	—	59	27
Missouri	—	1	39	51	26	7	—	1	1	51	48
Montana	—	1	1	2	20	—	—	—	—	—	—
Nebraska	—	1	7	6	60	2	—	—	—	1	11
Nevada	—	—	2	2	6	1	—	—	—	1	3
New Hampshire	—	—	—	—	1	—	—	—	—	—	—
New Jersey	1	—	16	—	2	105	2	3	—	1	2
New Mexico	—	—	1	15	2	—	—	—	—	4	13

New York	1	—	110	1	12	92	11	3	—	16	17
North Carolina	—	—	20	1	1	10	—	45	—	32	5
North Dakota	—	—	2	—	36	—	—	—	—	—	2
Ohio	1	—	—	4	5	57	3	2	—	37	13
Oklahoma	1	—	19	—	20	3	—	2	1	27	293
Oregon	—	—	2	3	—	2	—	—	—	—	7
Pennsylvania	—	—	161	—	3	—	3	5	—	11	17
Rhode Island	1	1	4	—	—	3	—	—	—	—	—
South Carolina	18	—	10	4	2	17	—	—	—	21	7
South Dakota	—	1	3	—	30	—	—	—	—	1	1
Tennessee	2	—	94	18	2	3	—	22	—	—	26
Texas	1	—	26	242	21	8	—	5	—	51	—
Utah	—	—	2	—	9	—	—	—	—	—	3
Vermont	—	—	2	—	—	1	—	—	—	—	1
Virginia	3	—	26	1	3	30	2	7	—	23	9
Washington	—	—	4	2	129	3	—	1	1	4	4
West Virginia	1	—	97	3	2	37	—	5	—	14	3
Wisconsin	1	—	10	2	7	1	—	1	—	2	3
Wyoming	—	—	—	1	9	1	—	—	—	—	5
U. S. possessions	—	—	—	—	—	—	1	—	—	—	—
Foreign countries	—	—	1	1	—	—	2	—	—	1	3

See footnotes at end of table.

Table 5.—State of Origin and State of Transient Bureau Registration of Migrant Families, June 30, 1935—Continued

State of origin	State of transient bureau registration						
	Utah	Vermont	Virginia	Washington	West Virginia	Wisconsin	Wyoming
Total	146	—	233	1,394	41	210	180
Alabama	—	—	3	1	—	—	3
Arizona	1	—	1	10	—	2	—
Arkansas	1	—	2	16	—	2	4
California	26	—	1	166	1	10	15
Colorado	10	—	—	86	—	3	16
Connecticut	—	—	2	2	—	1	1
Delaware	—	—	1	—	—	1	—
District of Columbia	2	—	6	5	1	3	—
Florida	3	—	6	5	1	1	2
Georgia	—	—	12	—	—	—	—
Idaho [2]	25	—	—	95	—	1	6
Illinois	3	—	2	24	2	51	6
Indiana	2	—	1	14	1	6	3
Iowa	—	—	—	25	—	8	6
Kansas	8	—	—	53	—	3	11
Kentucky	1	—	11	6	3	2	3
Louisiana	1	—	1	4	1	2	—
Maine	—	—	—	1	—	1	—
Maryland	1	—	13	2	2	—	1
Massachusetts	1	—	2	3	1	2	—
Michigan	2	—	7	23	—	16	3
Minnesota	—	—	—	53	—	23	—
Mississippi	3	—	2	1	1	4	—
Missouri	3	—	2	61	1	13	13
Montana	2	—	1	83	—	6	5
Nebraska	2	—	—	95	—	3	10
Nevada	1	—	—	3	—	—	5
New Hampshire	—	—	—	—	—	—	—
New Jersey	1	—	4	1	—	2	—
New Mexico	4	—	—	6	—	—	7

New York	2	—	13	10	1	9	5
North Carolina	2	—	51	3	1	5	1
North Dakota	1	—	1	117	—	6	1
Ohio	4	—	5	12	9	3	6
Oklahoma	2	—	1	51	1	3	19
Oregon	4	—	—	150	—	1	3
Pennsylvania	1	—	15	5	5	4	3
Rhode Island	—	—	—	—	—	—	—
South Carolina	—	—	15	—	3	1	—
South Dakota	7	—	1	88	3	2	1
Tennessee	2	—	18	6	3	3	11
Texas	6	—	—	21	2	—	2
Utah	—	—	—	11	—	2	1
Vermont	—	—	—	—	—	1	1
Virginia	1	—	—	2	2	1	—
Washington	2	—	1	—	—	2	3
West Virginia	—	—	34	6	—	1	—
Wisconsin	1	—	—	25	—	—	2
Wyoming	10	—	—	22	—	1	—
U. S. possessions	—	—	—	9	—	1	—
Foreign countries	1	—	—	12	—	3	—

[1] Division of Transient Activities, *Quarterly Census of Transients Under Care*, June 30, 1935, Federal Emergency Relief Administration, Washington, D. C. Families registered in State of origin are not included.

[2] Idaho transient bureau case load estimated on the basis of June 15, 1935, *Midmonthly Census of Transient Activities*. Origins of the Idaho case load estimated on the basis of the migrant family sample study.

Table 6.—Net Population Displacement and Reciprocated Movement Through Migrant Family Emigration and Immigration [1]

State	Migrant families		Net displacement		Recipro- cated movement
	Emigrating from	Immigrat- ing to	Gain	Loss	
Total [2]	29, 885	29, 885	10, 524	10, 524	19, 361
Alabama	596	417	—	179	417
Arizona	466	225	—	241	225
Arkansas	1, 161	693	—	468	693
California	1, 193	5, 996	4, 803	—	1, 193
Colorado	838	1, 847	1, 009	—	838
Connecticut	207	27	—	180	27
Delaware	53	48	—	5	48
District of Columbia	119	379	260	—	119
Florida	534	709	175	—	534
Georgia	690	393	—	297	393
Idaho	[3] 327	[3] 966	639	—	327
Illinois	1, 264	1, 515	251	—	1, 264
Indiana	685	315	—	370	315
Iowa	522	391	—	131	391
Kansas	1, 091	1, 368	277	—	1, 091
Kentucky	657	54	—	603	54
Louisiana	504	816	312	—	504
Maine	78	12	—	66	12
Maryland	209	272	63	—	209
Massachusetts	284	72	—	212	72
Michigan	799	676	—	123	676
Minnesota	334	358	24	—	334
Mississippi	609	128	—	481	128
Missouri	1, 818	1, 026	—	792	1, 026
Montana	264	97	—	167	97
Nebraska	809	288	—	521	288
Nevada	120	42	—	78	42
New Hampshire	19	126	107	—	19
New Jersey	592	537	—	55	537
New Mexico	369	714	345	—	369
New York	1, 074	1, 472	398	—	1, 074
North Carolina	409	48	—	361	48
North Dakota	318	11	—	307	11
Ohio	843	1, 479	636	—	843
Oklahoma	2, 633	606	—	2, 027	606
Oregon	503	755	252	—	503
Pennsylvania	1, 140	594	—	546	594
Rhode Island	59	48	—	11	48
South Carolina	299	193	—	106	193
South Dakota	521	5	—	516	5
Tennessee	687	918	231	—	687
Texas	1, 971	1, 070	—	901	1, 070
Utah	239	145	—	94	145
Vermont	86	—	—	86	—
Virginia	375	233	—	142	233
Washington	631	1, 373	742	—	631
West Virginia	341	41	—	300	41
Wisconsin	318	207	—	111	207
Wyoming	227	180	—	47	180

[1] Division of Transient Activities, *Quarterly Census of Transients Under Care*, June 30, 1935, Federal Emergency Relief Administration, Washington, D. C.
[2] 419 families emigrating from U. S. possessions or foreign countries are not included.
[3] Idaho transient bureau case load estimated on the basis of June 15, 1935, *Midmonthly Census of Transient Activities*. Origins of the Idaho case load estimated on the basis of the migrant family sample study.

Table 7.—Migrant Families [1] Emigrating per 1,000 Families in General Population 1930,[2] by State

State	Families in general population 1930	Migrant families emigrating from State	Migrant families emigrating per 1,000 families in general population
Total	27, 547, 200	29, 885	1. 08
Nevada	18, 730	120	6. 41
Arizona	91, 871	466	5. 07
Oklahoma	531, 183	2, 633	4. 96
Wyoming	48, 441	227	4. 69
New Mexico	89, 490	369	4. 12
South Dakota	146, 513	521	3. 56
Colorado	237, 936	838	3. 52
Idaho	95, 721	327	3. 42
Arkansas	410, 454	1, 161	2. 83
Nebraska	314, 957	809	2. 57
Kansas	446, 437	1, 091	2. 44
North Dakota	132, 004	318	2. 41
Montana	114, 679	264	2. 30
Utah	106, 621	239	2. 24
Oregon	231, 258	503	2. 18
Missouri	868, 115	1, 818	2. 09
Washington	371, 450	631	1. 70
Florida	332, 957	534	1. 60
Texas	1, 293, 344	1, 971	1. 52
Mississippi	436, 971	609	1. 39
Tennessee	567, 100	687	1. 21
Kentucky	573, 558	657	1. 15
Georgia	610, 083	690	1. 13
Louisiana	449, 616	504	1. 12
District of Columbia	108, 945	119	1. 09
Vermont	80, 197	86	1. 07
Alabama	556, 174	596	1. 07
Delaware	54. 155	53	. 98
West Virginia	353, 562	341	. 96
Iowa	583, 638	522	. 89
Indiana	779, 021	685	. 88
South Carolina	343, 562	299	. 87
California	1, 375, 607	1, 193	. 87
Virginia	493, 547	375	. 76
Michigan	1, 098, 010	799	. 73
Illinois	1, 789, 581	1, 264	. 71
North Carolina	615, 865	409	. 66
New Jersey	923, 613	592	. 64
Minnesota	560, 080	334	. 60
Maryland	356, 514	209	. 59
Connecticut	360, 764	207	. 57
Pennsylvania	2, 095, 332	1, 140	. 54
Ohio	1, 569, 544	843	. 54
Wisconsin	663, 089	318	. 48
Maine	177, 860	78	. 44
Rhode Island	153, 322	59	. 38
New York	2, 889, 889	1, 074	. 37
Massachusetts	940, 541	284	. 30
New Hampshire	105, 299	19	. 18

[1] Division of Transient Activities, *Quarterly Census of Transients Under Care*, June 30, 1935, Federal Emergency Relief Administration. Idaho emigration estimated on basis of migrant family sample study. 419 families emigrating from U. S. possessions are not included.
[2] Bureau of the Census, *Fifteenth Census of the United States: 1930*, Population Vol. VI, U. S. Department of Commerce, Washington, D. C., 1933, p. 36. 1-person families not included.

Table 8.—Migrant Families [1] Immigrating per 1,000 Families in General Population 1930,[2] by State

State	Families in general population 1930	Migrant families immigrating to State	Migrant families immigrating per 1,000 families in general population
Total	27,547,200	30,304	1.10
Idaho	95,721	973	10.16
New Mexico	89,490	714	7.98
Colorado	237,936	1,847	7.76
California	1,375,607	6,044	4.39
Washington	371,450	1,394	3.75
Wyoming	48,441	180	3.72
District of Columbia	108,945	379	3.48
Oregon	231,258	755	3.26
Kansas	446,437	1,372	3.07
Arizona	91,871	225	2.45
Nevada	18,730	42	2.24
Florida	332,957	717	2.15
Louisiana	449,616	820	1.82
Arkansas	410,454	693	1.69
Tennessee	567,100	919	1.62
Utah	106,621	146	1.37
New Hampshire	105,299	131	1.24
Missouri	868,115	1,027	1.18
Oklahoma	531,183	607	1.14
Ohio	1,569,544	1,480	.94
Nebraska	314,957	289	.92
Delaware	54,155	49	.90
Montana	114,679	99	.86
Illinois	1,789,581	1,525	.85
Texas	1,293,344	1,073	.83
Maryland	356,514	275	.77
Alabama	556,174	417	.75
Iowa	583,638	394	.68
Minnesota	560,080	359	.64
Georgia	610,083	393	.64
Michigan	1,098,010	679	.62
New York	2,889,889	1,746	.60
New Jersey	923,613	538	.58
South Carolina	343,562	193	.56
Virginia	493,547	233	.47
Indiana	779,021	316	.41
Rhode Island	153,322	51	.33
Wisconsin	663,089	210	.32
Mississippi	436,971	128	.29
Pennsylvania	2,095,332	594	.28
West Virginia	353,562	41	.12
Kentucky	573,558	54	.09
Massachusetts	940,541	80	.09
North Dakota	132,004	11	.08
North Carolina	615,865	48	.08
Maine	177,860	12	.07
Connecticut	360,764	27	.07
South Dakota	146,513	5	.03
Vermont	80,197	—	—

[1] Division of Transient Activities, *Quarterly Census of Transients Under Care*, June 30, 1935, Federal Emergency Relief Administration. Idaho Transient Bureau case load estimated on basis of June 15, 1935, *Midmonthly Census of Transient Activities*.

[2] Bureau of the Census, *Fifteenth Census of the United States: 1930*, Population Vol. VI, U. S. Department of Commerce, Washington, D. C., 1933, p. 36. 1-person families not included.

Table 9.—Urban-Rural Distribution of Place of Migrant Family Origin and Destination and Residence of Families in General Population of 1930 [1]

State	Migrant family origin [2]			Migrant family destination [3]			Families in general population 1930		
	Total	Urban	Rural	Total	Urban	Rural	Total	Urban	Rural
Total	4,216	2,934	1,282	3,882	3,185	697	27,547,200	15,975,874	11,571,326
	Percent distribution								
Total	100	70	30	100	82	18	100	58	42
Alabama	100	65	35	100	71	29	100	30	70
Arizona	100	66	34	100	93	7	100	36	64
Arkansas	100	38	62	100	58	42	100	22	78
California	100	89	11	100	94	6	100	76	24
Colorado	100	69	31	100	91	9	100	53	47
Connecticut	100	80	20	100	100	—	100	71	29
Delaware	100	71	29	100	65	35	100	51	49
District of Columbia	100	100	—	100	100	—	100	100	—
Florida	100	78	22	100	90	10	100	54	46
Georgia	100	62	38	100	81	19	100	33	67
Idaho	100	44	56	100	41	59	100	31	69
Illinois	100	91	9	100	94	6	100	74	26
Indiana	100	72	28	100	79	21	100	56	44
Iowa	100	66	34	100	82	18	100	41	59
Kansas	100	58	42	100	82	18	100	41	59
Kentucky	100	47	53	100	54	46	100	33	67
Louisiana	100	69	31	100	82	18	100	41	59
Maine	100	83	17	100	50	50	100	40	60
Maryland	100	56	44	100	89	11	100	61	39
Massachusetts	100	93	7	100	96	4	100	90	10
Michigan	100	85	15	100	86	14	100	68	32
Minnesota	100	72	28	100	96	4	100	51	49
Mississippi	100	47	53	100	46	54	100	18	82
Missouri	100	66	34	100	71	29	100	52	48
Montana	100	45	55	100	61	39	100	36	64
Nebraska	100	51	49	100	76	24	100	37	63
Nevada	100	69	31	100	83	17	100	42	58
New Hampshire	100	45	55	100	59	41	100	58	42
New Jersey	100	89	11	100	86	14	100	83	17
New Mexico	100	63	37	100	81	19	100	27	73
New York	100	93	7	100	97	3	100	84	16
North Carolina	100	68	32	100	71	29	100	27	73
North Dakota	100	26	74	100	60	40	100	18	82
Ohio	100	92	8	100	90	10	100	69	31
Oklahoma	100	57	43	100	57	43	100	37	63
Oregon	100	90	10	100	81	19	100	53	47
Pennsylvania	100	86	14	100	94	6	100	69	31
Rhode Island	100	100	—	100	100	—	100	92	8
South Carolina	100	78	22	100	83	17	100	23	77
South Dakota	100	15	85	100	100	—	100	21	79
Tennessee	100	67	33	100	77	23	100	36	64
Texas	100	72	28	100	79	21	100	43	57
Utah	100	76	24	100	93	7	100	55	45
Vermont	100	41	59	100	25	75	100	34	66
Virginia	100	59	41	100	83	17	100	35	65
Washington	100	72	28	100	83	17	100	59	41
West Virginia	100	58	42	100	32	68	100	31	69
Wisconsin	100	57	43	100	82	18	100	55	45
Wyoming	100	39	61	100	52	48	100	34	66

[1] Bureau of the Census, *Fifteenth Census of the United States: 1930*, Population Vol. VI, U. S. Department of Commerce, Washington, D. C., 1933, State table 5. 1-person families not included.
[2] 112 families, whose State of origin or size of place of origin was not ascertainable or whose origin was a foreign country or U. S. possessions, are not included.
[3] 446 families, without definite destinations, whose State of destination or size of place of destination was not ascertainable, or whose destination was a foreign country or U. S. possessions, are not included.

Table 10.—Size of Place of Origin and Destination of Migrant Families, by Year of Leaving Settled Residence

Type of residence change	Year of leaving settled residence								
	Total	Before 1929	1929	1930	1931	1932	1933	1934	1935
Total_____	4,074	143	139	141	167	269	486	1,346	1,383
	Percent distribution								
Total_____	100	100	100	100	100	100	100	100	100
To urban areas_____	76	64	60	68	64	58	71	82	82
To metropolitan cities___	53	32	31	35	36	33	48	61	61
From metropolitan [1] cities_____	24	15	19	20	18	18	23	24	26
From small [2] cities__	16	10	9	11	11	10	12	20	19
From villages [3]_____	7	4	2	1	3	4	7	8	9
From farms_____	6	3	1	3	4	1	6	9	7
To small cities_____	23	32	29	33	28	25	23	21	21
From metropolitan cities_____	8	11	14	15	12	11	8	6	5
From small cities____	8	11	9	10	10	8	8	7	8
From villages_____	4	7	2	6	4	4	5	4	5
From farms_____	3	3	4	2	2	2	2	4	3
To rural areas_____	17	21	30	23	26	33	23	14	12
To villages_____	10	11	20	12	15	19	14	8	6
From metropolitan cities_____	3	1	10	6	7	8	6	2	2
From small cities____	3	4	4	2	4	5	3	3	2
From villages_____	2	3	1	3	2	2	3	2	1
From farms_____	2	3	5	1	2	4	2	1	1
To farms_____	7	10	10	11	11	14	9	6	6
From metropolitan cities_____	2	2	4	5	5	7	2	1	1
From small cities____	1	1	2	3	3	3	2	1	1
From villages_____	1	2	2	—	2	*	1	1	1
From farms_____	3	5	2	3	1	4	4	3	3
No definite destination_____	7	15	10	9	10	9	6	1	6
From metropolitan cities_____	3	6	6	4	3	4	3	1	2
From small cities_____	2	6	1	3	5	3	2	2	2
From villages_____	1	*	1	2	1	2	*	1	1
From farms_____	1	3	2	—	1	—	1	*	1

* Less than 0.5 percent.

[1] Places of more than 100,000 population.
[2] Places of 2,500–100,000 population.
[3] Places of less than 2,500 population.

NOTE.—254 families, whose size of place of settled residence or destination and those for which the year of leaving settled residence were not ascertainable, are not included.

Table 11.—Place of Destination and of First Transient Bureau Registration of Migrant Families

Place of destination and of first transient bureau registration	Total	Migrant families	
		Urban destination	Rural destination
Total_____	3,896	3,190	706
		Percent distribution	
Total_____	100	100	100
Registered in place of destination_____	53	61	14
Registered in State but not at place of destination_____	8	6	19
Registered in State other than State of destination_____	39	33	67

NOTE.—1,593 families, which had no settled residence, had no definite destination, and whose State of destination or size of place of destination was not ascertainable, are not included.

Table 12.—Migrant Family and Unattached Cases Opened and Closed During Month and Number Under Care at the Middle of the Month in Transient Bureaus, February 1934—September 1935

Year and month	Migrant family cases			Unattached cases		
	Cases opened	Cases closed	Cases under care at midmonth	Cases opened	Cases closed	Cases under care at midmonth
1934						
February_____	5,911	4,045	10,522	92,417	88,465	60,577
March_____	6,612	4,933	11,585	136,088	129,812	70,483
April_____	6,929	6,316	13,458	179,660	174,835	76,934
May_____	8,444	7,475	14,289	209,136	200,870	78,771
June_____	9,568	8,204	15,885	240,716	231,079	86,369
July_____	11,301	9,160	17,346	291,148	286,451	96,687
August_____	13,925	11,149	19,235	345,031	335,988	104,789
September_____	12,885	11,886	22,275	302,439	308,984	108,134
October_____	13,999	11,789	24,044	298,262	285,786	116,289
November_____	13,875	10,687	27,391	271,941	260,973	128,686
December_____	12,734	11,071	30,216	213,739	213,506	136,823
1935						
January_____	13,070	11,184	33,124	212,894	210,145	135,051
February_____	11,505	10,930	35,414	207,189	208,272	134,170
March_____	12,967	13,576	35,254	279,632	283,653	132,562
April_____	13,961	14,118	35,019	303,941	312,594	129,249
May_____	14,769	15,174	32,727	310,642	317,035	120,224
June_____	15,122	16,179	32,669	298,034	308,168	112,958
July_____	16,848	17,716	31,791	295,999	298,334	110,094
August_____	15,945	16,588	31,112	275,090	281,814	105,174
September [1]_____	9,769	16,832	27,312	133,797	154,481	95,509

[1] Intake of new cases closed on September 20.

Source: Division of Transient Activities, Federal Emergency Relief Administration. Interstate cases only are included.

Table 13.—Size and Composition of Migrant Families During and Before Migration

Size	Total	Composition			
		Normal with or without children	Woman-children	Man-children	All other types
During migration	5,489	4,343	728	119	299
Before migration	5,489	4,476	589	105	319
	Percent distribution				
During migration	100	100	100	100	100
2 persons	35	35	42	43	15
3 persons	25	24	30	31	30
4 persons	17	17	14	12	19
5 persons	10	10	7	7	19
6 persons	5	6	3	4	8
7 persons	4	4	3	1	4
8 persons	2	2	1	—	2
9 persons	1	1	*	1	2
10 persons or more	1	1	*	1	1
Before migration	100	100	100	100	100
2 persons	32	32	41	37	13
3 persons	25	25	29	28	29
4 persons	18	18	15	13	19
5 persons	11	11	7	14	18
6 persons	6	6	4	6	9
7 persons	4	4	3	1	4
8 persons	2	2	1	—	3
9 persons	1	1	*	1	3
10 persons or more	1	1	*	—	2

* Less than 0.5 percent.

Table 14.—Age and Sex of Economic Heads of Migrant Families, of Heads of Resident Relief Families October 1933,[1] and Age of Male Heads of Families in General Population 1930 [2]

Age	Economic heads of migrant families [3]			Heads of resident relief families October 1933			Male heads of families in general population 1930
	Total	Male	Female	Total	Male	Female	
Total	5,480	4,725	755	204,100	174,042	30,058	26,093,416
	Percent distribution						
Total	100	100	100	100	100	100	100
16–24 years	13	12	19	7	7	5	5
25–34 years	36	37	32	22	23	17	23
35–44 years	29	29	27	27	28	25	27
45–54 years	15	15	14	22	22	22	22
55–64 years	6	6	7	13	12	16	14
65 years and over	1	1	1	9	8	15	9

[1] Division of Research, Statistics, and Finance, *Unemployment Relief Census, October 1933*, Report Number Three, Federal Emergency Relief Administration, Washington, D. C., 1935, p. 36. 1-person families are not included.
[2] Bureau of the Census, *Fifteenth Census of the United States: 1930*, Population Vol. VI, U. S. Department of Commerce, Washington, D. C., 1933, p. 9.
[3] 9 family heads, whose age was not ascertainable, are not included.

Table 15.—Age and Status in Family of Persons in Migrant Families

Age	Total	Economic heads [1]	Other principal members [2]	Children and other relatives [3]
Total	19,935	5,480	4,797	9,658
	Percent distribution			
Total	100	100	100	100
Under 5 years	15	—	—	31
5–9 years	14	—	—	28
10–14 years	11	—	—	23
15–19 years	8	1	8	12
20–24 years	10	12	22	3
25–29 years	10	18	20	1
30–34 years	9	18	15	*
35–44 years	13	29	21	*
45–54 years	6	15	9	*
55–64 years	3	6	3	1
65 years and over	1	1	2	1

*Less than 0.5 percent.

[1] 9 family heads, whose age was not ascertainable, are not included.

[2] In the majority of cases "other principal members" were spouse of economic heads. 2 other groups are also included: (1) parents of economic heads, where the economic head was an unmarried child; and (2) siblings (16 years of age and over) of economic heads.

[3] Includes brothers and sisters under 16 years of age, grandparents, nieces, cousins, aunts, uncles, etc.

NOTE.—43 persons, whose age was not ascertainable, are not included.

Table 16.—Citizenship Status and Color and Nativity of Economic Heads of Migrant Families

Citizenship status	Total	White		Negro	Other
		Native-born	Foreign-born		
Total	5,447	4,578	371	419	79
	Percent distribution				
Total	100	100	100	100	100
U. S. citizens	98	100	66	100	73
Naturalization in process	1	—	16	—	—
No U. S. citizenship	1	—	18	—	27

NOTE.—42 family heads, whose color, nativity, or citizenship status was not ascertainable, are not included.

Table 17.—Usual Occupation and Employability of Economic Heads of Migrant Families

Usual occupation	Total	Employability	
		Employable	Employable with handicaps
Total	4,729	2,995	1,734
	Percent distribution		
Total	100	100	100
White-collar workers	28	26	31
Professional and technical workers	5	4	5
Proprietors, managers, and officials (nonagricultural)	4	4	4
Proprietors, foremen, and overseers (agricultural)	8	7	10
Office workers, salesmen, and kindred workers	11	11	12
Skilled workers	23	25	21
Semiskilled workers	25	27	22
Unskilled workers	24	22	26
Laborers (nonagricultural)	8	7	8
Laborers (agricultural)	7	7	8
Domestic and personal service workers	9	8	10

NOTE.—760 economic heads of families, who were unemployable or who had no experience in any occupation and those whose usual occupation was not ascertainable, are not included.

Table 18.—Usual Occupation and Sex of Employable Economic Heads of Migrant Families

Usual occupation [1]	Total	Male	Female
Total	4,796	4,534	262
Inexperienced persons	67	9	58
White-collar workers	1,308	1,249	59
Professional and technical workers [2]	215	203	12
Actors	17	17	—
Artists, sculptors, and teachers of art	9	9	—
Chemists, assayers, metallurgists	3	3	—
Clergymen and religious workers	23	21	2
Designers	1	1	—
Draftsmen	2	2	—
Engineers (technical)	31	31	—
Lawyers, judges, and justices	1	1	—
Musicians and teachers of music	40	39	1
Nurses (trained or registered)	4	3	1
Physicians, surgeons, and dentists	6	6	—
Playground and recreational workers	4	4	—
Reporters, editors, and journalists	7	6	1
Teachers	13	9	4
Other professional workers	7	6	1
Other semiprofessional workers	47	45	2
Proprietors, managers, and officials (except agriculture)	180	179	1
Building contractors	12	12	—
Foresters, forest rangers, and timber cruisers	1	1	—
Hucksters, peddlers, and junk and rag dealers	19	19	—
Trucking, transfer and cab companies, and garages	8	8	—
Retail dealers and managers (n. e. c.[3])	51	51	—
Other proprietors, managers, and officials	89	88	1
Proprietors, foremen, and overseers (in agriculture)	383	382	1
Farm foremen, managers, and overseers	15	15	—
Farmers (owners, tenants, croppers, etc.)	368	367	1
Office workers	224	203	21
Bookkeepers, accountants, and auditors [2]	57	55	2
Cashiers (except in banks)	3	1	2
Clerks (n. e. c.)	98	91	7
Office machine operators	3	1	2
Office managers and bank tellers	5	5	—
Stenographers, stenotypists, and dictaphone operators	7	4	3
Telegraph and radio operators	16	16	—
Telephone operators	2	—	2
Typists	8	6	2
Other clerical and allied workers	25	24	1

See footnotes at end of table.

Table 18.—Usual Occupation and Sex of Employable Economic Heads of Migrant Families—Continued

Usual occupation [1]	Total	Male	Female
White-collar workers—Continued.			
Salesmen and kindred workers	306	282	24
Canvassers (solicitors, any)	31	26	5
Commercial travelers	28	28	—
Newsboys	3	3	—
Real estate agents and insurance agents	34	32	2
Salesmen and saleswomen (retail stores)	122	106	16
Other salespersons and kindred workers	88	87	1
Skilled workers	1,106	1,105	1
Skilled workers and foremen in building construction	664	664	—
Blacksmiths	25	25	—
Boilermakers	6	6	—
Bricklayers and stonemasons	19	19	—
Carpenters	128	128	—
Cement finishers	24	24	—
Electricians	59	59	—
Foremen: construction (except road)	11	11	—
Foremen: road and street construction	10	10	—
Operators or engineers: stationary and portable construction equipment	45	45	—
Painters (not in factory)	191	191	—
Paper hangers	2	2	—
Plasterers	13	13	—
Plumbers, gas and steam fitters	57	57	—
Roofers	10	10	—
Sheet metal workers	4	4	—
Stonecutters and carvers	4	4	—
Structural iron and steel workers	35	35	—
Setters: marble, stone, and tile	1	1	—
Other skilled workers in building and construction	20	20	—
Skilled workers and foremen in manufacturing and other industries	442	441	1
Cabinetmakers	6	6	—
Cobblers and shoe repairmen	15	15	—
Conductors: steam and street railroads and buses	4	4	—
Foremen (in factories)	18	18	—
Foremen and inspectors (except in factories)	22	22	—
Locomotive engineers and firemen	25	25	—
Machinists, millwrights, and toolmakers	63	63	—
Mechanics (n. e. c.)	171	171	—
Molders, founders, and casters (metal)	12	12	—
Sawyers	13	13	—
Skilled workers in printing and engraving	24	24	—
Tailors and furriers	11	10	1
Tinsmiths and coppersmiths	7	7	—
Metal workers (except gold and silver) (n. e. c.)	4	4	—
Skilled workers in manufacturing and other industries (n. e. c.)	47	47	—
Semiskilled workers	1,189	1,141	48
Semiskilled workers in building and construction	452	452	—
Apprentices in building and construction	1	1	—
Blasters (except in mines)	2	2	—
Firemen (except locomotive and fire department)	27	27	—
Operators of building and construction equipment	23	23	—
Pipelayers	2	2	—
Rodman and chainmen (surveying)	2	2	—
Truck and tractor drivers	327	327	—
Welders	28	28	—
Other semiskilled workers in building and construction	40	40	—
Semiskilled workers in manufacturing and other industries	737	689	48
Bakers	23	23	—
Brakeman (railroad)	18	18	—
Deliverymen	26	26	—
Dressmakers and milliners	7	—	7
Filers, grinders, buffers, and polishers (metal)	12	12	—
Furnacemen, heaters, smeltermen, etc. (metal working)	4	4	—
Guards, watchmen, and doorkeepers (except railroad)	12	12	—
Handicraft workers: textile, wood, leather, metal, etc	1	1	—
Inside workers (mines)	87	87	—
Operatives (n. e. c.) in manufacturing and allied industries	336	298	38
Chemical and allied industries	9	9	—
Cigar, cigarette, and tobacco factories	9	5	4
Clay, glass, and stone industries	9	9	—
Clothing industries	26	16	10
Electric light and power plants	1	1	—
Food and beverage industries	46	41	5
Iron and steel, machinery, and vehicle industries	65	64	1
Laundries and dry cleaning establishments	20	13	7
Lumber and furniture industries	22	22	—
Metal industries (except iron and steel)	6	6	—
Paper, printing, and allied industries	9	8	1

See footnotes at end of table.

Table 18.—Usual Occupation and Sex of Employable Economic Heads of Migrant Families—Continued

Usual occupation [1]	Total	Male	Female
Semiskilled workers—Continued.			
Semiskilled workers in manufacturing and other industries—Con.			
Operatives (n. e. c.) in manufacturing and allied industries—Con.			
Shoe factories	7	7	—
Textile industries	72	63	9
Miscellaneous and not specified manufacturing industries	35	34	1
Painters, varnishers, enamelers, etc. (factory)	15	15	—
Switchmen, flagmen, and yardmen (railroad)	15	15	—
Taxicab drivers, bus drivers, and chauffeurs	38	38	—
Other semiskilled workers in manufacturing and other industries	143	140	3
Unskilled workers	1,126	1,030	96
Unskilled laborers (except in agriculture)	357	357	—
Laborers in manufacturing and allied industries	68	68	—
Clay, glass, and stone industries	1	1	—
Iron and steel, machinery, and vehicle industries	19	19	—
Lumber and furniture industries	20	20	—
Other manufacturing and allied industries	28	28	—
Laborers except in manufacturing and allied industries	289	289	—
Mines, quarries, and oil and gas wells	32	32	—
Odd jobs (general)	19	19	—
Railroads (steam and street)	29	29	—
Roads, streets, and sewers	39	39	—
Stores (including porters in stores)	12	12	—
Laborers and helpers (n. e. c.) in building and construction	79	79	—
Longshoremen and stevedores	4	4	—
Lumbermen, raftsmen, and woodchoppers	21	21	—
Street cleaners, garbage men, and scavengers	3	3	—
Teamsters and draymen	9	9	—
Other laborers, except in manufacturing and allied industries (n. e. c.)	42	42	—
Unskilled laborers (in agriculture)	356	349	7
Domestic and personal service workers	413	324	89
Barber and beauty shop workers	51	49	2
Bootblacks	1	1	—
Cleaners and charwomen	8	6	2
Cooks and chefs (except in private family)	149	142	7
Elevator operators	10	10	—
Janitors, caretakers, and sextons	22	17	5
Laundresses (not in laundry)	4	—	4
Porters (except in stores)	11	11	—
Practical nurses, hospital attendants, and orderlies	25	13	12
Servants (hotels, boarding houses, etc.) (n. e. c.)	34	31	3
Servants (private family)	37	5	32
Waiters, waitresses, and bartenders	40	27	13
Other domestic and personal service workers	21	12	9

[1] The occupational classification used here differs from the classification in Bureau of the Census, *Fifteenth Census of the United States: 1930,* Vol. V, U. S. Department of Commerce, Washington, D. C., 1933. The basic code used in classifying the occupations was prepared by Palmer, Gladys L., *Occupational Classification,* Section 2, Division of Research, Statistics, and Finance, Federal Emergency Relief Administration, Washington, D. C., July 1935. The arrangement of occupations above is in the main comparable to that used by Hauser, Philip M., *Workers on Relief in the United States in March 1935,* Abridged Edition, Division of Social Research, Works Progress Administration, Washington, D. C., January 1937.

[2] Certified public accountants are excluded from professional and technical workers and are included with bookkeepers, accountants, and auditors.

[3] Not elsewhere classified.

NOTE.—693 economic heads of families, who were unemployable and those whose usual occupation was not ascertainable, are not included.

Table 19.—Industry of Usual Occupation and Sex of Employable Economic Heads of Migrant Families

Industry of usual occupation [1]	Total	Male	Female
Total	4,730	4,475	255
Inexperienced persons	67	9	58
Agriculture	761	753	8
Fishing and forestry	41	41	—
Fishing	8	8	—
Forestry	33	33	—
Extraction of minerals	203	203	—
Coal mines	73	73	—
Copper mines	4	4	—
Gold and silver mines	15	15	—
Iron mines	1	1	—
Lead and zinc mines	15	15	—
Other specified mines	1	1	—
Not specified mines	19	19	—
Quarries	10	10	—
Oil wells and gas wells	65	65	—
Manufacturing and mechanical industries	1,711	1,664	47
Building industry	658	656	2
Chemical and allied industries	43	42	1
Gas works	6	6	—
Paint and varnish factories	2	2	—
Petroleum refineries	17	17	—
Rayon factories	2	2	—
Soap factories	5	5	—
Other chemical factories	11	10	1
Cigar and tobacco factories	11	7	4
Clay, glass, and stone industries	19	19	—
Brick, tile, and terra-cotta factories	2	2	—
Glass factories	8	8	—
Lime, cement, and artificial stone factories	4	4	—
Marble and stoneyards	4	4	—
Potteries	1	1	—
Clothing industries	45	33	12
Hat factories (felt)	7	6	1
Shirt, collar, and cuff factories	3	2	1
Suit, coat, and overall factories	22	19	3
Other clothing factories	13	6	7
Food and allied industries	129	123	6
Bakeries	29	29	—
Butter, cheese, and condensed milk factories	5	4	1
Candy factories	15	13	2
Fish curing and packing	2	2	—
Flour and grain mills	12	12	—
Fruit and vegetable canning, etc	7	6	1
Slaughter and packing houses	46	45	1
Sugar factories and refineries	4	4	—
Other food factories	2	1	1
Liquor and beverage industries	7	7	—
Iron and steel, machinery, and vehicle industries	363	363	—
Agricultural implement factories	6	6	—
Automobile factories	71	71	—
Automobile repair shops	118	118	—
Blast furnaces and steel rolling mills	50	50	—
Car and railroad shops	16	16	—
Ship and boat building	17	17	—
Other iron and steel and machinery factories	79	79	—
Not specified metal industries	6	6	—
Metal industries (except iron and steel)	27	27	—
Brass mills	1	1	—
Clock and watch factories	1	1	—
Copper factories	4	4	—
Gold and silver factories	2	2	—
Jewelry factories	3	3	—
Tinware, enamelware, etc., factories	12	12	—
Other metal factories	4	4	—
Leather industries	14	14	—
Harness and saddle factories	1	1	—
Leather belt, leather goods, etc., factories	1	1	—
Shoe factories	10	10	—
Tanneries	2	2	—
Lumber and furniture industries	103	102	1
Furniture factories	29	28	1
Piano and organ factories	2	2	—
Saw and planing mills	60	60	—
Other woodworking factories	12	12	—

See footnotes at end of table.

Table 19.—Industry of Usual Occupation and Sex of Employable Economic Heads of Migrant Families—Continued

Industry of usual occupation [1]	Total	Male	Female
Manufacturing and mechanical industries—Continued.			
Paper, printing, and allied industries	73	68	5
Blank book, envelope, tag, paper bag, etc., factories	2	2	—
Paper and pulp mills	5	5	—
Paper box factories	2	2	—
Printing, publishing, and engraving	64	59	5
Textile industries	96	87	9
Cotton mills	48	43	5
Knitting mills	4	4	—
Lace and embroidery mills	1	—	1
Silk mills	8	7	1
Textile dyeing, finishing, and printing mills	1	1	—
Woolen and worsted mills	7	7	—
Other and not specified textile mills	27	25	2
Miscellaneous manufacturing industries	130	123	7
Button factories	1	1	—
Electric light and power plants	37	37	—
Electrical machinery and supply factories	14	14	—
Independent hand trades	31	25	6
Rubber factories	7	7	—
Turpentine farms and distilleries	1	1	—
Other miscellaneous manufacturing industries	28	27	1
Other not specified manufacturing industries	11	11	—
Transportation and communication	617	613	4
Air transportation	3	3	—
Construction and maintenance of streets, roads, sewers, bridges	154	154	—
Express companies	1	1	—
Garages, automobile laundries, greasing stations	50	50	—
Pipe lines	15	15	—
Postal service	5	4	1
Radio broadcasting and transmitting	1	1	—
Steam railroads	167	167	—
Street railroads	9	8	1
Telegraph and telephone	22	20	2
Truck, transfer, and cab companies	127	127	—
Water transportation	62	62	—
Other and not specified transportation and communication	1	1	—
Trade	579	553	26
Advertising agencies	19	19	—
Banking and brokerage	21	21	—
Grain elevators	1	1	—
Insurance	32	31	1
Real estate	14	12	2
Stockyards	1	1	—
Warehouses and cold storage plants	8	8	—
Wholesale and retail trade	482	459	23
Automobile agencies, stores, filling stations	50	49	1
Wholesale and retail trade (except automobile)	432	410	22
Other and not specified trade	1	1	—
Public service (n. e. c.[2])	63	61	2
Professional service	250	233	17
Professional service (except recreation and amusement)	111	97	14
Recreation and amusement	133	130	3
Semiprofessional pursuits and attendants and helpers	6	6	—
Domestic and personal service	438	345	93
Hotels, restaurants, boarding houses, etc	249	218	31
Domestic and personal service (n. e. c.[2])	154	99	55
Laundries	22	15	7
Cleaning, dyeing, and pressing shops	13	13	—

[1] The arrangement of industries is in the main comparable to that used by Hauser, Philip M. and Jenkinson, Bruce, in *Workers on Relief in the United States in March 1935*, Vol. II, A Study of Industrial and Educational Backgrounds. Division of Social Research, Works Progress Administration, Washington, D. C., (in preparation). Industries which were reported by no employable economic head of migrant families are not shown in this classification.

[2] Not elsewhere classified.

NOTE.— 759 economic heads of families, who were unemployable and those whose usual industry was not ascertainable, are not included.

Table 20.—Usual Occupation and Age of Employable Economic Heads of Migrant Families

Usual occupation	Total	Age			
		Under 25 years	25–34 years	35–44 years	45–64 years
Total_____	4,722	548	1,770	1,410	994
		Percent distribution			
Total_____	100	100	100	100	100
White-collar workers_____	28	18	24	30	37
Professional and technical workers_____	5	3	4	5	6
Proprietors, managers, and officials (nonagricultural)_____	4	1	2	5	7
Proprietors, foremen, and overseers (agricultural).	8	5	6	8	13
Office workers, salesmen, and kindred workers__	11	9	12	12	11
Skilled workers_____	23	11	23	27	26
Semiskilled workers_____	25	34	30	22	16
Unskilled workers_____	24	37	23	21	21
Laborers (nonagricultural)_____	8	10	7	6	8
Laborers (agricultural)_____	7	17	8	5	6
Domestic and personal service workers_____	9	10	8	10	7

NOTE.—767 economic heads of families, who were unemployable, who had no experience at any occupation, and whose usual occupation or age was not ascertainable, are not included.

Table 21.—Industry of Usual Occupation and Age of Employable Economic Heads of Migrant Families

Industry of usual occupation	Total	Age			
		Under 25 years	25–34 years	35–44 years	45–64 years
Total_____	4,656	543	1,752	1,384	977
		Percent distribution			
Total_____	100	100	100	100	100
Agriculture, forestry, and fishing_____	17	25	15	14	20
Extraction of minerals_____	4	4	4	5	5
Manufacturing and mechanical_____	37	30	37	39	37
Building and construction_____	14	8	14	16	16
Clothing industries_____	1	1	1	1	1
Food and allied industries_____	3	5	3	2	2
Automobile factories and repair shops_____	4	3	5	5	2
Iron, steel, and machinery industries_____	4	3	3	4	4
Textile industries_____	2	3	2	2	1
Lumber and furniture industries_____	2	2	2	2	3
Paper, printing, and allied industries_____	2	1	2	1	2
Other manufacturing industries_____	5	4	5	6	6
Transportation and communication_____	13	14	15	13	9
Trade_____	12	12	13	12	12
Public service_____	1	1	2	1	1
Professional service_____	6	5	5	6	6
Domestic and personal service_____	10	9	9	10	10

NOTE.—833 economic heads of families, who were unemployable, who had no experience at any occupation, and whose age or usual industry was not ascertainable, are not included.

Table 22.—Usual Occupation and Schooling Completed by Employable Economic Heads of Migrant Families

Usual occupation	Total	Schooling completed	
		8 grades or less	9 grades or more
Total_____	4, 687	3, 034	1, 653
	Percent distribution		
Total_____	100	100	100
White-collar workers_____	28	21	40
Professional and technical workers_____	5	2	9
Proprietors, managers, and officials (nonagricultural)_____	4	3	6
Proprietors, foremen, and overseers (agricultural)_____	8	10	4
Office workers, salesmen, and kindred workers_____	11	6	21
Skilled workers_____	23	24	23
Semiskilled workers_____	25	27	21
Unskilled workers_____	24	28	16
Laborers (nonagricultural)_____	8	10	4
Laborers (agricultural)_____	7	10	3
Domestic and personal service workers_____	9	8	9

NOTE.—802 economic heads of families, who were unemployable, who had no experience in any occupation, and whose occupation or schooling completed was not ascertainable, are not included.

Appendix B

SOME ASPECTS OF MINORITY-GROUP MIGRATION

FOREIGN-BORN

AMONG THE families with foreign-born white economic heads Italians formed the largest group with 20 percent of all foreign-born, followed in order by English (13 percent), Russians (9 percent), Canadians (9 percent), Germans (8 percent), Poles, Greeks, Austrians (each 6 percent), and Scandanavians (5 percent). The nationalities listed made up four-fifths of all the foreign-born family heads. Two-thirds of the foreign-born were citizens, and one-sixth had first papers.

State of Registration

The distribution of the 370 families with foreign-born economic heads was extremely uneven among the States. In New York the 308 families in the sample included 108, or 35 percent, foreign-born families. In contrast, the 320 families under care in Kansas included only 2, or less than 1 percent, foreign-born families. The proportion of foreign-born was consistently above the average (7 percent of all families studied) in Northeastern industrial States, such as New York, Massachusetts, Michigan, Pennsylvania, New Hampshire, and New Jersey, and consistently below the average in agricultural States, such as Kansas, Iowa, Oklahoma, and the entire Southeast.

State of Origin

The origin States of these families showed the same concentration. For example, 23 percent of the families whose last place of residence was in New York State were foreign-born, whereas only slightly over 1 percent of the families starting from Kansas were foreign-born. The same States that contributed and received the highest proportions of foreign-born migrant families are also the States that had the highest proportion foreign-born in their total 1930 population. Obviously, then, the movement represented by the foreign-born migrant family was between places of foreign-born concentration. Unlike native white migrant families the migration of the foreign-born was restricted to those communities where previous experience had shown that the conditions for absorption of the foreign-born groups were favorable.[1]

Reasons for Leaving Settled Residence

The reasons for migration reported by foreign-born families indicate that the economic forces operating on them were no less important than in the case of all migrants. Almost three-fourths of the foreign-born families were in economic distress when they set out to find a more favorable location. This ratio is slightly above that reported among all migrant families and is the result principally of the larger proportion of foreign-born reporting business failure as the reason for migration. Inadequate relief was a less important expelling force among foreign-born than among all families. A smaller proportion reported personal distress. Ill-health was the most important personal reason but was less frequently reported by foreign-born families than by all families.

Kind of Contact at Destination

The tendency of foreign-born families to migrate to places where there was already a concentration of the foreign-born is further illustrated in their choice of destinations. As compared with 80 percent of all families, 78 percent of the foreign-born had chosen a community where they had some kind of definite contact. Foreign-born families, however, showed a somewhat greater tendency to return to a place of previous residence than was found among all families. Chance selection of destination was reported only twice among the whole group of 370 foreign-born although rumor and advertising attracted 18 percent of them in contrast to 16 percent of all migrant families.

Reasons for Selecting Destination

As indicated by the reasons for leaving settled residence, economic betterment was the goal of the majority of the foreign-born migrants. Unlike all migrant families, however, a larger proportion sought business and farm opportunities. While 7 percent of all migrant families hoped or expected to obtain a farm or business, 11 percent of the foreign-born were motivated by this desire.

In summary, it may be said that although families with foreign-born economic heads were represented in comparatively small numbers

---

[1] For a discussion of the distribution of minority peoples in the United States, see Young, Donald. *Research Memorandum on Minority Peoples in the Depression,* Social Science Research Council, New York, 1935, ch. III.

among the depression migrants they migrated in response to forces similar to those operating on all transient families. The foreign-born tended to move to communities similar to the ones in which they had been living and showed a decided preference for the industrial States.

NEGROES

State of Registration

It was pointed out in chapter II that, in contrast with the prevailing westward movement of families, the movement from the South was to the Northeastern and North Central States.[2] The importance of the Negro family in this movement is evident in the greater than average proportions of Negroes registered in transient bureaus in such States as Illinois, New York, Ohio, Michigan, and Pennsylvania. Evidence of a movement of Negro families north along the Atlantic coast is found in the higher than average proportion of Negroes in the sample for the District of Columbia, Maryland, Delaware, and New Jersey. The 11 Southeastern States had only 9 percent of all Negro families under care.

State of Origin

The movement of families out of the Southern States, both from the deep South and the Mississippi Valley, included relatively large proportions of Negro families. Mississippi, Arkansas, Missouri, North Carolina, South Carolina, Kentucky, and Georgia were of outstanding importance as origins of Negro families. The 11 Southeastern States contributed 40 percent of all Negro migrant families.

With States in the southeastern section of the country contributing more than a proportionate share of Negro families to the transient relief population, and with States in the northeastern section receiving more than a proportionate share, it is clear that lines of Negro migration established during the 1920's were, in general, being followed during the depression. The attractive force during prosperity was industrial employment in the larger industrial centers. The pre-depression Negro migration undoubtedly influenced southern Negro families suffering from the depression to seek work in the northern cities where in many cases friends and relatives had preceded them.

Reasons for Leaving Settled Residence

Unemployment, domestic difficulties, inadequate earnings, and a desire to rejoin relatives were the more important reasons given by Negro families for leaving settled residence. Unemployment and ill-health were reported less frequently by Negroes than by all families or by the foreign-born; on the other hand, domestic difficulties, inadequate earnings, and inadequate relief were reported much more fre-

[2] See p. 40 ff.

quently by Negroes than by all families or by foreign-born white families.

Kind of Contact at Destination

Negro families had, on the whole, the same kinds of contacts in the community of destination as were reported for all families. The presence of relatives or friends in the place of destination, however, was decidedly of more importance among Negroes than among all families. "No definite entree" was reported somewhat less frequently by Negro families, and fewer Negro families were attracted by rumors and advertisements.

The conclusions to be drawn from this analysis of Negro families are (1) that the most important direction of movement was from South to North, with the large industrial centers as the principal destinations; (2) that economic causes were the chief expulsive forces, with domestic difficulties assuming more than average importance; and (3) that the presence of friends or relatives was an unusually significant factor in the choice of destination.

Appendix C

SCHEDULE AND INSTRUCTIONS

F. E. R. A. Form DRS–216A.

STUDY OF FEDERAL TRANSIENT FAMILY GROUPS

Date of interview_____ City and State of registration_____ Interviewer_____

Name of present head_____ Case number_____

Status of case: ( ) Under care; ( ) Intake.

1. Members of family group:

A	B	C	D	E	F		G	H	
					Place of birth			Education: Grades completed	
Line No.	Relation to head	Sex	Age	Color or race			Marital status		
					State	City or county		Grade and high school	College
1____	Present head_	_____	_____	_____	_____	_____	_____	_____	_____
2____	_____	_____	_____	x x	_____	_____	_____	_____	_____
3____	_____	_____	_____	x x	_____	_____	_____	_____	_____
4____	_____	_____	_____	x x	_____	_____	_____	_____	_____
5____	_____	_____	_____	x x	_____	_____	_____	_____	_____
6____	_____	_____	_____	x x	_____	_____	_____	_____	_____
7____	_____	_____	_____	x x	_____	_____	_____	_____	_____

(Enter below information for members usually included in family group but not now present)

8____	_____	_____	_____	_____	_____	_____	_____	_____	_____
9____	_____	_____	_____	_____	_____	_____	_____	_____	_____
10____	_____	_____	_____	_____	_____	_____	_____	_____	_____
11____	_____	_____	_____	_____	_____	_____	_____	_____	_____

2. Month and year of last marriage of normal head_____

3. Is normal head a U. S. citizen? ( ) Yes; ( ) No; ( ) First papers.

169

4. Residence history of family group since January 1, 1929, or since date of present marriage if later:

(*List in chronological order all places in which the family resided 1 month or longer, excluding periods when the family received transient relief*)

A Location		B Duration		C Nature of place (check one on each line)		
State	City or county	From (month and year)	To (month and year)	Farm	Village (under 2,500 population)	Urban (2,500 population or more)

5. Transient relief record since July 1, 1933:

(*List in chronological order all instances in which the family as a whole or 2 or more members of it were registered for transient relief as a family group*)

A Location		B Date of registration (month, day, and year)	C Length of stay	D Reason for leaving
State	City			

REASONS FOR FAMILY GROUP MOBILITY

(*This section applies to the entire period during which the family group has been in an unsettled condition, beginning before or after January 1, 1929*)

6. Last place in which the family lived a settled self-supporting life; that is, the place at which family group mobility began:

State _____ City or county _____ Date left _____

7. Reasons for leaving. State fully all the circumstances that caused the family to leave the place entered in question 6:

----

8. Destination at time of leaving place entered in question 6:

A. State _____ City or county _____

B. Reasons for selection of this place _____

_____

_____

_____

9. Present plans for future:
A. ( ) Formulated by family group.
   ( ) Formulated with assistance of Transient Bureau.

B. Nature of plans _____

_____

_____

OCCUPATIONAL HISTORY

10. Present employment status of *normal head*:
A. ( ) Not working; ( ) Working on transient relief projects.

   ( ) Other employment (specify) _____

_____

B. Interviewer's opinion as to employability of normal head:

_____

C. Employment handicaps of normal head (specify):

_____

_____

11. Usual occupations of *all employable persons 16 years of age and over* entered in question 1:

A	B		C	D	
Line number of person in question 1 (A)	Usual occupation		Total number of years experience	Last nonrelief job of 1 month or longer at usual occupation	
	Occupation	Industry		From (month and year)	To (month and year)
Present head _____					
Normal head _____					
Others _____					
_____					
_____					
_____					

12. Last nonrelief job of 2 weeks or longer held by *normal head* at any occupation:

A	B	C	
Occupation	Industry	Duration	
		From	To

INSTRUCTIONS FOR FILLING OUT SCHEDULE DRS–216A

Cases To Be Scheduled

1. Schedules are to be taken only for cases registered as family groups.

2. Schedules are to be taken only for cases classified as *Federal families* (i. e. Federal transients); *do not* schedule cases classified as *State families*.

3. Cases classified as "service only" are *not to be scheduled*.

General Instructions

An interview with a responsible member of the family group, preferably the head, will be necessary in all cases. For cases taken from current registrations, the entire schedule is to be filled by interview. For cases taken from among those under care, the case record will be helpful in providing some information, but an interview will be necessary to answer most of the questions on the schedule. The case record should also be of use in checking some of the information obtained from the interview.

At the time of the interview and before the person interviewed has left, the schedule should be checked to see that there are no omissions or inconsistencies.

Specific Instructions

Name of Present Head

The present head is the person who is registered by the Transient Bureau as the head of the family group.

1. *Member of family group.*

b. *Relation to head:* Enter on lines 1 to 7 the persons now registered as part of the relief case.

Enter on lines 8 to 11 persons normally a part of the family group but not now registered as part of the relief case.

The entries must be in terms of relation to the present head; e. g., wife, son, daughter, sister, friend, etc.

The entries must be in the following order: head, spouse, children in descending order of age, other persons.

If the person who is normally the head of the family group is not the person registered as the present head, enter his relation to the present head on line 8 and add "normal head"; e. g., husband (normal head).

In cases where the husband and wife are permanently separated or divorced, the husband is no longer a member of the family and should never be entered as the normal head.

c. *Sex:* Enter "M" for male, "F" for female.

d. *Age:* Enter age as of last birthday.

e. *Color or race:* Enter "W" for white, "Neg" for Negro, "Mex" for Mexican, and "Oth" for other races.

f. *Place of birth:* In all cases where the person was born on a farm, enter the name of the county followed by the abbreviation "Co."

If a person was born in a foreign country, enter the name of that country according to present day boundaries.

g. *Marital status:* Enter "S" for single, "M" for married, "Wid" for widowed, "Div" for divorced, and "Sep" for separated.

Separated means legally separated or separated with the intention of living permanently apart. The term must not be used to include temporary separation.

h. *Education—Grades completed.*

Grade and high school: Enter the highest grade successfully *completed* in grade and high school; e. g., for a person who completed eight grades in grade school and entered but failed to complete the third year in high school, enter "10."

For persons who entered school but completed no grade, enter "0."

For persons who have not attended school, enter a dash.

College: Enter the number of years successfully completed.

For persons who entered college but did not complete a year, enter "0."

Do not include attendance at so-called "business colleges."

2. *Month and year of last marriage of normal head.*

Enter the date when the normal head was last married. If inapplicable, enter a dash and explain.

3. *Is normal head a U. S. citizen?*

Check *First papers* for persons who have made formal declaration of intention to become U. S. citizens but who have not yet received their certificate of citizenship.

4. *Residence history of normal family group.*

List in chronological order all places in which the family has resided 1 month or longer since January 1, 1929.

Exclude periods when the family, or the two principal members thereof, were receiving transient relief.

If the family was formed after January 1, 1929, give the residence history from the time the principals were married.

a. *Location:* Enter the State and city for each residence.

If the residence was in open country, enter the name of the county followed by the abbreviation "Co."

b. *Duration:* Enter the month and year when each period of residence began and ended.

If at the beginning of 1929 the family was in a place where they had been living for some time previously, record the year their residence in this place began, regardless of the fact that it was prior to 1929. The earliest date entered here can never be earlier than the date of marriage of the normal head (Question 2) since that was the date the family was formed.

c. *Nature of place:* Determine for each period of residence the nature of the place in which the family was living.

Check one on each line.

Farm: If the family was living on a farm.

Village: If the family was living in or near a village with a population of less than 2,500, but *was not operating a farm.*

Urban: If the family was living in a place with a population of 2,500 or more.

5. *Transient relief record since July 1, 1933.*

Enter in chronological order all instances in which the family as a whole or two or more members of it were registered for transient relief as a family group. Include only relief given under the direction of transient authorities established under the provisions of the Federal Emergency Relief Act of 1933.

a. *Location:* Enter every place (State and city) in which transient relief was received.

b. *Date of registration:* Enter for each period of transient relief the date when the case was registered.

c. *Length of stay:* Enter the length of time the case was under care.

d. *Reason for leaving:* Enter the chief reason for the group's going off transient relief in each place listed.

Reasons for Family Group Mobility

This section applies to the entire period during which the family group has been in an unsettled condition, whether beginning before or after January 1, 1929.

6. *Last place in which the family lived a settled, self-supporting life.*

The purpose of this question is to determine the place and time at which family group mobility began.

Enter the name of the last place in which the family lived a settled, self-supporting life. That is, the place which the family considered its permanent place of residence and in which the family was entirely or mostly self-supporting. In cases where the family has moved several times in recent years careful interviewing will be necessary to determine the location of the place, because in one or more of these moves the family may have established a semipermanent residence which properly belongs to the period of family mobility. For example:

Family A—lived in Chicago, Ill., from June 1924 until August 1930. The head of the family was steadily employed there as a machinist. In August 1930 part-time employment had reduced the family income to a subsistence level. The head succeeded in finding a full-time job as field representative for a mill machinery company. The home in Chicago was given up and the family accompanied the head on his movements about the country. A year later the job ended when the family was in Houston, Tex., where the head found enough employment doing house painting to support the family for 2½ years. When this work failed, the family went to Richmond, Va. (birthplace of the head), where it obtained transient relief.

The proper answer to Question 6 in this case is "Illinois, Chicago, August 1930" and *not* "Texas, Houston, February 1934." Careful interviewing disclosed that although the family lived in Houston long enough to gain legal settlement, it did not consider Houston its home, nor its residence there as permanent, because the head could not obtain steady employment at what he considered adequate wages.

If the family has had no place of settled residence since marriage, enter "None" and explain.

If the last place of settled residence was prior to January 1, 1929, enter the name of this place and the date left.

7. *Reasons for leaving.*

Give a comprehensive explanation of all the circumstances which caused the family to leave the place entered in Question 6.

The answer to this question refers specifically to the place and time entered in Question 6 and is not to be conditioned by subsequent events.

Brief entries, such as "seeking work," "unemployment," "visits," "health," and "family trouble," are *not* adequate. The statement of reasons for leaving should be amplified to include both the primary and secondary factors which caused the family to leave a settled abode.

In no case is the answer to this question to be taken from the registration card (Tr–10).

8. *Destination at time of leaving.*

a. *State, city, or county:* The destination to be entered is the place to which the family planned to go *at the time* it left the locality entered in Question 6.

If the family had no definite destination, enter the general area into which it expected to go.

b. *Reasons for selection of this place:* Enter the reasons why the family selected this particular place rather than any other as its original destination.

9. *Present plans for future.*

State what plans for the future have been made by the family alone or by the family in conjunction with the transient relief agency.

Occupational History

10. *Present employment status of normal head.*

a. Check one item to indicate the employment status of the *normal head* at the time of interview.

Check *Other employment* if the normal head has any job other than a transient relief job. Include in this category persons on strike, persons going to a definitely promised job, and persons employed on nontransient work relief projects.

Specify what kind of work and in what industry; whether it is full time or part time; and whether the person is employed by others or working on his own account.

b. *Interviewer's opinion as to employability of normal head:* Enter here a statement of the interviewer's opinion as to whether the *normal head* is readily employable, or wholly or partially unemployable.

c. *Employment handicaps of normal head:* Specify all factors which would seriously handicap the normal head in securing and pursuing steady employment. It is particularly important to note such factors as permanent physical or mental disabilities, chronic illness, temporary disabilities, old age, personality difficulties, household duties, etc.

11. *Usual occupation of all employable persons 16 years of age and over entered in Question 1.*

a. Identify each person by the appropriate line number in Question 1a. If the present head and the normal head are the same, leave the second line blank.

b. *Usual occupation:* (See appendix for supplementary instructions for recording occupation and industry.)

The usual occupation is that at which the person has normally been employed, or the one which he considers has been his usual occupation by reason of experience or training.

If the person has worked at two or more occupations for short periods of time and considers none of them his usual occupation, enter "No usual occupation."

If the person has never done gainful work, enter "Never worked."

The occupation is the specific job or work performed (e. g., cook).

The industry is the specific industrial or business organization in which the job or work is performed (e. g., hotel).

c. *Total number of year's experience:* Enter the total length of time the person has worked at his usual occupation.

d. *Last nonrelief job of 1 month or longer at usual occupation:* Enter the dates of the beginning and ending of the last nonrelief job of 1 month or longer which the person held at his usual occupation Employment on PWA project is to be considered as nonrelief employment; employment on work relief projects is to be excluded.

12. *Last nonrelief job of 2 weeks or longer held by normal head at any occupation.*

This entry should report the *last* nonrelief employment at any job held by the normal head for 2 weeks or longer.

13. *Farm experience of normal head.*

a–b. The purpose of these questions is to determine the number of *normal* family group heads who have had some farm experience; and whether this experience was as farm laborer or as farm operator.

c. *Owner, manager, tenant, cropper.*

Farm owner: A farmer who owns all or part of the land he operates. Include squatters and homesteaders who are farming.

Farm manager: A person who manages a farm for the owner, assuming full responsibility for the crops and their cultivation and receives a salary for his services.

Farm cropper: A farmer who cultivates only rented land and to whom the landlord furnishes equipment and stock; i. e., he is a farmer who contributes only labor and receives in return a share of the crop.

Farm tenant: A farmer who cultivates rented land only, furnishing all or part of the working equipment and stock, whether he pays cash or a share of the crop or both as rent.

d. *Type of farm:* Indicate the type of farm; e. g., wheat, fruit, dairy, stock. In cases where there was little specialization, enter "general."

e. *Number of acres:* Enter the number of acres included in each farm, whether under cultivation or not.

f. *Location:* Enter the name of the State and county in which each farm was located.

g. *Number of years operated:* Enter the number of years each farm was operated.

h. *Date left:* Enter the month and year the person ceased operating the farm.

i. *Reason for leaving:* Enter the reason for giving up the farm; e. g., mortgage foreclosed, dispossession or eviction, drought, operated at a loss, moved to better farm, moved to city to obtain employment.

14. *Remarks on farm experience.*

If the normal head has had farm experience, but is not now capable of operating a farm, explain the circumstance, and specify whether there is some other member of the family group (e. g., son) who is capable.

15. *General comments on case.*

Make free use of this space to explain, amplify, or interpret entries on the schedule and to record other pertinent information.

Appendix D

LIST OF TABLES

TEXT TABLES

179

SUPPLEMENTARY TABLES

Index

INDEX